NEW YORK STATE
FOLKLIFE READER

NEW YORK STATE
FOLKLIFE READER
Diverse Voices

Edited by Elizabeth Tucker and Ellen McHale

University Press of Mississippi • Jackson

www.upress.state.ms.us

The University Press of Mississippi is a member of the Association of
American University Presses.

First printing 2013

Library of Congress Cataloging-in-Publication Data

New York state folklife reader : diverse voices / edited by Elizabeth Tucker
and Ellen McHale.
     pages cm
 Includes bibliographical references and index.
  ISBN 978-1-61703-863-1 (cloth : alk. paper) — ISBN 978-1-61703-865-5
(ebook) 1. Folklore—New York (State) 2. New York (State)—Social life and
customs. I. Tucker, Elizabeth, 1948–
  GR110.N7N495 2013
  398.209747—dc23   2013015808

British Library Cataloging-in-Publication Data available

CONTENTS

FOOD

DiDinga dancers. Photo: Geoffrey Gould.

INTRODUCTION

Under the blazing summer sun in July 2005, a small group of young Di-Dinga men performed a traditional dance as part of the social event called *gyrikot* in their homeland, Sudan, in northeastern Africa.[1] Most of the young men wore white T-shirts, blue jeans, and sneakers. Making percussive music with wooden spoons and aluminum pie pans, they shared their excitement with their audience. Soon men, women, and children were clapping in time to the music. These young singers had survived an arduous trip from Sudan, where civil war had devastated their villages and killed members of their families. Prevented from undergoing initiation to manhood because of this genocidal war, the young men had bravely walked many miles to a refugee camp. Citizens of Syracuse, New York, had invited the young men to make Syracuse their new home, and Felicia McMahon, research professor at Syracuse University, had invited them to perform at the Schweinfurth Memorial Art Center in Auburn, New York, along with members of two other ethnic groups with a history of overcoming severe challenges.

Children and parents who had recently arrived from Myanmar (formerly known as Burma) made up the second group. Wearing white robes symbolizing their national pride as young people from the Karen tribe, a group of children sang about their hopes for the future. Elders who introduced their performance explained that many of the seven million members of this ethnic minority group living in Myanmar had become refugees after Burmese soldiers destroyed their homes, crops, and livestock. After losing their family's way of life in Myanmar, they had begun a new way of life in New York State. To the side of their performance area, their mothers demonstrated their skill at traditional weaving (*tahtah*). While learning to be New Yorkers, these parents and children enjoyed sharing their Karen identity with people of various ethnicities.

The third group that performed in Auburn that sweltering afternoon represented the original population of New York State. Brenda Bush, a traditional artist of the Oneida Turtle Clan, quietly soaked cornhusks in preparation for creating "no-face" corn husk dolls. Nearby, John Webster of the Oneida Wolf Clan worked on elm-bark ceremonial rattles. Both of these kinds of craftsmanship have been important aspects of the state's folk culture for centuries. Although New York's Native people have undergone many changes and difficulties since the arrival of the first European explorers, their spirit remains strong, and their audience of non-Native people was eager to learn about their areas of expertise.

This book honors the diverse voices that have made New York's traditional culture so rich and intriguing. The term "voices" has a double meaning for the two of us who have edited the book, since it not only refers to individual and group expressions of folklore but also references the title of the publication *Voices: The Journal of New York Folklore*. Both of us have been members of the New York Folklore Society's executive board, and both of us feel proud of our society's publications that have appeared since 1944: not only *Voices* but also *New York Folklore Quarterly*, *New York Folklore Newsletter*, and *New York Folklore*. Through this volume, we hope to share the journals' insights with a larger audience.

New York and its folklore scholars hold an important place in the history of the discipline of folklore. Folklorists in New York are found both within academia and within public benefit institutions such as libraries, museums, and arts agencies, and many maintain dual appointments. In this volume, the works of New York's academic and public folklorists are presented together, since the two trunks of our discipline's growth are closely intertwined. The energy that generates all three aspects of folklore scholarship—teaching, fieldwork/research, and program administration—has produced memorable contributions to the field of folklore. With the beginning of government support for folklore scholarship through the granting mechanism of the New York State Council on the Arts and the leadership of Dr. Robert Baron of the Folk Arts Program, public folklore scholarship in New York saw its ascendency in the 1990s. Its focus on field-based studies has continued into the twenty-first century. Folklorists working in New York State have been given support for thoughtful, careful field research and for publishing their field studies in exhibition catalogs and program notes, and in the publications of the New York Folklore Society.

Folklore scholarship in New York has benefited from its close association with educational and social reform movements, and with American popular culture in the twentieth century. As described in this volume, campers at Camp Woodland, a progressive education camp that was based in the Catskill Mountains from 1939 to 1962, drew upon the folk culture of the Catskills to impart democratic principles and a sense of community to their young campers (Johnson 2002: 6). Similarly, the Foxfire Movement in Education, which focused on the study of Appalachian culture through hands-on interviewing by students, spawned several New York State–based programs in the 1980s and 1990s that were a direct result of this model.

Academic anthropologists also fostered the development of New York folklore studies. At Columbia University, Franz Boas and his students—Ruth Benedict, Margaret Mead, and others—inspired a generation of folklore scholars who looked to the urban core of New York City as well as to the rural portions of the state to conduct their field studies. Twentieth-century scholars who collected folk materials in New York State included Benjamin Botkin, Ruth Benedict, Frank Speck, Louis C. Jones, Elsie Clews Parsons, Edith Cutting, Agnes Underwood, Emelyn Gardner, and Zora Neale Hurston. These scholars significantly influenced the next generation of folklore and folk song collectors. The collective work of these major cultural anthropologists and folklorists helped to establish the New York Folklore Society in 1944.

The study of English literature also contributed significantly to the growth of folklore scholarship in New York and in other places. George Lyman Kittredge, a professor of English at Harvard University, studied with the pioneering ballad scholar Francis James Child, who had, in his own student days, attended lectures by the Grimm brothers. Having a deep appreciation for folk songs and folk literature, Kittredge conveyed that appreciation to his students. Among these students were Franklin D. Roosevelt, who initiated the Federal Writers' Project, and John Lomax, who preserved cowboy ballads and other significant forms of American folklore. These students were, as scholars, "great-grandchildren" of the Grimms, who had written the first European folktale collection in the early nineteenth century. While this lineage is just one of the threads that resulted in the New York Folklore Society's founding, it is an important one that links current respect for cultural diversity to the Romantic nationalism of 1812–1814.

The New York Folklore Society's founders, Harold Thompson and Louis C. Jones, had a profound influence on the shape and direction of folklore scholarship in New York State. Harold W. Thompson, affectionately known as "Tommy" by his colleagues and students, was a legendary professor of English in New York. In his tribute to Thompson in 1958, Louis C. Jones calls his mentor "one of the masters in the great art of teaching" (Jones 1958: 178). Thompson did not just lecture his students

Starting third from left: Louis C. Jones, Harold Thompson, Frank Warner, Dick Dorson, Anne Warner, Duncan Emrich, and Moritz Jagendorf. Reprinted with permission from the New York State Historical Association (NYSHA), Cooperstown, N.Y.

about folklore and literature; his Shakespeare students learned to sing the bard's songs, and his folklore students learned to sing folk songs. In 1934, Thompson began offering his course in American culture, marking, according to Jones, "the first time a course covering a large segment of our folk culture was given [to] undergraduates" (180). We are confident that the assertion holds true. Thompson taught at New York State College for Teachers in Albany from 1915 to 1940, then moved to Cornell University shortly after his book *Body, Boots, and Britches*, written for the edification and enjoyment of the general public, was published in 1939. His folklore archive of student papers, organized by regions of New York, provides an important resource for researchers. As a well-loved professor at the New York State College for Teachers, Thompson inspired a generation of New York State public school teachers who passed on a love of New York folklore to their young students in the years following World War II.

Thompson and Jones both graduated from Hamilton College in Clinton, New York, and shared a passion for folklore and literature. Jones taught English at New York State College for Teachers from 1934 to 1946. As the founding director of the Farmers Museum in Cooperstown, he served in that position from 1946 to 1972; he also taught seminars in

American culture and founded and directed the State University of New York's Graduate Program in Folk Culture at Cooperstown from 1964 to 1982. Although his teaching and administrative work kept him very busy, he found time to publish a number of important books, including *Things That Go Bump in the Night* (1959) and *Growing Up in the Cooper Country* (1965). With a strong interest in folklore of the supernatural that had grown through personal experience and interaction with students, Jones developed an extensive archive of ghost stories and other narratives.

On October 6, 1944, after some preplanning by Thompson and Jones, the New York Folklore Society was inaugurated at a lunch meeting at Trinity Methodist Episcopal Church in Albany. Thompson was elected president and Jones was elected editor. Other folklore notables at that first meeting included Grace Hudolwalski (who was later to become the president of the Adirondack Mountain Club and editor of their newsletter); collectors Frank Warner and Moritz Jagendorf; and Edith Cutting, a student of Harold Thompson's who was later to serve for many years as the society's secretary. Support for the society's new journal, *New York Folklore Quarterly*, came from Cornell University. Both the New York Folklore Society and its journal were, as Jones explained, "intended to reach not just the professional folklorists but those of the general public who were interested in the oral traditions of the State" (Jones 1958: 186). Believing that "sound scholarship could live at peace with sprightly literary style," Jones solicited articles for the *Quarterly* that were well researched, lively, and interesting (187).

This approach, which the New York Folklore Society still follows, has made the society's journal accessible to any reader who wants to learn about folklore and local history. In 1975, *New York Folklore Quarterly* became *New York Folklore*, a more academically focused journal with illustrations. Then, at the turn of the twenty-first century, *New York Folklore* became *Voices: The Journal of New York Folklore*, which combines research-based articles with interviews, narratives, reminiscences, and artwork from New York State. With its appealing design and accessible style, *Voices* represents a wide readership, not just academic and public folklorists.

Harold Thompson, Louis Jones, and others founded the New York Folklore Society so that they could give folk traditions back to the people of their state. Since then, various directors and executive board members have helped New Yorkers learn about their state's cultural heritage. The Internet has introduced exciting new forms of information sharing that continue to develop. Fifty years from now, New York folklore may be part of an interactive information system beyond any possibilities that we can currently imagine.

Unlike some folklore anthologies, this book does not follow an organizational plan based on regions or folklore genres. Because the New York Folklore Society has always tried to give folklore back to the people, we have decided to divide our book into sections about life processes that all New Yorkers share: memory, work, play, resistance, and food. At the book's end, we include a list of folklore archives and a calendar of New York's folk festivals.

Our book begins with five essays on various aspects of folk cultural memory: personal, family, community, and historical processes of remembrance expressed through narrative, ritual, and other forms of folklore. The first essay, Elizabeth Tucker's "Dynamics of New York's Folk Culture," places the development of folk traditions in the context of cultural ecology, with special attention to immigrants' folklife as well as social and political movements. Linda Rosekrans's "Oral Culture and History Today: Joanne Shenandoah and Jack W. Gladstone" reminds us that some of New York's earliest inhabitants, the Haudenosaunee (Iroquois), celebrate their historical memory in songs. According to Haudenosaunee singer Joanne Shenandoah, songs honor sacred sites and express principles for living; they also keep memories of important people alive. Some of these people are family members and friends of the singer, while others belong to Haudenosaunee history. The third essay, Michael L. Murray's "Cities within the City: Ben Botkin's New York," brings us back to the early twentieth century, when Ben Botkin first arrived in New York City. Appointed the national folklore editor of the Federal Writers' Project in 1938, Botkin directed the collection of folklore from Chinese, Greek, Ukrainian, Muslim, Hindu, and other immigrants to New York City. Jewish traditions have been integral to New York City's development. Barbara Myerhoff's "Ritual and Storytelling: A Passover Tale" eloquently examines the "Great Story" of the Passover seder, showing how this story expresses Jewish identity and connections to other Jews of the past and present.

The section's last two essays, Dee Britton's "Comfort in Cloth: The Syracuse University Remembrance Quilt" and Kay Turner's "Here *Was* New York: Memorial Images of the Twin Towers," explore the preservation of important memories at times of mourning. Britton explains how the creation of a quilt in 1998 helped members of the Syracuse University community come to terms with the loss of thirty-five students in the explosion of Pan Am flight 103 over Lockerbie, Scotland, as a result of terrorism in 1988. Total casualties from the incident represented the largest loss of life of American citizens through terrorism until the terrorist bombing of the World Trade Center and two other sites on September 11, 2001. Turner's essay sensitively portrays New Yorkers' vernacular representation of the 2001 tragedy through wall murals, shrines, graffiti, logos, costumes, window stickers, and other forms of remembrance. People's individual tributes to New Yorkers who died have become part of the historical memory of September 11 through folklorists' fieldwork and publications.

Our book's second section explores New Yorkers' pursuit of pleasure and balance through play. Robert Baron's "'I Saw Mrs. Saray, Sitting on a Bombalerry': Ralph Ellison Collects Children's Folklore in Harlem" presents and analyzes fieldwork on jump rope rhymes and other forms of children's play by author Ralph Ellison, who participated in the Federal Writers' Project in the 1930s. Because of Ellison's work, we have a detailed record of children's play in New York City at that time. Brian Sutton-Smith's "Cultivating Courage Through Play" analyzes children's stories collected by his students at Columbia University's Teachers College in Lower East Side schools from 1972 to 1974. Sutton-Smith finds that children's stories express stressful situations—attack, accident, uncleanness, alienation—that children must confront in order to maintain mental health. Through play, according to Sutton-Smith, children find an important kind of courage. Felicia McMahon's "Emerging Traditions: Dance Performances of the Sudanese DiDinga in Syracuse" explores young immigrants' efforts to adapt to daily life in their new homeland through the creative expression of their homeland's traditions. As mentioned earlier in this introduction, the DiDinga have become well known in both New York and other parts of the United States as courageous young performers. The next-to-last essay in this section, Elena Martínez's "Flyin' High: Kite Flying from the Silk Road to Roosevelt Avenue," compares Pakistani-American children's love of kite flying to mainstream American culture's passion for baseball. Noting that kite flying originated in India about five hundred years ago and that Pakistani kite flying festivals started in New York City in 1996, Martínez describes children's exuberance and delight in this creative form of play. Another popular New York City pursuit is petanque, a form of outdoor bowling that was invented in southern France toward the beginning of the twentieth century. Valérie Feschet's "Petanque in New York" identifies petanque as an inclusive sport counterculture that encourages anyone who enjoys competition to gather in shared urban spaces.

In contrast to the essays on play, essays in the third section, "Work," present diverse modes of gainful employment. Sometimes it can be hard to distinguish play from work, which can involve activities that are dear to the heart of the worker. Such is definitely the case in the work of Mexican *sonideros*, analyzed by Cathy Ragland in "Mediating between Two Worlds: The *Sonideros* of Mexican Youth Dances." Ragland explains that *sonideros*, who serve as disc jockeys at dances for Mexican young people, create a bridge between the old country and the new by encouraging dancers to compose salutations and dedications related to Mexican culture. Through their creative direction of the dances, these specialists keep dancers moving back and forth between their families' original homeland and their new home in New York. Similarly, Puja Sahney's "In the Midst of a Monastery: Filming the Making of a Buddhist Sand Mandala" describes the artistry of monks who live in a Buddhist monastery on the banks of the Hudson River in Wappingers Falls. Having adapted to life in New York by welcoming students of Buddhism to their monastery for retreats, the monks periodically create beautiful sand mandalas that represent the circle of life and death. After spending five days creating a mandala, the monks throw it into the river, expressing the Buddhist doctrine that nothing lasts forever.

The last three essays in this section examine work in specific parts of New York State. Tom van Buren's "Set in Stone: The Art of Stonework and Wall Building in Westchester County" traces the use of stone as a building material favored by immigrants from Europe. One of the masons in his study comes from Italy; the other comes from Ecuador. Although stonemasonry certainly exists in other parts of the state and nation, it has been especially popular in Westchester County. In a similar vein, professions connected with horse racing have come together in northern New York, in Saratoga Springs. Ellen McHale's "An Ethnography of the Saratoga Racetrack" identifies Saratoga Springs as an "intentional" community in which jockeys, exercise riders, trainers, and other workers share naming practices, speech, and concern about the uncertain outcome of horse races. When things can change very quickly, McHale observes, people find wisdom in the folk proverb "Chickens today, feathers tomorrow." The last essay in the "Work" section, Ryn Gargulinski's "Stand Clear of the Closing Doors! Occupational Folklore of New York City Subway Workers," also describes an uncertain work environment: the underground world of New York City's subways. In this network of train tracks where one false move can cause injury or death, folk narratives offer important words of caution. Besides horrifying and teaching listeners, these narratives entertain them with strange and sometimes gruesome details of life beneath the streets of New York City.

In the fourth section, "Resistance," we see New Yorkers' strength in opposing practices or attitudes that do not seem right to them. This section begins with Curtis Harris's and Leota Lone Dog's "Two Spirited People: Understanding Who We Are as Creation." This interview with two Native Americans in New York City by Deborah Blincoe focuses on their determination to increase New Yorkers' awareness of gay and lesbian Native people. Telling the stories of two ancestors, WeWah and BarCheeAmpe, Harris and Lone Dog refuse to accept stereotypes of Native people, or of members of the gay and lesbian communities. The second essay, Dale W. Johnson's "Camp Woodland: Progressive Education and Folklore in the Catskill Mountains of New York," explains a different kind of resistance: instruction in folk song, folk music, and other traditions of the Catskills at the progressive Camp Woodland, directed by the legendary leader Norman Studer, who had studied with the educational philosopher John Dewey. At this camp, children collected songs, stories, and other kinds of folklore from local residents. Because of the camp's integrated population and its progressive educational approach, some people found it to be subversive, and the camp was pressured to close in 1962. Welcoming ethnic diversity and valuing the preservation of New York folklife, Camp Woodland made a significant statement during the years that it operated. Also supportive of progressive politics were folk musicians Ruth Crawford Seeger and Zilphia Horton, profiled in Julia Schmidt-Pirro's and Karen M. McCurdy's "Employing Music in the Cause of Social Justice: Ruth Crawford Seeger and Zilphia Horton." Beginning her career in New York City, Seeger used folk songs to convey political concepts; in the American South, Horton taught folk songs to labor union and civil rights leaders. Both women died in the 1950s. The last essay in the "Resistance" section is Sandra Mizumoto Posey's "Burning Messages: Interpreting African American Fraternity Brands and Their Bearers." Posey examines physical branding practices at Omega Psi Phi Fraternity, which was founded in 1911 at Howard University; its Epsilon Chapter was founded in 1919 for African American men studying at universities in New York City. Some narratives in popular culture associate branding with slavery; however, Posey explains, members of this fraternity oppose these media narratives in reclaiming their bodies and expressing their identity as fraternity members. These fraternity members insist on expressing themselves on their own terms, using a folk practice that feels right to them in spite of opposition.

The "Food" section is an important part of this reader. Like any other state, New York has an array of cherished foodways. From hot dogs, hot chestnuts, and bagels in New York City to spiedies in Binghamton, hot chicken wings in Buffalo, and bullheads in the North Country, New York's foods are uniquely delightful. Some of these foods, like butter lambs sold in Buffalo at Easter, have a strong connection to holidays and festivals; others can be found at any time of year. A few traditions, such as hunting and serving wild game, remind us of the early settlement of New York State. Closely tied to a sense of family and community, the folklife of food has deep personal meaning and infinite variety.

New Yorkers have the opportunity to participate in their state's rich and diverse folk culture. We hope that this collection of New York's folklore and the work of New York's folklorists will inspire readers to seek out the lore found in their own communities. As North Country folklorist Varick Chittenden has pointed out, "It's everywhere you look."[2]

NOTES

1. Felicia McMahon's *Not Just Child's Play: Emerging Tradition and the Lost Boys of Sudan* (2007), which won the Chicago Folklore Prize in 2008, tells the young DiDinga men's story and shows how their recontextualized songs and dances have helped them to become adults as they have learned to handle day-to-day life in a new homeland. For an explanation of the informal social event *gyrikot*, see pages 129–130.

2. Exhibit: "Out of the Ordinary: Community Tastes and Values in Contemporary Folk Art, 1995," Varick Chittenden, Traditional Arts of Upstate New York.

WORKS CITED

Johnson, Dale W. 2002. "Camp Woodland: Progressive Education and Folklore in the Catskills Mountains of New York." *Voices: The Journal of New York Folklore* 28 (1-2): 6–12.

Jones, Louis C. 1958. "HWT: NYSCT: BBB: NYFS." *New York Folklore Quarterly* 14 (3): 177–188.

McMahon, Felicia. 2007. *Not Just Child's Play: Emerging Tradition and the Lost Boys of Sudan*. Jackson: University Press of Mississippi.

MEMORY

DYNAMICS OF NEW YORK'S FOLK CULTURE

ELIZABETH TUCKER

Through layers of historical and folk memory, we perceive New York's folk-cultural dynamics. Historical memory seems straightforward and detailed, but it does not tell the whole story of this part of North America. We can gain a fuller understanding of New York's past and present by studying various forms of folklore. The memory of folk communities and regions comes to us through origin tales, legends, songs, dances, rituals, customs, beliefs, games, quilt making, wall building, cooking, maple syrup production, and other kinds of lore. This essay examines dynamics of folk culture from the sixteenth century to the present, drawing upon both folk and historical memory.

New York's folk culture began with the area's first inhabitants: the Haudenosaunee (Iroquois) and Lenape people. The name "Iroquois" came from the French; "Haudenosaunee" means "People of the Longhouse." Because of its long heritage of oral narratives and records of political organization, Haudenosaunee culture has been well known to New Yorkers. Storytellers at many folk festivals and school assemblies have told the Haudenosaunee tale of the earth's creation, "The World on Turtle's Back." According to this story, our world began when a woman fell from the sky world to a water-covered world below. Helpful animals brought up mud from beneath the water's surface, gradually building an island on the back of a turtle so that Sky Woman could have a place to live. To honor the animals' work, we can call our earth "Turtle Island" (S. Thompson 1946: 312).

By the sixteenth century, or possibly earlier, the five Haudenosaunee nations—the Seneca, Cayuga, Onondaga, Oneida, and Mohawk people—had formed an alliance known as the League of Peace and Power. Their constitution, the "Sacred Tree of Peace," set a significant example of governance. At the eastern border of the Iroquois League, the Mohawk held the title "Keepers of the Eastern Door;" at the western border, the Seneca were

Dan Hill, silversmith and flute maker and player; Katie Thompson, basket maker; and Robin Lazore, Mohawk basket maker demonstrating their traditional crafts at the American Folklore Society Conference held in Rochester, N.Y., 2002. Photo © Martha Cooper.

known as "Keepers of the Western Door." In the eighteenth century, the Tuscarora became the sixth nation of the Iroquois. Although the French and Indian Wars (1754–1763), the loss of tribal territory, and the formation of reservations diminished the power of New York's Native people, their influence has continued to be substantial.

Among the first European explorers of the region that would become known as New York State were Giovanni da Verrazzano, who sailed as far as the bridge that now bears his name in 1524, and Henry Hudson, whose famous voyage in 1609 gave the Hudson River its name. Both Verrazzano and Hudson saw Lenape people paddling canoes. Hudson's crew member Robert Juet recorded descriptions of Lenape "Mantles of Feathers" and "great tobacco pipes of yellow Copper"; he also mentioned that the Lenape had sold the ship's crew some tasty "oysters and Beanes" (Jameson 1909: 18–27). The Lenape probably found Hudson's crew to be intriguing too, but we have no record of their reactions.

Later in the seventeenth century, explorers kept records of their travels through Native settlements. Harmen Meynertsz van den Bogaert, a Dutch traveler with some expertise in medicine, traveled as a member of the Dutch West India Company to Mohawk and Oneida country in the winter of 1634. His journal, the first of its kind in this region, offers details about language, foodways, etiquette, conflicts, musical instruments, fire making, burial customs, and healing rituals, as well as precise descriptions of long-houses and settlement patterns. Drawn to this region in search of beaver pelts, then fashionable in Europe, van den Bogaert and his companions enjoyed meals of bear meat, salmon, and beans, and received many beaver pelts as gifts. Toward the middle of their journey, they marveled at a cur-ing ceremony during which men "threw fire, ate fire, and threw around hot ashes and embers in such a way that [van den Bogaert] ran out of the house" (Gehring and Starna 1988: 18). Van den Bogaert and the other visitors left Mohawk country with vivid memories of Haudenosaunee folk traditions.

In 1614, the Dutch West India Company established a colony called New Netherland. Company director Pieter Minuit bought Manhattan Is-land from its Native inhabitants in 1626, giving them jewelry worth about sixty guilders, and founded Fort New Amsterdam on the island's southern tip. This new fort became the center for the Dutch West India Company's profitable fur trade, which also made use of Fort Orange (founded in 1615) on Castle Island near the current city of Albany. By the 1630s, settlers of diverse ethnic and religious backgrounds made New Amsterdam a lively place. Father Isaac Jogues, a visiting Catholic priest, wrote in 1646:

> On the island of Manhate, and in its environs, there may well be four or five hundred men of different sects and nations: the Director General told me that there were men of eighteen different languag-es; they are scattered here and there on the river, above and below, as the beauty and convenience of the spot has invited each to settle: some mechanics however, who ply their trade, are ranged under the fort; all the others are exposed to the incursions of the natives. (Jameson 1909: 259–260)

Father Jogues's observation shows that, even in its earliest days, the settle-ment later known as New York City had a highly diverse population. Since people from so many different backgrounds lived close together, there were sometimes misunderstandings and fights, but colony construction moved forward at a lively pace.

African slaves, who began to arrive in the 1620s, did much of the work of colony building in New Amsterdam and its environs. Slaves built fortifications, farmed, and protected the Dutch from attack by Native

Americans; for these important services, the West India Company gave some slaves their freedom. According to Thelma Wills Foote, author of *Black and White Manhattan* (2004), slaves made up about 20 percent of New Amsterdam's population in 1664, when the British captured the city. Foote suggests, "The Dutch colony builders were only dimly aware, if at all, that they were laying the foundations for an enduring social order predicated on the subordination of Africans and their descendants" (40).

Whether or not the Dutch intended to create a social order related to race, there were certainly tensions between slaves and colonists on Manhattan Island in the early eighteenth century. The New York Slave Revolt of 1712 resulted in the death of nine whites and the execution of twenty-five slaves. As a consequence of that uprising, the New York City slave code of 1731 prohibited slaves from carrying weapons and going out after dark, unless asked by their masters to do so. The Conspiracy of 1741, also called the Slave Insurrection of 1741, may or may not have involved plotting by slaves; apparently, rumors spread rapidly. After a series of fires broke out in the city, alarmed well-to-do white settlers concluded that slaves had joined forces with impoverished whites to take over the city. Hangings, burnings at the stake, and deportations took place as punishment for the fires (Foote 2004: 159–186). After this frightening series of events, slavery gradually diminished; it became illegal in New York State in 1827.

Early in the nineteenth century, poverty in Ireland motivated many Irish families to immigrate to the United States; the Potato Famine from 1845 to 1852 made farmers seek an alternative to starvation and suffering. Although there was initially some prejudice against Irish immigrants, the new Irish citizens of New York State worked hard and prospered. Irish Americans' involvement in New York State's development included construction of the Erie Canal.[1] Farmers, fishermen, seaport workers, and crafts specialists of Irish heritage made countless contributions to the growth of New York City and upstate regions.

Although memories of the Potato Famine have faded somewhat, the strength of Irish spirit reminds New Yorkers of the contrast between nineteenth-century privation in Ireland and twenty-first-century comfort in the United States. Saint Patrick's Day, which honors the saint who, according to legends, drove all the snakes from Ireland, provides a focal point for celebration of Irish heritage. The city of Binghamton in upstate New York has held an annual Saint Patrick's Day parade since 1967. "Everyone is Irish on parade day in Binghamton," according to a news report in 2010 (Jenereski 2010). On parade day, large crowds of Binghamton residents dress in green, wear funny hats, and visit taverns such as Fitzie's Irish Pub to drink green beer. In this jolly way, they celebrate Irish people's survival and prosperity in New York State.

Later waves of immigration brought increasing depth to the cultural diversity of New York State. The influx of northern Europeans from England, Ireland, and Scandinavia became a broader migration from other parts of Europe, including Germany, France, and Italy. Before Ellis Island opened in 1892, more than eight million immigrants had come to Castle Garden Immigration Depot in Manhattan; from 1892 to 1954, more than twelve million immigrants came to Ellis Island. During the peak immigration year, 1907, officials processed 1,004,756 immigrants. Each Ellis Island immigrant had to answer a series of twenty-nine questions. Although Ellis Island officials tend to deny that some immigrants received new family names during processing, the folklore of certain families retains memories of name changes ("Ellis Island" 2010).

Toward the end of the nineteenth century, eastern Europeans and Russians traveled in great numbers to the eastern United States. Although not all of them had positive experiences with relocation, many immigrants from that time period remembered the Statue of Liberty as an important, inspiring monument that represented their quest for better lives. Rose Chernin, for example, traveled to New York from Russia with her mother and siblings in 1914. Her daughter, Kim Chernin, relates stories from her mother's personal experiences during her own childhood days in Staten Island in her memoir *In My Mother's House*:

> Sometimes, on a Sunday, my mother or my aunt would make a lunch for us. Five cents for the trolley bought us a transfer to the ferry that crossed into New York. It went past the Statue of Liberty. No American, born in this country, could know the impression seeing this beautiful woman for the first time. We would crowd to the side of the boat, each time, to see her again. We felt she had been put there for us, we thought she was ours. (Chernin 1983: 37)

This moving narrative captures the beauty and meaning of the statue that had welcomed so many immigrants and would continue to welcome many more.

Before and during World War II, large numbers of German, Russian, and eastern European Jews came to New York City, leaving an indelible imprint on New York City's folk culture. Synagogues and shuls, stores, and kosher delis made New York a center of Jewish beliefs and practices. As Jewish adolescents came of age at their bar and bat mitzvahs, they celebrated a ritual of great importance to their faith (Bronner 2008–2009). Rituals for Yom Kippur, Chanukah, and Passover also expressed the strength of Jewish belief, both in New York City and in upstate New York. The "Utica issue" of *New York Folklore* (1983) includes articles about kosher cooking in Utica, as well as studies of Polish American food preparation and beliefs and other aspects of eastern European folk tradition.

Mid- and late-twentieth-century immigration to New York brought people from relatively nearby Caribbean islands as well as faraway Asian nations. Wars in Vietnam, Cambodia, and Laos resulted in the relocation of people from all of those areas; famine and civil war in Africa also motivated migration to the United States for those who could afford to make the journey. During the 1990s there was an unusually large wave of immigration, with 794,400 immigrants officially registered in New York City between 1990 and 1996. Most immigrants to New York City in the late 1990s came from the Dominican Republic, the former Soviet Union, China, Jamaica, Mexico, Guyana, Ecuador, Haiti, and Trinidad and Tobago (Groce 2004: 8).

The first decade of the twenty-first century has seen continuing waves of immigration. Although people typically arrive in planes at JFK or La-Guardia Airports rather than in ships sailing through New York Harbor, the immigrant experience continues to be intense, hope-filled, and anxious. Those who have come to New York State relatively recently, such as the DiDinga and Karen people who performed in Auburn in the summer of 2005, will make significant contributions to the state's folk culture, just as earlier immigrants did.

The wide range of immigrant cultures in New York State inspires reflection on the dynamics of folk-cultural expression and change. Since the publication of Gregory Bateson's *Steps to an Ecology of Mind* (1972), theorists have speculated about cultural ecology: the interdependence of people's daily lives—including folk traditions—with the natural environment. Cultural ecology applies in interesting ways to the interaction of people from diverse backgrounds. In mountainous areas, river valleys, and other landscapes in New York State, we can trace the development of folklore from people of varying ethnic and religious backgrounds.

The Hudson River Valley, for example, abounds in supernatural lore that has combined Native American, Dutch, English, and American elements. Washington Irving's *Sketch Book of Geoffrey Crayon* (1978) has made certain Hudson River ghosts famous, while oral tradition has nurtured other legends rooted in past migrations and conflicts. In her thought-provoking study *Possessions: The History and Uses of Haunting in the Hudson Valley* (2003), Judith Richardson explores intersections of supernatural lore with cultural history, economics, and land disputes. Drawing upon legends from the Louis C. Jones Archive in Cooperstown, Richardson suggests that the "brooding mountains" and "spooky woods" of legends in the Hudson Valley came from "an alchemy of physical, historical, and cultural factors, ranging from the local to the international: a terrain amenable to readings of inherent spookiness; a history troubled by restless change and contentiousness, which yielded haunting uncertainties; and a diverse set of cultural influences, from Native American spirit beliefs to transatlantic romantic aesthetics, which encouraged visions of ghostliness" (11). This analysis helps us understand the complex relationship of landscape with culture and economics during almost four centuries of adaptation and change.

My own legend study of another New York river valley region, *Haunted Southern Tier* (Tucker 2011), traces cultural influences from the time of European settlement to the present. Legends of haunted mansions, churches, parks, hospitals, and homes in the Southern Tier express the region's diverse ethnic and religious heritage. One of the Southern Tier's most famous ghost stories, "The White Lady," describes a vanishing hitchhiker dressed as a bride or prom queen who hovers near a dangerous curve called Devil's Elbow. This dramatic local legend has roots in southern Germany. Rod Serling, who grew up in Binghamton, based one episode of his popular television series *The Twilight Zone* on the "vanishing hitchhiker" legend cycle. In another episode of *The Twilight Zone*, a middle-aged man discovers his boyhood self on a carousel in a city park. Variants of the same ghost stories that fascinated Serling still circulate today in the Southern Tier, sending shivers down the spines of young people who listen carefully to their elders' stories.

Another kind of Southern Tier folklore shows the impact of landscape on folk traditions. Since the late 1970s, people have celebrated May Day at dawn at the confluence of the Susquehanna and Chenango Rivers. Following the well-known pattern of May Day rituals in Great Britain, these celebrations have involved Morris dancing,[2] singing, and passing of a flask of spirits from one person to another. Some years, participants have thrown homemade rafts of flowering branches into the rivers' confluence, signaling the end of winter and the beginning of spring. During some of

A white dress near a carriage suggests the presence of the White Lady of Devil's Elbow. Courtesy of Tioga County Historical Society. Photo: Geoffrey Gould.

those same years, a mysterious "Green Woman" wearing a tunic covered by artificial leaves and flowers has danced for an appreciative audience. While these May Day festivities have not been announced to the general public, informal invitations have drawn a good number of performers and onlookers, including Native Americans and members of Christian and neo-pagan religious groups. The confluence of these two rivers does not just bring together two waterways; it also provides a focal point for seasonal celebration by people of diverse backgrounds.

Viewing New York State as an ecosystem with limitless potential for growth and change, we can see it as an environment in which diverse groups have created a multitude of traditions. According to noted folk song scholar and archivist Alan Lomax, each culture has intrinsic value. Lomax's "An Appeal for Cultural Equity" states that cultural variation "has enabled the human species to flourish in every zone of the planet" and that folklorists have an obligation to preserve human life by supporting local cultures (1977: 125). This appeal has had a significant impact internationally. In November 2001, shortly after the terrorist attacks on New York City, UNESCO issued a "Universal Declaration on Cultural Diversity" that identified cultural diversity as an ethical imperative and defined cultural heritage as a "wellspring of creativity" (UNESCO 2001).

In relation to evolutionary biology, we can connect the development of multicultural New York folklore with the more gradual evolution of human beings. David Sloan Wilson (2007) and other biologists have studied cultural change, finding that it fits evolutionary patterns very well. Noting that "cultural variation is seldom in short supply," Wilson suggests that we should not be surprised by such variations, which happen in all complex systems (2007: 220). Folklore forms one important part of this process. According to folklorist John Suter, "A strong argument can be made that cultural evolution plays a critical role, supplementary to the much slower genetic transmission, in the evolution of the human species" (1999: 2). Suter finds that ecology and evolution provide "illuminating, if inexact, analogs to the dynamics of human cultures" (3). Citing patterns of conservation and change found in studies of evolution, he observes, "The rate of change in the environment is of critical importance for the survival of individual species and for the health of the ecosystem as a whole" (4).

Among all of the kinds of folklore that have generated local variations, one of the closest to people's hearts is food preparation. On the Lower East Side of Manhattan, for example, the family store Russ and Daughters has created a food empire from the Jewish tradition of eating bagels and lox, a cherished icon of New York City foodways. Folklorist Nancy Groce chronicles this historically significant store, founded in 1914, which offers customers "a stunning display of smoked salmon, lox, white fish, cream cheeses, and a kaleidoscope of colorful salads" (2010: 126). The store's emphasis on smoked fish reflects food preparation traditions from northern Europe and Russia, as well as among Native Americans. A statement from the current owner of Russ and Daughters, Mark Russ Federman, shows that diverse ethnic backgrounds and preferences still matter: "There are new guys on the block, and then there are little boutique smokers, and there's fish coming in from Scotland, or Ireland, or Norway . . . so we have to deal with a lot more people now" (133). Food, Federman suggests, is "the ultimate comfort when everything else fails us," and memories of visits to food stores with parents and grandparents provide solace as times change (134). Proudly considering his family's store's achievements, he states, "This is not just Jewish food anymore. The whole world wants smoked salmon. Right?" (135).

Another kind of folklore with fascinating variations is the game-song of contemporary African American girls. Ethnomusicologist Kyra D. Gaunt has found that such game-songs, many of which derive from popular music, teach children crucial lessons about African American music and identity. In *The Games Black Girls Play* (2006), she recalls learning the game-song "Candy Girl" from eight- and nine-year-old girls during an after-school program in Harlem. Based on the popular song "Candy Girl" from New Edition's 1983 album of the same name, the girls' game-song includes three dance steps. As the girls sing, "This is the way you do—the Janet Jackson," they dance "the Pepperseed"; as they sing, "This is the way you do—the Mike Tyson," they dance "the Fight"; and as they sing, "This is the way you do—the Bobby Brown," they dance "the Running Man" (Gaunt 2006: 74). This dramatization of famous persons through dance adheres to the centrality of dance in African American girls' games. According to Gaunt, "One could assert that the girls were performing the communal discourse, as well as a musical grapevine of blackness, through the body and their in-body formulas" (74). This eloquent explanation of game-songs' significance reminds us how important it is to preserve variants of folk tradition.

The development and study of New York State's folk culture have had a close relationship to certain political and social movements. During President Franklin D. Roosevelt's administration, catastrophic rates of unemployment led to the founding of the Works Progress Administration in 1935. One of the key divisions of the WPA was the Federal Writers' Project, which involved the collection of oral histories, local histories, and ethnographies. Among the best-known participants in this project were Ralph Ellison, Zora Neale Hurston, and Studs Terkel. The Federal Writers' Project, which ended in 1939, compiled an extensive collection of oral and local histories that enhanced New Yorkers' understanding of their heritage.

After World War II, the folk song revival emphasized the need to fight for human rights and oppose social injustice. Civil rights, workers' rights, and educational reforms were among the concerns that emerged in folk songs of the second half of the twentieth century. Certain concerts, such as Alan Lomax's Folksong '59 at Carnegie Hall in New York City, offered inspiring examples of traditional music along with folk revival songs performed by talented singers. Because of the political activism of some folk song revival singers, government agents suspected them of inclining toward communism. The Almanac Singers, who started performing together in 1941, were well known for their political activism. Among these singers were Pete Seeger and Lee Hays, who founded the singing group the Weavers in 1948; later members of the Almanac Singers included Woody Guthrie, Cisco Houston, and Bess Lomax Hawes. In 1955, Seeger and Hays had to testify before the House Un-American Activities Committee. The FBI investigated Alan Lomax's fieldwork and concert organization from the early 1940s to the late 1970s; a recent study by folklorist Susan G. Davis shows that prominent New York folklorist Ben Botkin underwent a similar investigation. Blacklisting of the work of certain performers made their lives difficult for a number of years. The folk song revival continued, however. Gradually, songs by Joan Baez; Bob Dylan; Peter, Paul, and Mary; the Kingston Trio; Arlo Guthrie; and other singers became mainstream hits; their popularity has continued into the twenty-first century.

Folklore scholarship in New York State both influenced and was influenced by American popular culture in the twentieth century. Benjamin Botkin, who served as the head of the Federal Writers' Project, became the head of the Archive of Folk Culture at the Library of Congress and chronicled the importance of folk culture within New York's urban life. Folklorist Zora Neale Hurston was an active member of the Harlem Renaissance and collected folk cultural material in New York State before relocating to Florida. Similarly, the malleable boundaries of folk and popular music were recognized by folklore collectors in New York State, with collectors such as Frank Warner and Herbert Haufrecht helping to record traditional musicians while at the same time popularizing the musical forms being collected. The work of New York music promoters and stylists such as Moses Asch, Oscar Brand, and Pete Seeger, as well as music historians Henry Sapoznik, Ruth Rubin, and Mick Moloney, profoundly influenced the expression and preservation of New York's folk culture, which has resulted in a treasure trove of music for all of us to enjoy today.

NOTES

1. Although oral tradition has held that most of the builders of the Erie Canal were Irish, some historians have asserted that the majority of the construction crew came from local recruitment; a number of those local recruits must have been Irish Americans (Shaw 1966: 90–91).

2. Morris dancing, traditional in England since the late fifteenth century, involves rhythmic steps, usually with musical accompaniment. Morris dancers may use sticks, swords, bells, and handkerchiefs in their performances. A good study of Morris dancing is John Forrest's *The History of Morris Dancing, 1483–1750* (1999).

WORKS CITED

Bateson, Gregory. 1972. *Steps to an Ecology of Mind.* Chicago: University of Chicago Press.

Bronner, Simon J. 2008–2009. "Fathers and Sons: Rethinking the Bar Mitzvah as an American Rite of Passage." *Children's Folklore Review* 31: 7–34.

Chernin, Kim. 1983. *In My Mother's House: A Daughter's Story.* New York: HarperCollins.

Davis, Susan G. 2010. "Ben Botkin's FBI File." *Journal of American Folklore* 122 (487): 3–30.

Dundes, Alan. 1965. *The Study of Folklore.* Englewood Cliffs, N.J.: Prentice Hall.

"Ellis Island Timeline." 2010. The Statue of Liberty–Ellis Island Foundation. Available at http://www.ellisisland.org/genealogy/ellis_island_timeline.asp. Accessed March 15, 2010.

Foote, Thelma Wills. 2004. *Black and White Manhattan: The History of Racial Formation in Colonial New York City.* New York: Oxford University Press.

Forrest, John. 1999. *The History of Morris Dancing, 1483–1750.* Cambridge: James Clarke.

Gaunt, Kyra D. 2006. *The Games Black Girls Play: Learning the Ropes from Double-Dutch to Hip-Hop.* New York: New York University Press.

Gehring, Charles T., and William A. Starna, eds. and trans. 1988. *A Journey into Mohawk and Oneida Country: 1634–1635.* Syracuse: Syracuse University Press.

Glassie, Henry. 1993. *Turkish Traditional Art Today.* Bloomington: Indiana University Press.

Groce, Nancy. 2004. "Local Culture in the Global City: The Folklife of New York." *Voices: The Journal of New York Folklore* 30 (1-2), 6–13.

———. 2010. *Lox, Stocks, and Backstage Broadway: Iconic Trades of New York City.* Washington, D.C.: Smithsonian Institution Scholarly Press.

Irving, Washington. 1978. *The Sketch Book of Geoffrey Crayon, Gent.* Edited by Haskell Springer. Boston: Twayne Publishers. First published 1819–1820.

Jameson, John Franklin, ed. 1909. *Narratives of New Netherland, 1609–1664.* New York: Scribner's.

Jenereski, Natalie. 2010. "St. Patrick's Day Parade Spreads Irish Cheer." WBNG-TV, Binghamton, N.Y., July 22. Available at http://www.wbng.com/closings/86724147.html. Accessed April 4, 2013.

Jones, Louis C. 1958. "HWT: NYSCT: BBB: NYFS." *New York Folklore Quarterly* 14 (3): 177–188.

———. 1959. *Things That Go Bump in the Night.* New York: Hill and Wang.

———. 1965. *Growing Up in the Cooper Country.* Syracuse: Syracuse University Press.

Lomax, Alan. 1977. "An Appeal for Cultural Equity." *Journal of Communications* 27 (2): 125–138.

McMahon, Felicia. 2007. *Not Just Child's Play: Emerging Tradition and the Lost Boys of Sudan.* Jackson: University Press of Mississippi.

New York State Council on the Arts (NYSCA). 2010. Available at http://www.nysca.org. Accessed March 10, 2010.

Oring, Elliott. 1986. *Folk Groups and Folklore Genres.* Logan: Utah State University Press.

Richardson, Judith. 2003. *Possessions: The History and Uses of Haunting in the Hudson Valley.* Cambridge: Harvard University Press.

Shaw, Ronald E. 1966. *Erie Water West: A History of the Erie Canal, 1792–1854.* Lexington: University Press of Kentucky.

Suter, John. 1999. "Thoughts on the Role of Folk Arts in the Ecology of Culture." *New York Folklore* 25: 1–16.

Thompson, Harold W. 1939. *Body, Boots, and Britches.* New York: Dover Books.

Thompson, Stith. 1946. *The Folktale.* New York: Holt, Rinehart and Winston.

Traditional Arts in Upstate New York (TAUNY). 2010. Available at http://www.tauny .org. Accessed April 12, 2010.

Tucker, Elizabeth. 2011. *Haunted Southern Tier.* Charleston, S.C.: History Press.

United Nations Educational, Scientific and Cultural Organization (UNESCO). 2001. "Universal Declaration on Cultural Diversity." Available at http://portal.unesco.org/ en/ev.php-URL_ID=13179&URL_DO=DO_TOPIC&URL_SECTION=201.html. Accessed March 3, 2010.

Wilson, David Sloan. 2007. *Evolution for Everyone: How Darwin's Theory Can Change the Way We Think about Our Lives.* New York: Delacorte Press.

ORAL CULTURE AND HISTORY TODAY

Joanne Shenandoah and Jack W. Gladstone

LINDA ROSEKRANS

Between Earth and Sky—You will hear me.
Between Earth and Sky—You'll dance beside me.
I am the wind—I am the water—I am your Son—I am your daughter.
And will they listen to the stories—will they hear our ancestors call?
Will they realize what we've sacrificed to keep our music alive and well?
—JOANNE SHENANDOAH, "EARTH AND SKY"

Between earth and sky lies the understanding of what is sacred.

There are several things that need to be said by way of beginnings for this paper. Joanne Shenandoah and I spoke in August 2005. Acknowledging that I am not Haudenosaunee, she reminded me that one fundamental concept in Haudenosaunee tradition is the "Good Mind—a willingness to come together, to try to understand each other, to leave what's troubling us, personally or otherwise, behind the door" for an unclouded discussion. To establish this agreement, I want to define how the sacred will be viewed in this paper. In *The Sacred Hoop: Recovering the Feminine in American Indian Traditions*, Paula Gunn Allen (Laguna Pueblo) writes, "The word *sacred*, like the words *power* and *medicine*, has a very different meaning to tribal people than to members of technological societies. . . . There is a spirit that pervades everything, that is capable of powerful song and radiant movement, and that moves in and out of the mind. This spirit, this power of intelligence, has many names . . . the necessary precondition for material creation . . . the spirit that informs right balance, right harmony" (72). Originally, "sacred ways and practices were at the heart of living and survival. There was not a part of life that was not touched by these traditions. . . . Great respect is held for those who protect sacred ways and help them grow" (Beck et al. 1977: 4–5).

Peggy Beck and her coauthors continue, "In discussing the sacred, it might be said there are two sides to it: the personal, . . . and the part of the sacred that is shared and defined year after year through oral histories, ritual, and other ceremonies and customs" (6). That which is truly sacred to a culture remains within that culture and is not written or spoken for the public. Although I cannot and would not speak of those things sacred, I see worth in celebrating Native American artists as they gift their audiences with their celebration of the spiritual in life—that which is of the spirit—and that which is held in highest regard as most important to the teachings of the culture. Such sacred things include one's home place, language, and concept of the eternal—a concept that is at the very core of a culture's understanding of itself, through sacred teachings and stories and in traditional (sacred) language.

Today's literary canon has expanded to encompass writing recognized as both creative and critical to an expression of culture. Native American literature pushes the conventional boundaries of the canon to include oral transmission of information and events, pictorial renderings, and stories created to teach principles: ledger art, wintercount (pictorial history), oratory, and song. The Native literary tradition was historically, and remains today, oral. One of the most important literary phenomena of the last decades is a conscious decision by Native artists to render—for an audience immersed in written culture—communication in traditional ways, through structure, story, and song. Song is an ancient, continued medium of orality, transmitting traditional principles, culture, and history in first languages and English, blending words and music and old and contemporary. Two such successful Native artists are Joanne Shenandoah (Oneida) and Jack W. Gladstone (Blackfeet).

According to Shenandoah, writing/creating "is a sacred process," as well as being as necessary to her "as eating or breathing. It operates on a time frame in which everything is potentially past, present, and future." She writes "to influence in a positive way, to change lives, to effect in profound ways, to heal. Writing also communicates; it is an expression of who we are, who's influenced us, done or said something. We also write to tell stories. Stories are the backbone of who we are. Telling is part of the mission to preserve the earth, to make a peaceful and safe place for our children and their children" (2005b). I asked whom she writes for, thinking of the obvious "Native and non-Native" answer. Her response touched me deeply: It is "a responsibility for everyone to use the gifts the Creator has given." It is a choice much like "the choice a physician has in an airplane

Joanne Shenandoah. Photo: Harry Diorio.

when a passenger goes into cardiac arrest: does one use one's gift, or deny it?" Given the name Tekaliwha:kwha, or She Sings, Shenandoah is "grateful for the gift" each time she "asks and the gift of a song is given" (2005b). Song, she says, in every culture, "is what moves the earth, the heartbeat of the human spirit. It is connected to every movement made. Without it there would be no dance, no life." Music she sees as the embodiment of the spiritual self, the embodiment of one's entire being. Song—an oral tradition never interrupted—is her vehicle for preserving and honoring those stories she has heard since childhood, of communicating important principles, and of "healing the earth and those who live with it" (2005b).

From Shenandoah's earliest work, the songs she has been given have shared sacred principles of the traditional Haudenosaunee, affirming them for those within the culture and educating those of us outside it. "We Are the Iroquois" celebrates the persistence and longevity of the culture, the spiritual values that remain vibrant:

We are the Iroquois,
We're proud, we are strong,
We've held onto our culture now, Oh, for so long.
Though times have changed,
We remain the same.
We listen to our elders now,
They know the way.
Ceremonies, social dances,
Songs that we sing,
Being proud of our tradition we all feel within . . .
There are many lessons in the legends that are told.
(Shenandoah 2001)

Haudenosaunee sacred history, which provides context for "how we got here," is seen in the lyrics from the song "Beneath the Great White Pine" as well as in her album *Peacemaker's Journey* (2000). Songs in this album are sung in the Oneida language. The liner notes translate the songs and tell the story of the Peacemaker's journey—re-created by Shenandoah and her husband, historian Doug George-Kanentiio, in English—explaining its significance to the Haudenosaunee culture. At the end of the Peacemaker's journey, the notes recount:

> The People of the Longhouse raised a tall eastern white pine next to Onondaga Lake . . . the Great Tree of Peace, the branches of which touched the sky for all to see. Its four gleaming roots extended to each sacred direction around the earth. . . . An individual or nation seeking an end to war may follow the roots to the Great Tree where they were to receive shelter. On top of the Great Tree he placed a mighty eagle who was to cry out if danger approached the people. Beneath the Great Tree the leaders of this confederacy of nations formed a circle by holding hands, pledging to uphold the Great Law of Peace for all time. (Shenandoah 2000)

Another song that celebrates the history of the Haudenosaunee, as important to teaching sacred principles as is Biblical history to the teaching of Christian sacred values, is Shenandoah's composition honoring Ganondagan, a sacred Seneca site just south of Rochester (2005a). Her composition relates the historic change in the Haudenosaunee as the Peacemaker united the nations, creating the confederacy and establishing an order followed today. That the Haudenosaunee and all First Nations people continue to believe in their sacred relationship with the land is evident in the song "Treaty." Dedicated to Faithkeeper Oren Lyons, "Treaty" speaks with Haudenosaunee voices, confronting government officials with a powerful message of permanence.

> So when you seat your council, who will come to speak
> For the Buffalo, the Eagle, the forests, and the trees. . . .
> Hear me Mr. President,
> This is sacred ground.
> (Shenandoah 2001)

In the liner notes to *Covenant*, Shenandoah writes, "When our ancestors first encountered the Europeans, they made a covenant with the colonists . . . signifying that all people were to respect each other's cultures and traditions while not interfering in their respective affairs. . . . Silver was used to indicate that this peace agreement, a sacred pledge, would last forever" (2003a).

Principles for living and explanations of one's place in this world have traditionally been passed on through story, a critical component of oral culture. As elders and storytellers pass down the stories, Native writers and composers widen the circle through song. Shenandoah has set a number of traditional tales, in addition to the *Peacemaker's Journey* album, to music. Among my favorite songs are "The Seven Dancers" and "One Silver, One Gold," as I have also heard each told by elders in story circles. Retelling stories sacred to the culture allows the stories to "breathe again," as Alyce Spotted Bear aptly put it (2005). Widening the circle serves to provide an additional oral medium through which members of a culture and outsiders can both learn sacred stories. Shenandoah has extended her retelling to include a book for children called *Skywoman*, coauthored by Doug George-Kanentiio, followed by the album *Skywoman: A Symphonic Odyssey of Iroquois Legends* (2005a).

Another reemergence of the sacred manifests itself in a return to one's first language in song composition. Language holds culture; many important concepts just do not translate and, more importantly, should be expressed in their own sacred voice. According to Shenandoah in the liner notes to *Orenda*, "Ceremonial songs restore the balance between the physical and spiritual worlds. These songs are restricted to the longhouses and exclusively for the Haudenosaunee" (1998). Some, like the Thanksgiving

Address, are learned and carried in their own language and translated into other languages for educational purposes. The opening song on Shenandoah's *Covenant* (2003a) features Mohawk chief Jake Swamp delivering this prayer in both Mohawk and English. The liner notes to the album explain:

> Chief Swamp, like his traditional colleagues, has spent his adult life as an advocate for preserving the spiritual and moral values of the Haudenosaunee. He believes it is principles such as cooperation, eco-spirituality, humility, adherence to natural law, multigenerational planning, love of family, respect for elders, and compassion for other species which will ultimately come to be accepted by all nations.

Several of Shenandoah's albums—*Orenda, Covenant*—feature songs in traditional language. Says Shenandoah, "I believe that a language must be used in order to survive" (2005b). Of the meaning of "Prophecy Song" on the *Orenda* album, Shenandoah writes, "This song is to remind us to be aware of our place upon the earth and to fulfill our obligations to ourselves, our families, nations, the natural world, and to the Creator. The words say we are to awaken, stand up and be counted, for you are being recognized in the spirit world" (1998).

Shenandoah's *Matriarch* album collects traditional Oneida women's songs sung in Oneida to pay tribute to the women important in her life. In a blending and layering of several sacred traditions, another recent album, *Sisters*, records Christian hymns sung in Oneida by Shenandoah's mother, Clanmother Maisie Shenandoah, and her aunt, Elizabeth Roberts. During our interview, Shenandoah observed:

> Christianity was a significant part of our history, too much so to be ignored. The Iroquois managed to survive [the seventeenth century] with much of their indigenous culture intact, including a tradition of spiritual tolerance. One important practice was to blend ancestral social customs with Christian. To this day, many church services are conducted in Native language. (2005b)

Shenandoah explains in the liner notes to *Sisters*, "We know how vital our songs of thanksgiving are to the human heart. . . . By raising our voices in song, we extend words of gratitude to every living thing. This is the very essence of what it is to be Ukwehe:we, a True Human Being" (2003b).

Jack W. Gladstone (Blackfeet) is of the same mind: "All that is, is sacred, the great mysterious" (2005). Most captivating in his work is the constant presence of the spiritual—the sacred—the awareness that we are spiritual beings among other spiritual beings. For Gladstone, great-great-grandson of Chief Red Crow, the sacred is "the air, the oxygen, the atmosphere in which everything is placed, the wind, what informs this motion, the energy of Creation" (2005). Sharing this through song came to Gladstone as a call. In his song "Into a Child's Eyes" from the *Blackfeet Storysmith* double album (itself a collection of stories told by his father and mentor, Wallace J. Gladstone), Jack Gladstone writes, "Earth and sky are unified in story" (2004b). The stories—and awareness of their importance—were passed down through his family, centrally by his Blackfeet grandmother. She recounted the stories of her life and the mythology of their Blackfeet Indian people, something Gladstone holds sacred to this day. In his song "Legends of Glacier" from the 2004 album *Tappin' the Earth's Backbone*, he recounts:

> Grandmother's stories ignited the spark,
> Now warming the heart of a man.
> Fantastic odysseys, requested dreams,
> Were part of our first human clans.
> Elders have summoned the auras of old
> Remembered and treasured through time.

His work embraces many aspects of the sacred—retelling traditional Blackfeet tales, honoring those stories sacred to Blackfeet and other nations' cultural histories, restoring oral history through oratory (what he calls "storatory")—everything in language that reminds us that all life is fundamentally spiritual. Says Gladstone, "We sing, we heal, we grow" (2000b).

One of Gladstone's early songs, "Dyin' for a Metaphor," takes a hard look at the absence of the sacred in consumer America, responding with compassion for the plight in which this leaves Americans: "Lost we weave our way through mall-faced stores / Dyin' for a Metaphor." He continues, "What is the proper way to express what can't be seen, / For our senses grasp only a glimpse of the mystery between." But "words tumble short to say" (1992). Gladstone reminds that for the "most sacred, there are no words" (2004c), so we are "resigned to weave our way through the forest of word lore" (1992). He wishes for us, "May your love reflect the spiritual

Jack W. Gladstone.
Photo: Karen Vaughan.

into your point of view," and encourages us to "explore the metaphor to inspect what can't be seen" (1992) to "align ourselves with the eternal" (2004c). The spiritual and eternal, for Gladstone, are understood in a traditional way:

> In a bottomless sea of timeless space
> In the center of a trillion stars
> There's a circle from which we all have come
> That reflects who we are.
> From this circle we hear her seasons change
> In four scene harmony
> And from this song we know her love
> In all the Earth receives.
> From the snow pack in the highlands

Her blood flows with the Spring
Forever the Sun's lover
A songbird choir sings.
(1992, "Circle of Life")

This spiritual platform provides the context for most other songs on his albums, including but not limited to "Last Best Place," "The Sun Loom of Creation Has Spun Our Heart a Home," "Celebrate Relation with Creation," and "Tappin'," which refers not only to dancing and drumming but also to drawing strength from the Earth and the mountains—the sacred below, as well as above. In "For Those Who Cried," "miracles still work within the heart and in the mine of the human soul, where ancient rhythms flow" (2000a). "Faces the Blizzard" honors the bison, sacred to the Blackfeet, "the heart of the circle Nature formed / A covenant born" (1997). In the title song to the *Buffalo Cafe* album, we are told we will learn "about the land that taught us to talk, / With Mother's hand we learned to walk." This world is "Sun's creation"; a "symphony on waving grass / Was composed by sun and cast . . . Our Creator's voice was the thunder roll / All of creation shared one soul" (1997).

Sacred language characterizes Gladstone's expression of sacred themes and concepts—within a traditional framework, a blend of sacred language familiar from a Christian perspective. *Buffalo Cafe* invites listeners to "Nature's anointed play." In "Faces the Blizzard," the word "covenant" has meaning within a Biblical context. In lines addressed to the buffalo, "But for you, my black-hooved brother / whose flesh through us was reborn," the listener hears of the buffalo's importance as a source of food and survival, but as Gladstone reminds, "A deeper reading recognizes the Catholic sacrament of the Eucharist, where one is reborn through partaking. It is, in its deepest form, language of reverence and identification, and reaffirmation in the telling" (1997). The bison, "blackfooted, is connected to the Blackfeet, people of the buffalo," observes Gladstone (2005). The older, soft "thee"—familiar from the King James translation of the Bible—graces both Gladstone's early love songs and the last track on the *Storysmith* album, "Into a Child's Eyes," which speaks of one important moment of the sacred: passing from this mortal world to the next. A song honoring Western artist C. M. Russell takes its title from his painting "When the Land Belonged to God," called by Gladstone an "epiphany of spirit" (1997). At the end of the song, at the end of mortal life, "as we choose our trail up the Great Divide to an unknown stage on the other side," the "land belongs to God" (1997). On this mortal plane, European "cashiers and surveyors" subdued and transformed Western landscapes, but in sacred time all life is still properly aligned. "Legacy," a song set in the Pacific Northwest, recalls an "earlier year, when cedars brushed the sky and the land was in line with God" (1998). Of the blend and sometimes juxtaposition of images Christian and traditional, Gladstone reflects that he is "realigning with sacred imagery and language learned as a Catholic, applied to something more relevant" to himself as a person (2005).

Jack Gladstone reminds us that "mythos, 'myth,' means original or sacred words" (2004c). Sacred stories place one in the fabric of one's life; the storyteller weaves the fabric. Gladstone grew up hearing traditional stories from his grandmother. In each album he returns to the oral telling of these Blackfeet stories, sometimes as ballads: of Poia, "who ventures to the Lodge of the Sun to win the love of a girl" ("Noble Heart"); the Bear Who Stole the Chinook; the girl who was taken by the Sun to be his bride and the boy who loves her ("To Marry the Sun"); and Kut-oy-is, "Blood Clot Boy," an ancient Blackfeet superhero. Stories of Napi (Old Man), Blackfeet trickster and culture hero, "contain principles" (Gladstone 2005), lessons to build character, as Napi attempts to understand another species by asking to transform to become a wolf:

In the long ago time in this homeland of mine
Old Man roamed far and alone
His fascination led to the tale of Napi Becomes a Wolf.
"As we all grow old, it's through choice we grow wise,
Napi listen close if you can,
Through this transformation you may realize the love that binds our
    wolf clan."
And then by choice Napi fell under his medicine spell
He woke behind eyes of different sheen.
His new ears heard the world and each moment unfurled
The Sacred within every living thing
When Napi Became a Wolf.
(Gladstone 1997, "Napi Becomes")

In a contemporary song about the history of Dineh (Navajo) codetalkers, to provide the proper cultural context for the codetalkers' decision to contribute the gift of their language to U.S. military efforts, Gladstone sets a portion of the Dineh creation story—the Changing Woman Suite:

In the beginning First Man and First Woman lived as one
The first couple forged the Sun. . . .
On a cradleboard of sunrays and rainbows came a girl
She nursed on dew and pollen from her mom
Changing Woman.
(1995, "Codetalkers")

This segment creates, the composer explains, an "ethereal, dreamlike oasis in the midst of the horrible turbulence of war; it opens the sky with Creation, . . . stalking the spirit to capture it, placing it into melodic and rhythmic form as a gift to the people" (2004c). A lighter but far from irreverent lesson about a traditional spiritual being is Gladstone's "Thunderman" on the *Tappin' the Earth's Backbone* album. Prepared for the moment that "Thunderman gets his own TV series," Gladstone brings to a popular setting knowledge of "Thunder Chief, . . . a personification of the ultimate power" and giver of the Thunder Medicine Pipe to the Blackfeet people (2004a).

Gladstone also honors the sacred by restoring sacred history told through oratory, oral again in song. In "Beneath Another Sky," Gladstone restores voice to Heinmot Tooyalakekt, Chief Joseph of the Nez Perce:

From the corner of the universe, my soul has found a pen,
For I believe this story must be told again,
Not by some historian, not by some bleeding heart,
But by the man who saw the web of justice spun apart.
In the year of eighteen sixty-three, according to their Lord. (1997)

In "Colter's Run," Gladstone gives voice to a new narrator. Both invoking and inverting the Christian story of Genesis, oral historian Adam, Old Man's son (not the first man), tells a revised version of the story of mountain man John Colter, this time from the Blackfeet perspective:

My name is Adam, Old Man's son,
I've seen four hundred springs.
I'm what you'd call an oral historian
By nature do I sing.
And now it's time to set the record straight about John Colter's run
The tale that spun forth from his lips was stitched with buffalo chips.
(1997)

Awarded the Montana State University Human Rights Award for Outstanding Community Service as a bridge builder between cultures, Gladstone builds sacred bridges. His early song "Spiritual Brothers," written in 1990 with cowboy musician Rob Quist and included in *Legacy* (1998), celebrates their deep friendship—brothers from different cultures, approaching Montana from different backgrounds but together in spirit:

> Many years, we have lived
> Across the river of fears
> My father rode a brand new country
> Your father rode a trail of tears . . .
> For a Spiritual Brother of a different color
> Isn't always easy to find
> And the time has come
> For the children of the ones who survived
> To leave that river behind.

At a time when we most needed compassionate spirits, Jack Gladstone penned a song with Ken Flint, "Letter to the World," calling for us to remember that, although theologically divided, we are all "children of God." In the days after September 11, 2001, as Gladstone says he "struggled to transcend fear and anger," he both reminded America that this was not new—that earlier terrorist attacks had been perpetuated against Native villages by the U.S. military—and called for healing through "selflessness within" and the care of a "loving mother and children" (2004a).

In an earlier song rereleased on the *Storysmith* album, about culture hero Kut-oy-is, Gladstone set all into perspective:

> We're awake in the twenty-first century
> Inside a hungry beast
> Of our own righteous design.
> Be it a system or addiction
> Or a serpent in a tree
> It's the heart that we must listen for
> It's the heart that we must find
> Through legends and lore.
> "Earth and sky are unified in story." (2004b)

Through story in song, both Joanne Shenandoah and Jack Gladstone provide for First Nations and non-Native audiences the cultural bridges and the spirit of healing to celebrate the sacred in all, for all. Their work is of paramount importance among the sacred stories of Native America.

RECORDINGS

Joanne Shenandoah
(www.joanneshenandoah.com)
All recordings by Silver Wave Records. *Joanne Shenandoah* (1989); *Matriarch* (1996); *Orenda* (1998); *Peacemaker's Journey* (2000); *Eagle Cries* (2001); *Covenant* (2003a); *Sisters* (2003b); *Skywoman: A Symphonic Odyssey of Iroquois Legends* (2005a).

Jack W. Gladstone
(www.hawkstone.com)
All but one recorded by Glacier Pacific Productions. *Buckskin Poet Society* (1992); *Noble Heart* (1995); *Buffalo Cafe* (1997); *Legacy* (Hawkstone Productions, 1998); *Buffalo Republic* (2000a); *Tappin' the Earth's Backbone* (2004a); *Blackfeet Storysmith* (2004b).

WORKS CITED

Allen, Paula Gunn. 1992. *The Sacred Hoop: Recovering the Feminine in American Indian Traditions*. Boston: Beacon Press.
Beck, Peggy V., et al. 1977. *The Sacred*. Tsaile, Ariz: Navajo Community College Press.
Gladstone, Jack W. 2000b. Interview by Linda Rosekrans, November. Transcript.
———. 2004c. Interview by Linda Rosekrans, February. Transcript.
———. 2005. Interview by Linda Rosekrans, August. Transcript.
LaDuke, Winona. 2005. *Recovering the Sacred: The Power of Naming and Claiming*. Cambridge, Mass.: South End Press.
Shenandoah, Joanne. 2005b. Interview by Linda Rosekrans, August. Transcript.
Spotted Bear, Alyce. 2005. Interview by Linda Rosekrans, August. Transcript.

"Oral Culture and History Today: Joanne Shenandoah and Jack W. Gladstone" first appeared in *Voices: The Journal of New York Folklore* 33, nos. 3-4 (Fall–Winter 2007): 35–40.

CITIES WITHIN THE CITY

Ben Botkin's New York

MICHAEL L. MURRAY

> "Al Smith made the sidewalks of New York popular," said a Sawkill poultry farmer to me, "but we sent them in from here." He was referring to the Ulster County [New York] bluestone, quarried by Irish workers toward the middle of the last century, and worn by the feet of immigrants who came here expecting instead to find streets paved with gold.
>
> —BEN BOTKIN, *NEW YORK CITY FOLKLORE*

Although born in Boston, Benjamin A. Botkin was sometimes more comfortable with his New York identity than with his New England roots. As an undergraduate at Harvard, he confronted and overcame his childhood struggles against anti-Semitism and Brahmin attitudes, and he remained proud of this experience throughout his life (Hirsch 1996). Yet New York City represented his cosmopolitan ideal, and it would become both a rich inspiration for his scholarship and his home. Botkin first came to New York in 1920 to earn a master's degree in English literature at Columbia University, and he returned to the city in 1923 to spend two more years teaching "Americanization" and English to immigrants. In 1938, he traveled to New York as the national folklore editor for the Federal Writers' Project. And later, when he decided to pursue a career as a freelance writer, Botkin returned again to the city (Botkin 1946). Settling in Croton-on-Hudson, a northern suburb, he routinely traveled into the city, writing about it, collecting its lore, and considering its role in the folk culture of the Middle Atlantic region.

As a scholar, Botkin allied himself with regionalism and its efforts to explore the local character of American culture. This interest, including his appreciation for Lewis Mumford and his understanding of the role of the metropolis in regional culture, deeply influenced Botkin's own studies

A Russian dancer in lower Manhattan celebrates the American Bicentennial in 1976. Photo: Katrina Thomas.

of the folklore of his adopted urban place, New York City (Botkin 1935). Many years before academic folklorists began to consider the folk culture of urban spaces (Dorson, Dégh, and Moss 1970), Botkin looked to the unique character of life in New York City and saw the ways in which the urban experience both provided a place of union between the indigenous and the metropolitan and inspired the emergence of new traditions that expressed the reality of modern life. With his regionalist's attention to the relationship between art and place, Botkin turned many times in his scholarship to the nature of life in New York City. He considered all aspects of urban and suburban life in his attempt to uncover the personality of New York and to characterize the folklore of what, for him, became the quintessential urban place.

As Jerrold Hirsch notes, Botkin never attached to New York City the same "symbolic importance" he afforded his tenure at Harvard. Nevertheless, the city had a deep impact on his understanding of folklore and modernity in the urban world (1996: 315). New York was the city where the intellectual richness of modern life became a reality. It was home to new works of literature composed and published within the city, as well as Old World tales brought directly from Old World nations.

Botkin, well before others in the discipline, understood that modernity was not a threat to traditional culture but rather an important influence on existing and emerging folk expressions. As Bruce Jackson wrote, he "refused to distinguish between what people wrote, what happened in a movie, and what was said on a street corner. For him, the stuff and process of folklore were truly protean" (1986: 29). Botkin's theory of folklore was ideally suited to the protean nature of New York City's streets. He often wrote about the character of urban life in his *New York Folklore Quarterly* column, "Downstate, Upstate," explaining in 1953 the difference between the state's folklorists as typified by the diverse and ever-growing qualities of urban culture. "The real difference between Downstate and Upstate folklore and folklorists," he wrote, "is the difference between the 'sounds of our times' and those of other times" (Botkin and Tyrrell 1953: 232). The folklore of urban and suburban New York City was something emerging in time, realized in the daily lives of a cosmopolitan folk; rural folklore echoed traditions that emerged from a historical landscape.

In this contrast, the metropolis becomes a unique place that requires attention to the forces of change defining its folklore. The specific character of life in the metropolis shapes and colors the lives of its inhabitants in all the forms and places of that expression. Carrying this concept into practice, Botkin saw the exploration of New York City's folk culture as a natural extension of his research into America's regional culture. He would break up the metropolitan regions—the various neighborhoods and quarters of the boroughs and the metropolitan area—and consider how the culture in each was shaped by occupational, neighborhood, and ethnic affiliations.

In the introduction to *New York City Folklore* (1956), his collection of folklore and folk-say[1] from the city, Botkin illustrates this process by mapping New York City as a "circle or wheel whose center or hub is Manhattan and whose radii or spokes are the boroughs of the Bronx, Brooklyn, Queens, and Richmond radiating into the metropolitan hinterland" (xvi). In his visualization, he translates the city's geographic reality into a figurative image. The rigid right angles of the urban grid are transformed into the circles and spokes that make up the wheel. Botkin saw the neighborhoods as cities within the city and was fascinated by the ways in which New York's streets, buildings, and people were known and navigated in terms of a sense of urban space.

On the sidewalks of New York, Botkin recognized a relationship between culture and space that was later echoed by Michel de Certeau, who wrote that New York City's reality exists somewhere on the streets "below the thresholds at which visibility begins" (1984: 93). Walking, for de

Certeau, is the fundamental form by which the New Yorker experiences the city. In the bustle of everyday life, city dwellers make their way through a metaphorical place, which sits transparently on the literal and readable city. The reality of this experiential city is realized through *practice* rather than geography or geometry. The walkers in the city are at work building a myth of the city, charting its spaces based on routines of navigating and dwelling within its landscape (de Certeau 1984: 93, 102). Botkin understood and valued this experiential connection to urban space and urban life, and he stressed to his WPA fieldworkers in New York City that they would learn of the "relation between art and life, between work and culture" almost naturally "on the sidewalks of New York skipping rope and bouncing ball" (Botkin 1939: 7). Botkin developed a strategy of urban ethnography, which took into account the city's unique personality, created by the lives and lore of its people and the shape, smells, and sounds of its physical form. Eventually, he worked this theory of urban culture into his own writing on New York in his efforts to define the city's personality through its lore.

When Botkin came to New York City to train his WPA fieldworkers, he examined the city through his regionalist's lens. Thinking of the neighborhoods as regions within the metropolis, he suggested a modified regional approach to their study. He instructed his fieldworkers to travel to the places where New Yorkers lived and worked and played to uncover the relations between place, art, and life. He wrote, "We learned early in the game that you cannot collect folklore by simply walking the streets of the city. Folklore is not on the surface" (1958: 193). Rather, folklore dwells within the spokes of New York City's wheel. It is latent in the neighborhoods, the cities within a city, which produce unique expressions in and of unique urban habitats. If the "key to living lore" is, as Botkin wrote in his *New York Folklore Quarterly* essay of the same name, "the relating of the foreground, lore, to its background in life," then the places his informants lived would naturally be an excellent point of departure (1958: 191).

A WPA fieldworker quoted by Botkin characterized the relationship between art and life in the city as a business of "bread and song." The phrase emerged from an interview with a Yugoslavian tailor who tried to sing a song for the fieldworker but was frustrated and unable to concentrate. The tailor tells the fieldworker, "We ought to live, too. Something happen if this keep up. . . . If I could only put my head to it for a few hours, I could make a few songs." The fieldworker replies first by placing herself within the tailor's New York: "Oh, don't be worried. I understand. You see,

The San Gennaro Day feast on Mott Street in Manhattan's Little Italy is New York's largest and longest "street party," usually lasting about ten days. The greased pole climb is no longer performed because of liability issues; this image was taken in 1978. Photo: Katrina Thomas.

I don't come from Park Avenue either." Persistent in recording a song, she eventually embraces her own statement of solidarity and confesses,

> My, how you lied! You certainly didn't sing when you had no bread! You couldn't remember your own name, never mind about where you lived four years ago. And your voice was so weak the relief investigator told you to take a couple of sips of water to moisten your throat! . . . Great thing this bread and song business! Messy world, messy world! We're all in the same boat—Yugoslav, Mayflower descendant, all mixed up on this bread and song thing. (quoted in Botkin 1939: 7)

For Botkin, research into urban experience required fieldworkers to establish this degree of empathy with the folk of the city and pay attention to the nature of life in the depressed streets of the WPA era. As much as this particular fieldworker was occupied by "this bread and song thing," she connected with the tailor as a fellow laborer struggling in a city where Park Avenue represents a foreign land, and the city's social cacophony blurs lines of ethnicity and is obscured by sentiments of neighborhood and labor.

Botkin later noted that for the WPA projects, the neighborhood approach did not succeed in practice. He and the fieldworkers found the city's map sometimes too difficult to decipher, its many neighborhoods and streets too complex an entrée into the culture, even though he acknowledged the importance of place in studying the city. This, however, was a practical matter that did not alter Botkin's conviction that folklore should broaden its focus to include the contemporary, the industrial, and the urban worlds (Mangione 1983: 269–270). His attention to the living lore and folk-say of New York City, in the summer of 1938 and later, suggested a new way of conceptualizing folklore in the urban experience and a new way of studying it. In his introduction to the 1954 collection *Sidewalks of America*, Botkin wrote, "For years American Folklorists from the cities have been going into the Kentucky mountains and other remote places to gather folk songs and stories, while all the time folklore was all around them on the sidewalks of America" (vii). When Botkin's main sounding boards, the *New York Folklore Quarterly* and the New York Folklore Society, were formed in 1945, many of the founding members were teachers and professors who lived in New York City and had been introduced to the WPA's new way of viewing urban culture.

Other folklorists publishing on the city in *New York Folklore Quarterly* also focused on this characterization of the urban as possessing a personality. From Bayrd Still's 1958 *New York Folklore Quarterly* essay "The Personality of New York City," we learn that part of the folklore in and of the city is a reflection of its distinctive personality. This personality is based on the city's corporeal features—the towering profile of the New York City skyline, the odors of car exhaust and roasted chestnuts filling Times Square in the winter. Another element is the stamp on the landscape made by its inhabitants, their daily lives, and their personal histories. As Keith Basso writes of a sense of place, it is a product of becoming aware of one's attachment to "features of the physical world" (Basso 1996: 55). Still explained, "few will deny that cities, like people, have distinguishing features—personalities if you will—which make one urban community different from another" (1958: 83). Life in the city and the city itself are intertwined in the popular imagination such that the identities of its citizens come to publicly represent the metropolis, as do its corporeal features and sensual characteristics. Still once noted in an interview, "the city has a 'unique and heady essence,' blended . . . of 'the dry, astringent odor of

ozone and gasoline' and 'the scent of open spaces caught up in the towering metropolis'" (1958: 84). In writing about the personality of New York
City, Still acknowledged the city as a unique place that required a different
sort of investigation.

His reading suggests that although the countryside, too, has landscapes,
smells, and sounds that could suggest a personality, that personality is
stable in the memories of its inhabitants. The city, on the other hand, is
different: memories of it are never stable, buildings emerge overnight, and
citizens from entirely different lands arrive by the boatload every morning. The result is a New York City that for Still and Botkin was defined by
its constant change (Still 1958: 90). Art critic Lucy Lippard would later observe this same sense of a dynamic urban space, noting how the city's nervous state of excess exponentially increases the "social cacophony" within
it (1997: 200). The city is said to have a dizzying effect on its inhabitants,
who are constantly presented with new and unrecognizable forms.

Raymond Williams, referring to industrialized England, suggested that
the urban citizen in such a context could do one of two things: "we can
retreat, for security, into a deep subjectivity, or we can look around us for
social pictures, social signs, social messages, to which, characteristically,
we try to relate as individuals but so as to discover, in some form, community" (1973: 295). Central to Botkin's study of New York City folklore
was recognition that these two strategies for life in the urban environment
produced a different form of folklore, which required a different frame for
investigation by folklorists. Interest in urban culture sparked a conversation on the differences between the rural folklife of upstate New York and
the cosmopolitan and ethnic folklife of downstate.

According to Botkin, any separation between the two comes from the
antiquarian nature of the rural experience versus the lived and emergent
character of the urban experience. The city has a unique personality, created by the lives and lore of its people and the shape, smell, and sounds
of its physical presence, and this personality becomes defined by the constant shifts in these elements. The urban place's lore is thus characterized
by creative force and emergence from a rapidly changing experience.

In his notes at the end of the 1953 downstate issue of *New York Folklore
Quarterly*, Botkin compares the character of urban folklore studies with
their rural counterpart:

But the real difference between Downstate and Upstate folklore and
folklorists, as I see it, is the difference between the "sounds of our

times" and those of other times, between complicated and confused ways of life and "ways of life followed by those who live simple, unnoticed lives." . . . An interest in the "sounds of our times" implies not a break with the past but a quest for continuity and for what might be called a "usable present." And that is not to negate what we can learn from the old-timers, such as helping us to know our place in the long stream of cultural tradition. (Botkin and Tyrrell 1953: 232)

The nature of life in the city, with its complicated interactions of many different cultures and its constantly shifting possibilities of experience, produced for Botkin a type of lore that is conspicuously a "sound of our times." In this characterization, the downstate folklorists approached folklore as the fantasies, games, and stories that emerge from the unique character of city life.

One of *New York Folklore Quarterly*'s most compelling analyses of the urban experience comes from Botkin's essay in the 1965 New York City issue. In this piece he introduces Fanya Del Bourgo's essay "Love in the City," a transcription from an interview conducted by Botkin. During the interview, Botkin was exploring the upstate-downstate dichotomy; he asked, "How did love in the city differ from love in the country?" Although she had no experience of the country, Del Bourgo, a dance instructor in Croton-on-Hudson, laid out an autobiographical account that linked her coming of age to the city's many places. "She told how and where young people got together," Botkin wrote in his introduction, "in the East Side, in Brooklyn, in Coney Island, on a Bear Mountain boat, in a Catskill summer camp, in Greenwich Village in the Jazz era. And what their romantic customs and diversions, attractions and interests, freedoms and restrictions were at various stages of growing up, from the time she first learned about sex on the East Side docks to her 'intellectual life' in the Village where 'It was all very poetic'" (Del Bourgo 1965: 165). Although he intended to discuss with her the differences between rural and urban experience, Botkin noted that she couched her current suburban identity in her urban experiences and that much of that urban life history must be couched in her immigrant childhood.

Here Botkin makes an effort—rarely made before in essays concerning New York City—to place a storyteller within the context of her social and cultural history (Botkin 1965). In this analysis, the city is at once—as Barbara Kirshenblatt-Gimblett (1983) would later call it—the locus and the focus; it is the place where Del Bourgo lives, making her story a New York City experience, but it is also a history of life in New York City as it affects the formation of a personal identity. In this essay Botkin echoes a statement he made about the nature of the city in his collection *Sidewalks of America*: "The hero of this book—the city—has many faces and many voices" (1954, vii). In nominating the city to hero status, Botkin suggests that the folklore of the city is shaped by the relationship between its citizens and their environment. The city has many faces and many voices, each constructing narratives—whether about a secluded spot for an assignation on Riverside Drive or a spiel to would-be customers in Times Square. The city is indeed the hero of Botkin's book, as it is the force responded to in the folklore of New Yorkers.

PHOTOGRAPHING NEW YORK'S NEIGHBORHOODS

When Congress passed new immigration laws in 1965 admitting many nationalities that had been excluded, freelance photographer Katrina Thomas, whose photographs accompany this article, sensing that the United States was not truly a "melting pot," decided to document the traditions that immigrant groups were celebrating in their new country.

Her photographs capture the full range of New York City's rich diversity, from Chinese New Year and nationality days and parades in the five boroughs to Italian, Greek Orthodox, Russian, and Ukrainian feast days. Less well known are celebrations of Buddha's birthday, the Eid (Muslim), Diwali (Hindu), and Baisahki (Sikh).

Secular festivals that Thomas has photographed include the parade of Caribbean cultures on Brooklyn's Eastern Parkway in September, in which West Indians wearing elaborate costumes proceed on roller skates to the accompaniment of steel bands; Irish hurling in Gaelic Park in Manhattan; and Puerto Rican teams playing softball and baseball in Central Park.

Her project coincided with a surge of interest in ethnic identity. No longer ashamed of speaking imperfect English, newcomers were demonstrating pride in their culture. By 1976, the melting pot had given way to a "cultural mosaic." On the Fourth of July of the Bicentennial, New York City, like many cities across the country, celebrated its ethnic heritage by building platforms and stages for performers and folk dance groups. Public festivals were soon being held in parks and plazas around the year. Katrina Thomas has contributed her collection of images to City Lore, 72 East First Street, New York, NY 10003, 212 529-1955.

NOTES

1. Botkin's term "folk-say," coined in 1929, went beyond academic terminology to indicate that folklore involves a dynamic, contemporary linguistic process in which storytelling is very important.

WORKS CITED

Basso, Keith. 1996. "Wisdom Sits in Places: Notes on a Western Apache Landscape." In *Senses of Place*, 53–89. Edited by Steven Feld and Keith Basso. Santa Fe: School of American Research Press.

Botkin, B. A. 1935. "We Talk about Regionalism: North, East, South, and West." *The Frontier: A Magazine of the Northwest* 13 (May): 286–296.

———. 1939. "WPA and Folklore Research: 'Bread and Song.'" *Southern Folklore Quarterly* 3 (1): 7–14.

———. 1946. "Living Lore of the New York City Writers' Project." *New York Folklore Quarterly* 2 (3): 252–263.

———. 1954. *Sidewalks of America: Folklore, Legends, Sagas, Traditions, Customs, Songs, Stories, and Sayings of City Folk*. Indianapolis: Bobbs-Merrill.

———. 1956. *New York City Folklore: Legends, Tall Tales, Anecdotes, Stories, Sagas, Heroes and Characters, Customs, Traditions, and Sayings*. New York: Random House.

———. 1958. "We Called It 'Living Lore.'" *New York Folklore Quarterly* 14 (3): 189–201.

———. 1965. Postscript to "Love in the City." *New York Folklore Quarterly* 21 (3): 231–233.

Botkin, B. A., and William G. Tyrrell. 1953. "Upstate, Downstate: Folklore News and Notes." *New York Folklore Quarterly* 9 (3): 231–238.

De Certeau, Michel. 1984. *The Practice of Everyday Life*. Translated by Steven Rendall. Berkeley: University of California Press.

Del Bourgo, Fanya. 1965. "Love in the City." *New York Folklore Quarterly* 21 (3): 165–178.

Dorson, Richard M., Linda Dégh, and Leonard W. Moss. 1970. "Is There a Folk in the City?" *Journal of American Folklore* 83: 185–228.

Hirsch, Jerrold. 1996. "My Harvard Accent and 'Indifference': Notes toward a Biography of B. A. Botkin." *Journal of American Folklore* 109 (433): 308–319.

Jackson, Bruce. 1986. "Ben Botkin." *New York Folklore* 12 (3-4): 23–32.

Kirshenblatt-Gimblett, Barbara. 1983. "The Future of Folklore Studies in America: The Urban Frontier." *Folklore Forum* 16 (2): 175–233.

Lippard, Lucy R. 1997. *The Lure of the Local: Senses of Place in a Multicentered Society*. New York: The New Press.

Mangione, Jerre. 1983. *The Dream and the Deal: The Federal Writers' Project, 1935–1943*. Philadelphia: University of Pennsylvania Press.

Still, Bayrd. 1958. "The Personality of New York City." *New York Folklore Quarterly* 14 (2): 83–92.

Williams, Raymond. 1973. *The Country and the City*. Oxford: Oxford University Press.

"Cities within the City: Ben Botkin's New York" first appeared in *Voices: The Journal of New York Folklore* 29, nos. 1-2 (Spring–Summer 2003): 34–38.

RITUAL AND STORYTELLING

A Passover Tale

BARBARA MYERHOFF

INTRODUCTION BY STEVE ZEITLIN

I was privileged to meet anthropologist Barbara Myerhoff on two occasions prior to her untimely death at the age of fifty in 1985. The first was when my wife, Amanda, and I invited both Myerhoff and Barbara Kirshenblatt-Gimblett to a consultants' meeting at our Washington, D.C., apartment for a project called the Grand Generation. I can vividly recall Myerhoff's remarkable beauty and her humor—and I fondly recollect these two brilliant women bragging to one another about the bargains they had gotten on various items of clothing they were wearing at the time.

I met Barbara Myerhoff again at a second meeting after I had moved to New York. She was already an iconic figure, having written *Number Our Days* and completed a film with the same title, which won an Academy Award in 1976. I remember asking her if success had changed her. She said, you know, it's at the point now where I walk into the restroom at the university, and students follow me in and keep talking right through the stall. Today, as her students, we're still doing that: continuing the conversation across death. I also remember her telling me that people in academe put so much emphasis on writing and not enough on talking—and talking is so important.

Myerhoff's astonishing talk, "Ritual and Storytelling: A Passover Tale," published here in an abbreviated version, captures the rhythm of her words and her vivid and distinctive train of thought, bringing the reader into the classroom of one of the discipline's finest lecturers. As an anthropologist with a poet's gift for language, she utilizes the tools of ethnography—a remarkable ethnographic eye—to explore the familiar: a Passover seder. In adapting the piece for magazine publication, I had to cut Myerhoff's essay in half; I urge all of you who enjoy this abridged version to buy the book from which it is excerpted, *Stories as Equipment for Living: Last Talks and Tales of Barbara Myerhoff*, where you may read it in its entirety.

Some months after Myerhoff's death in January 1985, we held an event in her honor. It was City Lore's first public event, and Myerhoff's ideas of "re-membering" and her vision of the way culture is transmitted set forth in this essay informs our work, always.

Barbara Myerhoff's talk was given at the Brookdale Center on Aging at Hunter College on June 6, 1983. It was part of a series of public lectures on late-life creativity, organized by Marc Kaminsky at the Brookdale Center's Institute on Humanities, Arts, and Aging and funded by the New York Council for the Humanities.

I would like to talk to you about a ritual that is built around storytelling. It is what we would call a meta-story—that is, a story about telling the story, about passing on to the progeny the experience of the ancestors, and it's a familiar one to many of you. I like working with familiar materials because there are almost always elements whose specialness and profundity we have overlooked, and I think that looking at familiar materials retrieves them and gives them to us with a freshness that makes them more intense and more effective. The ritual I'm going to talk about is Passover. . . .

The work I'm going to describe comes out of a longer study of *yiddishkeit* called the "Transmission of an Endangered Tradition." A number of us at the University of Southern California studied the transmission of yiddishkeit through various means—ritual, story, performance, and folk art. We videotaped many events and then proceeded, over the course of two years, to look at them and look at them and look at them. This, then, is what I'm going to tell you: the story of a Passover seder that we videotaped. It's a four-hour-long tape that we looked at again and again to try to figure out what was going on there. What makes this so important is that this is, indeed, the study of the transmission of culture. . . . We look at their world as a set of meanings, a web of understandings, that they somehow have to animate. And this, then, becomes our task: to see them seeing themselves.

Now as we looked at this ritual—this storytelling ritual, this performance of a story—trying to figure out what was going on and how to tell other people what was going on, what quickly became apparent to us was that we were struggling to tell two stories at the same time. One is the chronological story of the ritual, which has a certain set of procedures, of fixed events that have to occur in a given order, and the other is the story of the family that is performing the ritual. And every family performs it differently, and every year it is performed differently, although one of the great myths about ritual is that it is always the same. This is the essence of ritual. It is the story that says: This is always the same.

But of course it isn't. Common sense—which ritual banishes, and which it is supposed to banish in order to induce belief—tells us that, if we look at it immediately, every ritual has to be different. There are different performers, it's a different world, a different year. And yet we accept the claim to perpetuity that ritual makes. Because it is rhythmic, because it is repetitive, because it uses a special vocabulary, all ritual takes ordinary things and makes them extraordinary. The means it uses are everywhere the same. Whether it's an African initiation ceremony in Botswana or a Jewish storytelling session in Los Angeles, ritual sets the ordinary apart by its use of language, gesture, costume, posture—sensuous things. And those sensuous things are very persuasive and invite us to suspend disbelief, exactly as we do in a theater. . . .

Now let me briefly say what Passover is. This is a formal holiday celebrated each spring by Jews since the time of the dispersion from Palestine, after the destruction of the Temple. They are admonished to assemble to retell the story of their deliverance from Egypt and from slavery. This is the heart of the story: the release from affliction, the release from oppression. This leads to a reaffirmation of the wandering through the desert where, at the end of forty-nine days, they receive the Covenant on Mount Sinai, and the Torah is given, and the Jews come into being as a constituted entity. The Bible requires that this account of exodus and freedom be repeated. The parents tell it to the children every year when the children are told to ask, "Why do we assemble?" They are asking: What's special about Passover, in addition to that historical or mythical event, so that this is the only formal holiday of this seriousness that takes place in the home, instead of the synagogue? Friends are there, family members are there, personal ties give the whole thing its context. It takes place among one's primary group, so that sacred beliefs are again put in touch with the ordinary people of one's life, and those ordinary people take on an extra dimension. They become the characters in the great drama itself. And this revitalizes family relations. It doesn't always make them harmonious or even affectionate, but it certainly intensifies them. . . .

Let me tell you about the text. It is called the Haggadah, which means, literally, "the telling." There are many versions of this book. Now people write their own to suit their present circumstances. Different families have their own version, and they don't like the others. Within families, there are often arguments about which version to use. If the critical one got lost, this is a big problem. But no matter what the version, there is always some written text called the Haggadah, which will always be followed. And that is what you call, in anthropology, part of the Great Tradition. This is the allegedly permanent, official, written record of how the story is to be told, with stage directions: Now you drink a glass of wine. Now you hide a piece of matzoh.

Then there is the oral tradition that goes alongside this. "Well, this is the part we leave out." "That's where Aunt Sadie put in this other part." "Aren't you going to do this one?" "No, we don't have time for that. Let's do this one instead." Often the agreements that come out of these differences get penciled in. And so a family's history can be read in and through its Haggadah. We have a group of people who are doing this together year in and year out. The participants are always changing somewhat. Someone has died, someone has been born, someone is out of town, someone brings a guest. But there is some stable group of people who are always present year after year, and they, in effect, become the elders who guard the tradition.

So their family story over the years, their oral stories, their particular histories go along with this Great Tradition. The Little Tradition of local people on the ground, alive in time, goes along with the Great Story, and they intermingle, contradict one another, and jog along more or less side by side, hopefully ending at the same time. So these two stories, then, are simultaneously told: the Great Story, which is in the Haggadah and which is written down, the written tradition and history of how the people came out of Egypt and received the Covenant, and the individual family story. And these become inseparable, because you cannot understand the one without the other. You are reading both stories at the same time. The seder is contrapuntal.

The other thing that makes this a special event, a particular kind of ritual, is that the children must be present. The whole point of it is for one of the children—allegedly, the youngest son—to ask the leader, "Wherefore is this night different from all other nights?" This is the first of the Four Questions, which the child asks at the beginning of the seder. This is a marvelous piece because it permits the child to say, "Why are we doing this? What's this ritual for? Why do we lean tonight? Why do we eat bitters? Why do we eat of unleavened bread?" All these questions are saying:

What's all the specialness for? And this is a set-up. You can almost hear the voice of the Great Tradition say: Ah, I thought you'd never ask. It's what makes the whole thing happen. . . .

Children are obviously very symbolic. They represent many things: the future, innocence; above all, they are symbols of perpetuity. So the children have to be present throughout the seder. Ideally, they should be awake, but because the seder goes on a long time, it's not guaranteed. So various devices are put in to make sure the children are awake throughout. There are songs, there are riddles, and there are all sorts of opportunities and invitations for misbehavior. It is understood that the children will get drunk because everyone present has to drink four cups of wine. The children usually tipple throughout the evening. They spill and they drink, and they spill and they drink. There is an opportunity, which I will describe later, when they are actually encouraged and allowed to spill. This is quite a thrill. And then there is an actual ransom of a piece of matzoh.

Now matzoh, which is unleavened bread, is the symbolic food that is eaten during the eight days of Passover. There is a very important piece of matzoh called the *afikoman*, which is understood as dessert, and it is broken. The ceremony cannot be completed until its two halves are reassembled. So it has become the custom for the leader to break this piece of matzoh and put it in a conspicuous place where a child will see it and steal it and hide it. And the child holds it for a ransom. After dinner, when there is more ceremony to do—by then it is usually very late, and everyone is very tired and impatient—the seder cannot be completed, and the Messiah will never come, unless the afikoman is recovered. But the child does not give it back until the leader pays for it, and the payment varies with the times and the economic community. It can be a bicycle, and it can be a quarter—it all depends on what you can get away with. . . .

All this brings us to a particular Passover, the four-hour one we taped. It was a four-generational ceremony. It took place in the home of an old couple—East European, Yiddishists, not Orthodox people. Arnold was then ninety-two, Bella was eighty-nine. He was something of a poet and a writer, a philosopher. She in old age had become an artist, and a rather serious one. Their daughter, who is my closest friend and my age, was then in her middle forties. Deena is a feminist, a poet herself, divorced. Her two sons, Marc and Greg, were twenty and nineteen at the time. A non-Jewish girlfriend of one of the boys was present. They were both religiously ignorant, with the same nostalgia, yearning back to the tradition but feeling they did not really possess it—really lost as to their own way, but full of desire for something Jewish that was their own. I was present with my husband and my two sons, who were then six and nine. There were a bunch of older people who dropped in during the course of the evening, Yiddishists, all of them, who had carried on a long conversation, day in and day out, with the old couple. . . .

So there we were, all assembled. Now for many a year—I have been going to these seders for many a year—Arnold has been flirting with some essence: he has begun the seder by saying, "This will be my last seder." And that is difficult to receive on many levels. It has to be treated with respect and also with a measure of skepticism. He announced it this year as he had in the past. . . .

Arnold was very aware that his grandsons didn't know anything Jewishly, and he wanted this tradition passed on. So after saying the opening prayers, he introduced his older grandson and said, "My grandson Marc will lead the seder." Greg had been given a chance to lead the seder a couple of years before. So Marc was expecting this, and he said under his breath as he came into the house, "If he tells me to lead it and breaks in and interrupts it and takes it over, I want you to know I'm leaving." He said this to his mother as we all went in. So we were all very tense. This combination of intentions does not make for a relaxed evening, but seders are never relaxed.

It was a sacrifice for the old man to give up leading the seder because it was something he loved to do, but he was doing this to assure that his grandsons would be prepared to carry it on. What happened during the course of the evening was that the boy slowly changed into a man. You could see it happening before your eyes—this is the wonder of working with videotape—and it became a rite of passage for him. It was the bar mitzvah that, in a sense, he had never had. He began the seder as an ignorant, unsure boy, and by the end of the evening he was commanding the situation with a good deal of authority.

It so happened that by the end of the evening, he was rather drunk as well. So the videotape has this wonderful mixture of authority and slippage. When his grandfather put him in charge of the seder, he began to take a lot of wine because he was very nervous, and his grandfather turned to him and said, "You can't do that, you're supposed to have four cups." The grandson said, "Look, these are my sacred cups, and then over here I have my other cup. I'm drinking from that one, and I do the required four cups at the right time." And the grandfather said, "That's an interesting idea. Do you think I could do that too?" And so an innovation was made that you knew was going to get passed down, and that generations from now in this family they would tell the story of how this came about. . . .

I said before that anthropologists and others have not studied the transmission of culture systematically. We have a rather mechanical view—we get it from the secular world—that education is something like a bag of potatoes in a relay race. One generation hauls it forward, and the children pick it up and continue with it, as if it were a mechanical thing that you thrust onto the youth, and they take it and continue it. But this is simplistic and erroneous.

What happens when we view the transmission of tradition in the context of this Passover seder? Mind you, we are dealing here with family and with sacred materials. Again, I say "sacred" meaning a form of authority that does not come from God; I mean what carries authority because it goes to the heart of what makes you a human being, it's what you carry with you all your life. And that isn't something you take dutifully and receive, and then you say "thank you" and go on. Anyone who is a parent knows this. That is not the way you teach your child to be a *mentsh* or the way you teach your children to do what you do or teach them what you believe in. Not at all, on the contrary. Common sense tells us that socialization—which is the teaching of sacred things—is ambivalent, it is a struggle. And the problem is how to get the children to receive what you have to teach in some form that you consider valid and recognizable, and to take that version and make it their own. That is the struggle of the parent or the one who is passing it on.

The struggle from the children's point of view is how to take that stuff and make it have something to do with their lives, how to adapt it, how to make it useful, how to make it speak to the world around them. If either of these tasks fails, the whole thing fails. If the children take the traditions and change them, bowdlerize them, alter them too profoundly, so that the older people say, "I don't understand what's going on. I don't recognize this, it has nothing to do with us," then from the parents' point of view this has been a failure, they don't care any more. If, on the other hand, the children have had something imposed on them that doesn't speak to them, that is not vital to their lives, then it's a mechanical act of obedience, and it's useless.

So that means there is a built-in tension, a built-in antagonism between the generations about the sacred word that has to be passed on. So there has to be some negotiation. Both parties have to give something up, and both parties have to agree in the end that they recognize what it is that has been given and received. This is a very different model from the mechanical one that goes "here it is" and "thanks." This, again, is a dialectic. And that is why Passover is such a useful thing to study as an example of socialization. The children come in and say, "What is going on here?" And working that out, then, becomes what the evening is for.

The first fight that took place was a fight about language. This issue is probably a very common one, the issue of what language to have the ceremony in, anyway. "Is this in Hebrew or in English?" The older people, of course, want to do it in Hebrew, which is the sacred language, the language of their sacred youth, and the children don't understand Hebrew, so there is a struggle. On the videotape, we hear the grandson who is leading the seder saying, "I have to do this in a language I understand." And Greg, the younger brother, who turns out to be more of a traditionalist, saying, "But I don't like the sound of it in English, it doesn't sound like what even I remember when I was a kid. Even if I don't understand it, I still want to recognize the sounds." And the old man saying, "What kind of seder do you call this if it's not in Hebrew, if the prayers aren't in Hebrew?" So there's a tussle about language.

Meantime, the older man and the older woman, whenever they come to a stumbling point and they want to have a little argument aside, talk in Yiddish. This brings in all their cronies from their own generation, and all the children are then left completely in the dark. They are very annoyed; they say, "Come on, come on, let's have this in English, we want to know what you're talking about." So there are three-way struggles there. . . .

Then came the issue of the ten plagues. This is the recitation of all the afflictions that the Lord visited upon the Egyptians. Deena said, "Now we get to my favorite part of the seder, and I see that my father has just crossed it out. He wants to leave it out for all the right reasons because we don't want to talk about the suffering of our enemies here. But I must say that I always liked this part because it keeps us from being sanctimonious, it reminds us that we are all in symbolic Egypt, we are all suffering, and I really feel this should be put in."

A big argument develops around this question: What does it mean to talk about these plagues, anyway? And they are terrible plagues: they are vermin and boils and locusts and cattle disease and blood and slaying of the firstborn—really horrible things. So a big discussion ensues: What are we doing when we talk about all this? Deena's son Marc says, "Look, there is nothing wrong with including this. All we are doing is saying that these things happened to our enemies, and because they happened, we do not fully rejoice." Now what happens when you say the names of the plagues is, traditionally, you put your finger in your cup of wine and take out a drop, and you drop it on your plate for each one of the plagues, as you recite them: "Boils . . . murrain . . . locusts . . . frogs . . ." So Marc says, "We're not celebrating these afflictions; we are simply making our own rejoicing less, we are making our cup less full because our enemies suffered." He is moved by the nobility of this. And Greg says, "I don't think that's what we're doing here at all. We are rejoicing. We are saying: 'Look what we did! Look what happened to our enemies!'"

This went into a discussion of who are the Egyptians. Who is the "us" and who is the "them"? This is the point in the seder where we acknowledge that our enemies are part of humanity—they are like ourselves—and that is why we are diminishing our cup: what happened to them happened to us. This, then, is the "humanism versus particularism" issue.

As soon as it is raised, someone inevitably chimes in and says, "Yes, and we also diminish our cups for the Vietnamese." Someone else says, "South Vietnamese or North Vietnamese? Or all the Vietnamese?" "What about South Africa?" "What about people of color here in America?" "And women!" All those present bring in their favorite groups of the oppressed. "Students! . . . Children!" My children always say that to be a child is to be oppressed. And what happens is that this list of the oppressed enlarges and enlarges until it finally verges on being absurd, then everyone pulls it back in. But before they do, there has been a big, very big, discussion of boundaries, and the boundaries have been moved by force of these questions: Who is "them" and who is "us"? Are we Jews? Are we human beings? Who are our co-sufferers? . . .

While the boundaries between Jews and Egyptians are shifting and thickening and dissolving in discussion, the camera is wandering back and forth across the table and comes to rest on my six-year-old son Matthew. He's doing the plagues. And seeing him do the plagues on videotape, I understand exactly why the plagues will never be eliminated. There he is, sticking his finger in the cup and flinging the wine, so that it hits the tablecloth—the white linen tablecloth, on which the others have been accidentally spilling their wine. But he is allowed to do it—he is even encouraged to do it. He is reciting these plagues in Hebrew and putting these drops of wine on his plate, and some of it gets flung elsewhere. You see why there will always be resistance to making certain changes in ritual, you absolutely see that this is a moment of great excitement and satisfaction for a child. There is this overlay of "yes . . . yes . . . friends . . . enemies . . ." But what he is really going to remember, besides getting a present and getting drunk, is spilling the wine on the tablecloth and not being scolded for it.

When I moaned and groaned about how badly behaved my children were at this, as at all other seders, a wise friend of mine said: Don't you understand when you read the text that *this* is what it's about, that it has always been this way? From the times of the Temple, as long as there has been a Passover ceremony, it is to keep the children awake, it is to keep them involved. It's because they're not behaving themselves and the adults aren't rebuking them that they really know this night is special, different from all other nights, and they're given additional energy by this permission. It's because they do grow sleepy after all the wine and talk that you have to bring them back, to complete the ceremony. So for the ceremony to succeed, the children must be allowed to mess up. This misbehavior— this space for the children's spontaneity and innovation—is at the heart of the Passover story, which is the story of a family getting its children to pay attention, and this is always difficult. I found this very wise and very consoling. . . .

The evening is by then over. There is a good deal of chaos, and then some silence when everyone realizes it has come to an end, very inconclusively. Enough has been successful so that the grandparents have recognized what has happened, even if they say it isn't theirs. They have compromised. The children have compromised, and they recognize that this seder has something to do with their lives. The exchange has taken place. We have seen these people for four hours passionately arguing about what is going on there. Every single one of the major people, during the course of the evening, has said, "This is a terrible seder. This is not my kind of seder. I would never do it again. Next year I have other plans." You know that they'll all be back. You know that much of this will occur again.

Ritual has the power to generate its own need to be redone. It's never the mythology that was wrong, it's not the Haggadah. The family didn't do it right. So next year you get to do it right. When a medicine man loses a patient—and this is as true of our medicine men as of Indian medicine men—it is never the mythology or the germ theory of disease that is at fault. The question of whether the gods do indeed hear our calls never arises. There is always some reason that explains why it was the practice that was wrong and not the theory or the mythology. So here, too, they don't look at the Haggadah and say, "There's something wrong with this text." They say, "Next year we'll do it better, we'll do it different, we'll do it right."

And so they conclude. Spoken into the tense silence that then occurred, probably the only little silence that occurred during the evening, are the words that Marc says, somewhat lamely and very touchingly: "Next year in Jerusalem." This is as close to an agreement and a success as any ritual needs to come. Its very imperfections require that it be done again—differently, better—the following year, and somehow "next year in Jerusalem" will never come, need never come, should never come. And so it is that human beings struggle to reinvent the reason for coming together and performing the great stories that tell them who they are, why they are located in history and in the moment as they are, and what their individual lives with their struggles and their confusions have to do with the great stories of their people.

"Ritual and Storytelling: A Passover Tale" was published in *Voices: The Journal of New York Folklore* 34, nos. 3-4 (Fall–Winter 2008): 10–14. Barbara Myerhoff's talk was included in *Stories as Equipment for Living: Last Talks and Tales of Barbara Myerhoff* (Ann Arbor: University of Michigan Press, 2007), edited by Marc Kaminsky and Mark Weiss in collaboration with Deena Metzger, and is reprinted here with permission from the University of Michigan Press.

COMFORT IN CLOTH

The Syracuse University Remembrance Quilt

DEE BRITTON

On the evening of December 21, 1988, Pan American Flight 103 flew into the winter solstice skies over London's Heathrow Airport as it began the final leg of a journey that originated in Frankfurt and was to conclude at New York's JFK Airport. The plane carried 259 people; in addition, its cargo hold carried a suitcase that contained a radio cassette player filled with Semtex explosives. The bomb exploded at 7:03 p.m., breaking the plane into pieces. Passengers, their personal effects, and flaming debris rained onto Lockerbie, a small village in southern Scotland. All on board were killed, as well as 11 Lockerbie residents who died when one of the plane's wings incinerated their neighborhood. Beyond the private tragedies of 270 dead, the Lockerbie air disaster was politically significant. Pan American World Airways was globally perceived as the American flagship carrier, even though it was in actuality a private carrier. Although the bombing of Pan Am 103 was a continuation of a number of terrorist attacks on U.S. interests, this attack was the first time in modern history that a large group of American civilians were the direct target of a terrorist attack. The bombing of this plane resulted in the United States' largest death toll from a terrorist attack until September 11, 2001.

Three thousand miles from the flames and wreckage of Lockerbie, Syracuse University faced its own devastation. Thirty-five students of this central New York university were on board Pan Am 103, returning from a semester's study in Europe. On the evening of December 21, the plane was filled with youthful passengers: the median age of all the victims was twenty-nine years, and the mode age was twenty years. Although many colleges and universities lost students as a result of the bombing of Pan Am 103, Syracuse University's loss of thirty-four undergraduates and one graduate student was one of the largest simultaneous student death tolls in U.S. collegiate history. This extensive loss of life ensured that the university would publicly commemorate their students. On the evening of the disaster, students, faculty, and staff joined in a candlelight vigil. Over subsequent years, the university held memorial services, constructed a Place of Remembrance, and instituted a Remembrance Scholars program. Each year, thirty-five seniors are designated Remembrance Scholars and charged with creating activities and traditions that commemorate the lives of the thirty-five SU students lost on Pan Am 103.

Colleges and universities have unique temporal contexts. Department curricula rely upon historical knowledge and disciplinary understanding. Collegiate traditions and rituals provide a group identity that transcends normal temporal boundaries. Yet colleges and universities are transitory in nature; students flow into and out of the university community as they matriculate and then graduate. In 1998, although the bombing of Pan Am 103 was a defining event for the school, it was "history" to undergraduates who were between the ages of eight and twelve when the disaster occurred. Maurice Halbwachs, the first sociologist to use the term "collective memory," explained that all collective memory is constructed and organized by social groups; individuals then do the actual work of memory (1950). Halbwachs also noted the difference between autobiographical and historical memory. Autobiographical memory is memory of events that a person has experienced, which tends to fade and disappear unless group members occasionally meet and reinforce those memories. Consequently, Halbwachs concluded that autobiographical memory is "rooted in other people. . . . Only group members remember, and this memory nears extinction if they do not get together over long periods of time" (Coser 1992: 24). Historical memory occurs when one does not have personal experience of an event; it is created through discourse, visual imagery, rituals, and celebrations that commemorate the event. Historical memory is thus a memory that is stored and reproduced by social institutions. The annual Remembrance Week at Syracuse University creates and reinforces both autobiographical and historical memory.

As the 1998 Remembrance Scholars gathered to discuss potential commemorative activities for the upcoming tenth anniversary, one of the scholars convinced her peers to create a remembrance quilt. There are many types of quilts, including patchwork, crazy, mourning, victory, and friendship quilts. Historically, quilting has provided a sense of social solidarity and group identity. Remembrance quilts began to appear in the United States in the early 1800s. Individual blocks were made by the women of a community and were stitched together to create a quilt for

Syracuse University Remembrance Quilt, which commemorates the thirty-five Syracuse students lost in the 1988 bombing of Pan Am 103. Photo: Dee Britton.

someone who was leaving the community. In essence, the remembrance quilt was to remind the owner to remember those left behind as a result of a life transition.

The remembrance quilt concept was transformed by the advent of the NAMES Project's AIDS Memorial Quilt in 1987. Cleve Jones, a gay activist from San Francisco, created the first panel for his best friend. As organizer of the NAMES Project, Jones wanted to create grassroots communities of local support, as well as a national memorial that would visually represent the immense toll of the AIDS epidemic. The three-by-six-foot panels have been made by friends, family members, lovers, and strangers to commemorate those lost to AIDS. A number of people with AIDS have created their own panels prior to their death (Sturken 1997: 188). The AIDS quilt was composed of 1,920 panels the first time it was displayed in Washington, D.C., in October 1987; currently, there are more than 46,000 panels. The Syracuse University Remembrance Quilt is different from traditional remembrance quilts, since those remembered were unable to make their own blocks. Just as the majority of the AIDS quilt panels were created by community members to commemorate their dead, the Syracuse community gathered together to quilt individual blocks in order to remind themselves of those who had been lost from the community.

In a letter dated September 14, 1998, Remembrance Scholar Kimberly Hamilton described the quilt project to the parents of the Syracuse victims and requested "information such as a favorite color, special talent, or long-time hobby. . . . We would also encourage you to send any items, fabrics, or photographs you would like incorporated in the quilt. No suggestion is out of the realm of possibility." None of the Remembrance Scholars had quilting experience; they did not realize the immensity of the task that they had assumed. The quilt was to be presented at the tenth anniversary memorial service that would be held a mere three months and one week from the date of the letter sent to the parents. "Had I not been naïve about quilting," Hamilton later recalled, "I might never have proposed the idea. It has taken much more work than I ever imagined and at times has been very emotional" (Bédy 1998).

Boxes containing a variety of personal objects began to arrive on campus. Several family members sent single earrings that were found in the wreckage; their matches were never found. Another family sent an intramural field hockey shirt that had been recovered from the debris. Prior to its return to the family in 1989, the shirt had been washed multiple times by women in Lockerbie to remove the fuel and mildew that was embedded in the material. A mother sent fabric that she had purchased with her daughter in London; they had planned to use it in a quilt project when her daughter returned. Photos abounded. Another mother sent a piece of wallpaper from her daughter's childhood bedroom. Pajamas, a favorite shirt, a dusty Boston Red Sox cap, a cassette tape of a song written for one of the victims—all of these items were entrusted by grieving families to be incorporated into the quilt.

The Syracuse University Remembrance Quilt is not only a memorial for the bereaved and the university community but also a work of art. Howard Becker claims that the existence, form, and representation of all works of art are determined by cooperating networks that make up various "art worlds" (1982). Although many public commemorative projects are created in an environment of conflicting intentions, the Syracuse University Remembrance Quilt was created in an intensely cooperative art world of beginning and experienced quilters. The Remembrance Scholars approached two Syracuse University staff members who were longtime quilters, as well as a group of quilters that met in the university chapel. A flyer inviting students, faculty, and staff was distributed throughout the campus. Twenty-nine students, six staff members, and a faculty member's spouse answered the initial call. Individual quilt blocks were designed using the information and artifacts sent by the victims' parents. Students and staff worked to sew and then quilt each individual block. One staff member decided that she wanted to place at least two stitches in every student's block. A janitor worked on a block representing a young man from his hometown. Ten women who were members of a local quilting guild volunteered to devote an entire December day to completing the quilting, although they had no direct relationship with Syracuse University and had not known any of the students lost on Pan Am 103. Their participation was symbolic of the social cohesion that resulted from the loss of so many students and is typical of the quilting community.

The quilt's finished size is 87 by 91 inches. The quilt is composed of a center panel measuring 36 by 58 inches, surrounded by thirty-six individual blocks. The design of the center panel is based on an illustration created in 1989 by art student Jonathan Hoefer. A dove of peace is formed by the names of the thirty-five students. The Remembrance Scholars approached a university staff member who was an experienced quilter to create the center panel. Initially, she was hesitant, reasoning:

> This is a painful thing for all of us, I have grieved privately for the thirty-five students who were lost in that terrorist attack. One side of me shies away, saying, "It's time to let it rest, it's history, why bring it up again?" And the other side of me understands that those families do not want their children to be forgotten. What a tragic thing to have so many talented young lives so cruelly thrown away, and what agony those families have had to endure. This is too worthwhile to ignore, and I can see they need a lot of help to pull this off. I just wish they had started last February, not in mid-October!

The machine-appliquéd work took her more than eighty hours, over a period of twenty-four days, to complete.

Detail of the quilt's center panel. The names of the students form a dove of peace. Photo: Dee Britton.

Thirty-five blocks are individual commemorations of the students, arranged alphabetically by surname. Letters that family members sent in response to the quilting project are folded accordion style and sewn into light orange borders adjacent to the student's block. A local sewing store volunteered to embroider the students' names on the blue lattice beneath the blocks. The individual blocks are poignant reminders of the vibrant interests and activities that filled the lives of the students who were killed in the bombing. A pocket of a favorite shirt holds a cassette tape. Favorite authors and quotations are interspersed with athletic logos, flowers, musical instruments, and theatrical symbols. In the upper right-hand corner of the quilt, two blocks are intertwined by blue and red bandanas tied together. Eric and Jason Coker were twins. When they were small, their mother dressed Eric in blue and Jason in red in order to identify them at a distance. As college students, they continued this differentiation when they donned blue and red bandanas while they worked for a landscape company. Although they had matriculated at different colleges, they both chose to study in the Syracuse University London Program during the fall 1988 semester. To mark their semester together, they decided to receive symbolic tattoos; Eric chose the symbol for the English pound, while Jason selected the British flag. Those tattoos were used after the crash to identify the twins, so that their bodies could be returned to their family. These important symbols are included in their quilt blocks. Their childhood is also embedded in their quilt blocks. Eric and Jason grew up with a beloved dog, Shad, and a representation of his doghouse crosses their blocks. Eric and Jason were individuals who had strong personal interests and talents, yet they were tied together in both life and death, as surely as the two bandanas unite their blocks.

The quilt's thirty-sixth block is an embroidered dedication, using words borrowed from the university's permanent memorial to the victims:

> This Remembrance Quilt is dedicated to the memory of the 35 students enrolled in Syracuse University's Division of International Programs Abroad who died with 235 others as the result of a plane crash December 21, 1988, caused by a terrorist bomb.

The dedication's wording is not the only component borrowed from other memorials for the Pan Am 103 victims. Steve Berrell's and Karen Hunt's quilt blocks include quotations that are also found on their plaques at Lockerbie's Dryfesdale Cemetery. The quilt block of Wendy Lincoln, who was a dancer, includes her same silhouette that marks the headstone in her hometown cemetery. Cindy Smith's block includes an angel representing the mahogany angel that was carved in her memory, and is used every year in her hometown's crèche.

The quilt was completed in time for the tenth anniversary memorial service. Its usual home is Hendricks Chapel at Syracuse University, but it has traveled to a number of different sites. After an exhibition in Lockerbie in 2000, a local representative wrote the following in the remembrance book that accompanies the quilt:

> "Remember us when you see these blocks." During its three week stay with us the Remembrance Quilt has brought with it an enormous wealth of feelings, thoughts, information, and love. The love contained within it is overwhelming and is tangible. We in Lockerbie wish to include our love into the quilt's embrace and so with our love we send it back to you.

The Syracuse University Remembrance Quilt celebrates the individual lives lost on that winter solstice evening. The comfort and warmth that the quilt provides to family members and the Syracuse University community is unmatched by the many other memorials to the tragedy that dot the United States and Scotland. As Shannon Davis's mother stated during an exhibition of the quilt shortly before the fifteenth anniversary of the downing of Pan Am 103, "Looking at the quilt and knowing it's coming close to the fifteenth anniversary, of course, my heart still aches for Shannon not being with us. But when I see the quilt, I understand something bigger than us is at work" (Bodwicz 2003).

WORKS CITED

Becker, Howard. 1982. *Art Worlds*. Berkeley: University of California Press.
Bédy, Zoltan. 1998. "Personal Artifacts Form Remembrance Quilt." *Syracuse Record*, December 7.
Bodwicz, Marty. 2003. "Shelton Woman Finds Comfort in Quilt." *Huntington (Conn.) Herald*, August 13.
Coser, Lewis. 1992. "Introduction: Maurice Halbwachs, 1877–1945." In Maurice Halbwachs, *On Collective Memory*, 1–34. Edited and translated by Lewis Coser. Chicago: University of Chicago Press.
Halbwachs, Maurice. 1950. *The Collective Memory*. New York: Harper-Colophon.
Sturken, Marita. 1997. *Tangled Memories: The Vietnam War, the AIDS Epidemic, and the Politics of Remembering*. Berkeley: University of California Press.

"Comfort in Cloth: The Syracuse University Remembrance Quilt" was first published in *Voices: The Journal of New York Folklore* 34, nos. 3-4 (Fall–Winter 2008): 3–6.

HERE *WAS* NEW YORK

Memorial Images of the Twin Towers

KAY TURNER

To mark the fifth anniversary of September 11, 2001, Brooklyn Arts Council (BAC) Folk Arts mounted an exhibition, "Here *Was* New York: Memorial Images of the Twin Towers," in eleven Brooklyn galleries from September 7 to 30, 2006. Consisting of 350 photographic images by 175 photographers, the exhibit was an homage and a counterpoint to "Here Is New York," a photo exhibit (titled as a play on E. B. White's famous essay in praise of the city and organized by Alice Rose George, Gilles Peress, Michael Shulan, and Charles Traub) that opened immediately after the attacks in 2001. Held in a makeshift gallery in SoHo, that remarkable project made it possible for anyone to hang photographs recording the events of September 11. Hundreds did so, and thousands came to see the pictures.

Acting upon the same democratic principles as its predecessor, the "Here *Was* New York" project invited the public to submit photographs of the Twin Towers as they persist in symbolic form throughout the New York metropolitan area. Recording vernacular representations and acts of informal and ephemeral remembrance that continue to appear in our communities, the photos show depictions of the Towers in wall murals, shrines, custom painting on trucks, logos, graffiti, tattoos, merchandise displays, window stickers, and more.

In the immediate aftermath of September 11, makeshift shrines and memorials made from ephemeral materials and objects filled the cityscape. In those days, the burden of the ephemeral was particularly acute. Those fragile assemblages of candles, photos, flowers, messages, and mementoes—many of them incorporating images of the Twin Towers—were called upon to speak for those, living and dead, who were muted by the disaster. With color and collage, they filled the void with something to see, to smell, to touch, and to say: they filled the anxious space of incomprehensibility. Ground Zero burned with the stench of annihilation; one mile

Immediately after September 11, most scheduled street fairs, festivals, and other events were canceled. One of the first public events held after the attacks was the annual West Village Halloween Parade, where a number of New Yorkers took the opportunity to comment on the tragedy with their homemade costumes. Photo © Martha Cooper.

An offering of flowers placed in the fencing that surrounds Ground Zero in Lower Manhattan. The photo above the flowers, part of an exhibit at the site, shows the World Trade Center area before 9/11. Photo: Elena Marrero.

Detail of Olga Bruh's 9/11 home altar. Photo: Elena Marrero.

Brooklyn neighborhood handball court painted with the names of those lost on 9/11. Bill Brown Memorial Playground, Avenue X and Bedford Avenue, Sheepshead Bay (2006). Photo: Sonja Shield.

Memorial wall painting behind the counter at Anthony's Deli in Brooklyn. Photo: Geoff Rockwell/ Deborah Field.

north, Union Square burned with thousands of candles and reeked, but of flowers, incense, and melting wax.

Those ephemeral memorials are long gone, but the need to remember, to insert the past into the present, continues. And remarkably, one way that New Yorkers choose to remember is by a continuous reassertion of the past, keeping the Twin Towers symbolically visible and alive: not at Ground Zero, but painted on the side of a restaurant in Queens, tattooed on a shoulder or forearm, or worn as a costume in the annual West Village Halloween parade. Walk down Humboldt near Metropolitan Avenue and you encounter New York Heating's testimonial mural painted on their metal drawdown. On your morning drive to work you pass a slow-moving truck on the Brooklyn-Queens Expressway; on its fender you spot "9/11 Never Forget" ornately hand-lettered over an airbrushed rendering of the Towers. These public apparitions are everywhere. Inside homes and businesses, the memorials are also found. At Anthony's Deli in Williamsburg, all manner of delicious Italian food is served across a long counter backed by a hand-painted mural of the Towers; in Olga Bruh's living room in the Bronx, a home altar is dedicated to those lost and to the place lost with them.

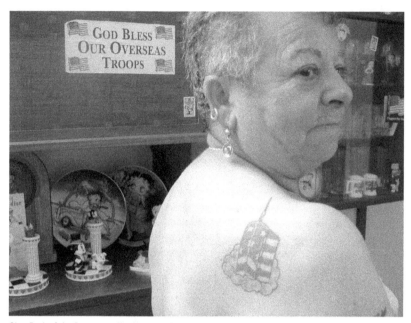

Olga Bruh of the Bronx proudly shows her flag-wrapped Towers tattoo. Photo: Elena Marrero.

In Brooklyn, New York City Heating's cityscape mural features the Brooklyn Bridge and the Twin Towers encircled with a memorial ribbon. Photo: Justine Raczkiewicz.

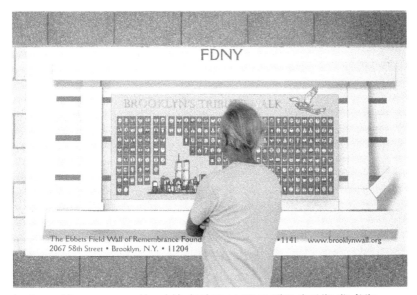

Local memorials, some sponsored by neighborhood groups, are seen throughout the city. At the Brooklyn Cyclones baseball field on Coney Island, a man looks at a 9/11 memorial sponsored by the Ebbets Field Wall of Remembrance Foundation. Photo: Sonja Shield.

Five years after the bombing, collapse, and disappearance of the World Trade Center, ephemeral vernacular arts still play a central role in memorializing the tragic loss of life and landscape. Perhaps these images serve as a placeholder until the official memorial is finally completed in Lower Manhattan.[1] Perhaps they imply that "never forget" refers not only to that single infamous day, but to all the days that preceded it, when the Towers loomed large and were affectionately called the Twins.

NOTES

1. The official memorial for the victims of September 11 was completed and opened to the public in 2012.

"Here *Was* New York: Memorial Images of the Twin Towers" was first published in *Voices: The Journal of New York Folklore* 33, nos. 3-4 (Fall–Winter 2007): 24–30.

PLAY

"I SAW MRS. SARAY, SITTING ON A BOMBALERRY"

Ralph Ellison Collects Children's Folklore in Harlem

ROBERT BARON

Along Harlem streets, in housing projects and on playgrounds, Ralph Ellison employed his formidable gifts for observing and rendering speech play as a collector of children's folklore. His collecting for the Federal Writers' Project (FWP) in 1939 represented one dimension of a lifelong engagement with African American folklore. This engagement extended from traditions acquired in his youth in Oklahoma City through works of fiction employing multiple folkloric genres and essays discussing the centrality of folklore for the African American experience and its indispensable role in cultural resilience. Collecting at a time of heavy African American migration from the South, Ellison researched folklore that embodied both a Southern heritage of largely rural character and traditions adapted to a new urban environment.

As a New Yorker who moved permanently to Harlem in 1938, Ellison experienced firsthand the struggles of recent arrivals adjusting to a vastly different social and cultural situation. Remarking on these challenges in 1948, he wrote of how "American Negroes are caught in a vast process of change that has swept them from slavery to the condition of industrial man in a space of time so telescoped . . . that it is literally possible to step from feudalism into the vortex of industrialism simply by moving across the Mason-Dixon line." In Harlem, the "folk personality" was "caught in a process of chaotic change" (1995a: 321, 325). Writing on "Harlem's America" eighteen years later, Ellison saw continuity as well as change in Harlem's folklore, where "you see the transformation of the Southern idiom into a Northern idiom," in "a place where our folklore is preserved, and transformed" and "the body of Negro myth and legend thrives" (1966: 28).

The modern and the traditional were also at play in Ellison's fiction. He was one of the great modernist writers and, without contradiction, infused folklore throughout his work. Influenced by existentialism and writing surrealistically, counting Eliot, Dostoyevsky, Faulkner, and Malraux among his literary "ancestors" (1995c: 158), Ellison all the while incorporated folklore in his work at least as much as any of his peers. Writing in 1958, he stated, "I use folklore in my work not because I am a Negro, but because writers like Eliot and Joyce made me conscious of the literary value of my folk inheritance," and he found early in his career that the "Negro American folk tradition became precious as a result of an act of literary discovery" (1995b: 111, 112). A few years after seeing that "in both *The Waste Land* and *Ulysses* ancient myth and ritual were used to give form and significance to the material," Ellison came to "realize that the myths and rituals which we find functioning in our everyday lives could be used in the same way" (1995d: 216). The "grist for my fictional mill" included "details of old photographs and rhymes and riddles and children's games, church services and college ceremonies, practical jokes and political activities observed during my prewar days in Harlem" (1994: xxvii).

As an FWP cultural worker, Ellison collected personal narratives, researched local African American history, and took to the streets to collect children's folklore. The FWP folklore researchers were supervised by folklorist Herbert Halpert, who instructed them to "look for children's rhymes, making specific note of the nationality of the reciter, the place of collection, and any comments made by the children. Since the workers were untrained, a questionnaire . . . was prepared" (Halpert 1946: 5). In all, about a thousand items of children's folklore were collected, and Ellison contributed approximately one hundred different items. He observed children at play and noted contexts while recording texts, conducted interviews with both adults and children, probed memory culture, and even contributed folklore remembered from his own childhood.

Ellison collected mainly folk rhymes. They included texts retained from Southern tradition as well as others transformed and localized to New York City. While many were maintained largely or entirely within African American tradition, with some exhibiting African derivations, others were part of repertoires shared by New Yorkers of diverse ethnic backgrounds. In his master's thesis, "Folk Rhymes of New York City Children," which included rhymes collected by Ellison, Halpert singled out African American and Puerto Rican children as each having "unique" rhymes, while noting that they also perform variants of nearly all the rhymes he collected elsewhere in New York City. However, he found that rhymes introduced to Harlem by migrants from the South are not disseminated elsewhere in New York City (1946: 15). He suggested that a "large part of the stock of rhymes and games . . . held in common by White and Negro children dates from before World War I," when the "color barrier" was not as strong, and the African American population was smaller (16).

Whatever their source, the rhymes Ellison collected were distinguished by their innovative and improvisatory qualities, features often noted by him and consonant with the high value placed upon innovation within tradition in African American folk culture. According to Halpert's proposal for a book based upon the New York City FWP children's folklore collection, "Children's Rhymes and Games," "old English rhymes make their appearance" in African American children's folklore "[more] than in any other group, but there [is], on the other hand, considerably more innovation and invention." They were also distinguished by "a greater variety of subject matter and rhythmic pattern" than the rhymes of other groups in the FWP New York City collection (n.d., n. p.).[1]

Ellison provided much information about his collecting process. We see the collector at work as he observed, interviewed, and recorded texts. At times, variants and versions of a folklore item were collected. Ellison had a keen eye for observing creativity in process through improvisation, and delight in wordplay suffuses the collection. He recognized the musicality of the rhymes, noting "polyphony" on one occasion, and referred to performance as "chanting," implying that they could be viewed as being somewhere between speech and song. The rhymes contained influences from popular culture, specific local references, topical references, and content reflecting harsh urban realities like problems paying rent and gun violence.

Much of Ellison's field research occurred near his home at 25 Hamilton Terrace. The October 13, 1939, report offered especially detailed, multilayered descriptions of the collecting situation. He presented multiple dimensions of text, context, and performance rarely before provided in collections of children's folklore.

One group of children demonstrated improvisation and individual creativity as they performed a taunt, followed by improvised lines to a "jingle" and a riddle. Ellison describes their performance of folklore as an emergent process rather than as repetition of a fixed text. We see what Dell Hymes has called a "breakthrough into performance" as interviewees move from *reporting* folklore to spontaneous *performance* (1981: 79–86):

Buster Brown
When you see a guy got on brown pants you say:
Buster Brown
Went down town
With his britches hanging down.

When the above was given, other members of the group chimed in with the following. While most of the jingles appear to have a set formula, there were many attempts at improvisation. Each voice followed the other in rapid succession, giving an antiphonal effect as varied as the colors named.

"Yellow, yellow
Kiss a fellow."
"Blue, blue
I love you"
"Black, black
Sit on a tack"
"Green, green
Eat ice cream
Stick your nose in kerosene"
"White, white,
You can fight"

Hey Mister, if you shut up in an iron house without any windows
    and you didn't have nothing but a baseball bat?

In an *iron* house?

Yeah, yeah that's right. Come on sister, what'll you do?

Well, I guess I don't know.

Gee, don't you know how to play baseball? Anybody who can play
    baseball knows how to get outta there.

Well how would I get out?

Three strikes and you out, Mister . . .

You see what he means, THREE STRIKES AN YOU OUT![2]

Thickly describing these performances, Ellison anticipated the approach to folklore as emergent performance and situated small group interaction that developed in folklore studies three decades later.[3] One actually sees folklore as it is created, as "living lore," which FWP national folklore editor Benjamin A. Botkin saw as "living speech . . . responsive to the mood of the moment," still being created in urban as well as rural areas (1958: 190). As Jerrold Hirsch indicates, Botkin's *Manual for Folklore Studies* instructed collectors to "submit complete field notes from every interview together with a personal history of the informant" (1988: 58). While Ellison regrettably submitted minimal personal information about almost everyone he interviewed, his field notes, at their best, provide highly textured accounts of the collecting of folklore in, and as, performance. In his later fictional writings, he would vividly render the performative and improvisatory qualities of speech and verbal art. These writings embody a "collaboration . . . between oral and literary techniques and traditions; between performance and composition," which John F. Callahan sees as intrinsic to *Invisible Man* (1994: 89). While Ellison scholars have long emphasized the influence of improvisation in jazz upon his fiction, his folklore collecting demonstrates an emphasis on improvisation, emergence, and performance in folklore that reemerges in subsequent literary works.

Ellison's field research involved both close observation of children at play and interviews. He drew reports and performances of folklore from tradition bearers young and old:

> Mrs. Julia Fisher of 2816 Eighth Avenue sung the following words to a slightly varied melody of "Little Sallie Walker." Mrs. Fisher learned this version as a child in Key West, Florida:

> Little Sallie Water
> Little Sallie Water
> Sitting in a saucer,
> Crying and weeping for a young man
> Oh, rise, Sallie, rise,
> Wipe your weeping eyes,
> And turn yourself to the water front
> And tell them who you love the best.

At the same collecting session on October 13, 1939, a group of girls demonstrated singing games substantially maintained from Southern folklore, embodying the creolization of traditions. One game included a refrain, "Sail

Away, Sail Away, Sail Away," well known in Anglo-American folk song. A tap dance, perhaps a new element, was introduced in another game. Had moving images and/or sound recordings also been used, African cultural sources for these games might be adduced, since, as Bess Lomax Hawes commented in her notes to the film *Pizza Pizza Daddy-O*, African American singing games "stylistically, especially in terms of musical and kinesic elements . . . seem equally clearly African, or at least Afro-American" as "British" or "American" (quoted in Sanches and Kirshenblatt-Gimblett 1976: 69). At times, such as in the following accounts of "Buckeye the Rabbit" and "Lady in the River," Ellison demonstrates how the singing games of African American girls involve a tight interrelationship between song and movement, which Kyra Gaunt sees as "embodied musical practices" (2006: 2) incorporating "intrinsic" relationships between movement and music (7).

"Buckeye the Rabbit," in another variant, appears in *Invisible Man* when the narrator experiences electroshock treatment after the factory accident. Asked "Who is Buckeye the Rabbit?" the narrator responds in a manner both "giddy" (1972: 183) and grounding, which, Keith Eldon Byerman contends, brings out "cultural history," which "prevents his total loss of identity" (1985: 27). The narrator in *Invisible Man* remembers that "*I* was Buckeye the Rabbit . . . or had been, when as children we danced and sang barefoot in the dusty streets" (1972: 184). In Harlem, Ellison had observed children dancing as they sang in this children's singing game played in both the North and the South:

Buckeye the Rabbit
I'm riding through Kentucky
I'm riding through the sea,
And all I catch behind me
Is a buckle on my knee
Buckeye the Rabbit,
Shake it
Shake it
With a buckle on my knee,
I swing to the bottom
I swing to the sea
And all I catch behind me
Is a buckle on my knee
So Buckeye the Rabbit
Shake it

Shake it
So Buckeye the Rabbit
Shake it
Shake it
With a buckle on my knee.

The worker observed this game played by a group of five girls, four of whom joined hands and formed a circle around the fifth. All five took part in singing the above verses up to the line "Buckeye the Rabbit" upon which the girl in the center began dancing steps from a tap dance routine. One girl, Mary Suarez of 259 W. 139th St., sung the following words as she continued to dance after the others had finished one of the songs.

"You jump to the front
And you jump to the back
And you do the snake-hips 1, 2, 3
A riding to the sea."

The others joined in:

"So Buckeye the rabbit,
Shake it shake it" etc.

Upon finishing this, girls took her place in the circle and one of the others took her place, whereupon the same routine began again. The game is flexible and allows for the use of varied dance steps. The worker was informed that this game was learned from other children, while one girl, Catherine Mason, said she learned it in Richmond, VA.

Lady in the River (a game song)
There's a lady in the river
Sail away, sail away, sail away
There's a lady in the river
Sail away,
Looking for her lover
Sail away, sail away, sail away.
Then she found her lover

Sail away, sail away, sail away
Then she found her lover
Sail away, sail away, sail away.

This game was not played for me but the lyrics were sung.

Helen Lewis offered what she claimed was an original, collectively created "taunt" during the same day of collecting. It expresses the competi-
tiveness and fierce identification that many New Yorkers have felt for their
own block. In *City Play*, Amanda Dargan and Steven Zeitlin note that
streets, like public schools, buildings, and playgrounds, are often identified by number in New York City, but can be the subjects of great pride.
They describe play about such places, indicating that while "identified
by number, seemingly anonymous places in a crowded city are rendered
meaningful through play" (1990: 10). This "taunt" contains, like older
rhymes of Southern provenance collected by Ellison, the formulaic refrain
"buckeye the rabbit" along with newer content.

"When the 134th Street girls get together we all say this rhyme, we
made it up ourselves."

Take off your shoes and stockings,
and let your feet go bare.
For we are the girls from One hundred-thirty-four
So don't you dare come near.
So, buckeye, the rabbit,
Shake, shake
Buckeye the rabbit
Shake, shake
So don't you dare come near.

Ellison recorded a number of ball bouncing rhymes found in other
New York City neighborhoods and ethnic groups. He asked about acquisi-
tion and observed that the traditions were learned from other children
rather than adults—a characteristic of children's folklore that folklorists
have noted wherever it is collected:

The following are rhymes chanted by little girls while bouncing their
balls and were collected at the corner of 141st Street and Hamilton

Terrace, Manhattan. None of the children questioned were able to tell where they learned the rhymes. In each instance they replied that they had been taught by "another girl," or "another kid." Sometimes the writer was told that certain rhymes were the original creations of the child involved, but in no case was I able to obtain a rhyme which had been taught a child by his parents.

One Two Three a Nation
One, two, three a nation,
I received my confirmation
In the Church of the Annunciation
One, two, three a nation.[4]

One, two, three a nation
Doctor, doctor here's a patient
Waiting for an operation,
One, two, three a nation.[5]

One Two Three O'Lerry
One, two, three, O'Lerry,
I saw Mrs. Saray
Sitting on a bombalerry
Just like a chocolate ferry.[6]

I Had a Little Monkey
I had a little monkey,
I sent him to the country
To buy a loaf of bread.
Along came a choo choo
And knocked my monkey coo coo
And now my monkey's dead
With a bullet in his head

Charlie Chaplin
Charlie Chaplin went to France
To teach the ladies how to dance
This is what he taught them:
"Heel and Toe, Clap your hands and over you go."[7]

Public School 89 was the subject of two rhymes. In his book proposal, "Children's Rhymes and Games," Halpert indicated that there were few rhymes in the entire New York City FWP collection referring to schools, with the exception of derogatory ones (like the ones Ellison collected). In this collecting situation, Ellison noted the effect of his presence upon the performance:

> Most of the rhymes in this group were collected in the vicinity of Public School #89 and in every instance the informant was a boy. The following rhyme reveals one boy's attitude toward P.S. #89; the first version before he knew the words were to be taken down, and the second, more respectable version, when he saw the pencil put to paper.

> Remember the Eight
> Remember the Nine
> Remember that "City Dump" 89

> Remember the Eight
> Remember the Nine
> Remember that "White House" 89

Ellison's remarks about his impact as a collector on the content of these rhymes reflect his awareness of the dynamics of subject/object relationships in fieldwork. He became at once both subject and object of his research when he acted as his own informant. Interspersed among texts collected in Harlem are several items remembered from his Oklahoma childhood. Ellison, after all, was part of the great migration of African Americans to Northern cities, retaining childhood traditions even while moving in literary circles and beginning his writing career in New York.

Ellison remembered a "choosing rhyme" from 1925. Other versions of this counting out rhyme have been reported from Canada, England, Scotland, and the United States:

> My mother and your mother
> Were hanging out clothes
> My mother hit your mother
> Right in the nose
> O-U-T Spells Out!

Ellison remembered a "taunt" from 1920, when he was about six years old:

Patty on the brooms tick
Patty on the sea
Patty tore his britches
And layed it on me

Another taunt, from 1922, was "used to taunt white children as well as for the choosing of sides":

Enny meany minny moe
Catch a white peck by the toe
If he bites you let him go
Enny meany minny moe!

Both Ellison's texts and children's folklore collected from non–African Americans in New York City for the FWP include a number of taunts of other ethnic groups. Coming across these taunts came as no surprise to me, having grown up in the Bronx in the 1950s and 1960s and remembering folklore performed by members of white ethnic groups referring disparagingly to other groups, most viciously about African Americans. Taunts, whether with ethnic reference or not, are a widespread genre of children's folklore. They have long been pervasive among American children, and Jorgensen notes that as "forms of victimization," they represent "behaviors that children are likely to experience at almost any time and in any place" (1995: 213–214). One taunt Ellison collected, about "crackers," was both pithy and pointed. William and Eddie Freeman reported, "that's what we used to say when the white boys made us mad." They learned it on a visit to relatives in Charleston, South Carolina:

Cracker, cracker ring the bell
Cracker, cracker go to hell!

Children who "cannot read well" felt the signifying sting of another taunt:

Can you read
Can you write
Can you smoke your daddy's pipe?

An overweight child was the target of another taunt:

> Fat and skinny had a race
> Fat fell down and broke his face
> Skinny said I won the race
> Fat said that ain't fair
> Cause I lost my underwear

"Delaware" rhymed easily with "square" and "fair" (for the 1939 World's Fair) in a taunt for "strangers":

> Look at them squares
> From Delaware
> They musta got left
> From the World's Fair

Ellison noted that the following version was recited "when a stranger or out-of-town license on a car driven by Negroes, is noticed." The last two lines were recited by Herbert Lambert, sung to the tune of "Shave and a Haircut":

> I'm a square from Delaware
> Just in town to see the Fair
> Boom da dee ah dee
> Boom, boom!

Topical references appear in other items. The Opies categorize such rhymes as "topical rhymes" because "the era in which [they belong] is immediately apparent," but caution that they may be versions of much older rhymes (1959: 98). Halpert found widespread reference to "contemporary events, personalities and institutions" in rhymes collected during the 1930s (1946: 14). Joe Louis appears in the following rhyme, with a notation in Ellison's hand about the "trucking" dance:

> <u>Joe Louis and Bob Pastor</u>
> Bob Pastor was on his knees
> Said, "Joe,
> Don't hit me please,
> Just go on trucking on out the ring."

This rhyme tells the story of the Pastor-Louis fight, which took place in 1939. The term "trucking" refers to a dance step popular at that time; a version of which was inspired by Louis' peculiar, shuffling footwork.

According to Halpert, children "quickly became adept exponents of truckin', introducing it in a number of songs and games" (1946: 114). He indicated that "truckin'" rhymes were not known outside of Harlem, viewing them as a kind of emergent folklore, as mainly "recent compositions either based on older rhyme forms or composed from scratch" (15–16).

Only a few jump rope rhymes were collected by Ellison. Halpert, in his proposal, "Children's Rhymes and Games," speaks of how specific words may be used to indicate actions. In the first of the two rhymes that follow, the jumper is expected to either straddle the rope or miss her turn, allowing the jumper to avoid a "faux pas." These rhymes are found extensively in Anglo-American and British tradition:

I know a lady
By the name of miss
Sat by the fire and gave me a kiss
All of a sudden
She missed like this![8]

Johnny on the ocean
Johnny in the sea
Johnny broke a windowpane and blamed it on me
I told ma
And ma told pa
And Johnny got a beating and ha ha ha[9]

This "gag" collected by Ellison was also recited in my own childhood in the northwest Bronx, with the addition of a "the" before "ice":

Ladies and gentlemen
Take my advice
Pull down your pants
And sit on ice.

A very short verse collected by Ellison was labeled a "baseball rhyme." Short verses were found widely among New York City children—Halpert speaks in his proposal, "Children's Rhymes and Games," of the "distinctly New Yorkese rhyme which is short, snappy and to the point."

> In and out
> Three strikes and out

Some rhymes were uncategorized by Ellison. The text of a rhyme that improvised on a popular song was followed by a note about continuities between African American folk songs and "commercial" songs:

> Margie is a swimming pool
> All around the house
> But never in the pool
> Well allright then . . .

> The above rhyme is an improvised lyric to a popular song, origi-
> nating in Harlem, the title of which is "Well All Right Then." This title,
> which gives the tune its refrain, is nonsensical as far as actual mean-
> ing is concerned. And as is typical of such Negro songs, the pattern of
> "WELL ALLRIGHT THEN" is very elastic in order to allow for such
> improvisations; a characteristic which comes out of the folk period of
> Negro music and which has been carried over into the commercial.

African American children's rhymes and singing games have continued to incorporate popular music. Kyra Gaunt shows that this relationship
works both ways in an ongoing circulation between folk and popular traditions, citing many examples of rhythm and blues, blues, and hip hop songs
appropriating children's game songs (2006: 2–3, 68–69, 89–110). Ellison
saw how such use of popular song underscores the fluid, improvisatory
character of African American music, characteristic of both a "folk period," when it consisted largely of folk music, and his own time, when com-
mercially produced popular music strongly shaped cultural preferences.
In referring to continuity and change in African American music, Ellison
speaks to transformations in Black American culture occurring during the
interwar period, when he collected traditions brought by migrants from
the South and maintained in Harlem. These traditions were often adapted,
localized, and changed by children, who also performed traditions maintained as well by other ethnic groups, and practiced emerging folklore
newly created in New York.

These children experienced both tradition and change through folklore as in other aspects of their lives. In his own life at this time, Ellison was experiencing personal and professional transformations as a migrant as well as a writer. Like other FWP folklore workers, Ellison collected during the day and wrote in the evening (O'Meally 1980: 35–36), working for the first time as a full-time cultural worker.

Robert O'Meally indicates that Ellison perceived Southern sources "even when the Harlem lore seemed indigenous," and he would sometimes "recognize a remnant of a saying or rhyme he had heard in the South reduced to a 'mumble' or nonsense phrase in Harlem." Discussing Ellison's suggestion that they bridged Southern tradition and African ancestry, O'Meally cites Ellison as stating that their "tradition goes way back to the South, and some of it goes back to Africa" (1980: 34). While much of the children's folklore collected by Ellison was distinctively African American in provenance and current practice, some of these traditions were also practiced by whites. The critical essays and fiction of Ellison embody his views of the creative genius and cultural distinctiveness of African American cultures, the importance of Southern roots, and the Americanness of African Americans, all characteristics evident in the children's rhymes he collected early in his career.

Ellison's collections of children's folklore for the FWP incorporated traditions distinctive to African Americans as well as traditions shared by New Yorkers and other Americans. While Ellison did not note that many of these traditions were also practiced by non-blacks, their provenances reflected the interactions of blacks and whites as well as the distinctive contribution of African Americans to American life, themes running throughout Ellison's writings. In his scathing critique of LeRoi Jones's *Blues People*, Ellison contends that "Jones has stumbled over that ironic obstacle which lies in the path of anyone who would fashion a theory of American Negro culture while ignoring the intricate network of connections which binds Negroes to the larger society. To do so is to attempt delicate brain surgery with a switchblade" (1995e: 283). He saw mutual influences between African Americans and other Americans as continuous and ongoing, with folklore embodying "the close links which Negro Americans have with the rest of the nation . . . constantly influencing the larger body of American culture and in turn influencing them" (292). While recognizing reciprocal cultural influences, Ellison viewed African American folklore as a hallmark of their cultural genius, asserting humanity and creativity over centuries of oppression.

While Ellison's FWP folklore collections have enduring significance as a foundation for both his fiction and nonfiction, they also have substantial but unrecognized value as folklore collections on their own terms, drawing from multiple cultural sources while demonstrating creativity in the creation of emerging traditions. Reading Ellison's field notes and texts of seventy years ago from the standpoint of a folklorist trained in the performance-centered approach to folklore study, I am struck by his accounts of performance situations, his sensitivity to performance styles, and the contextual details he provided. Contemporary folklorists should also be impressed by his frequent notes about the uses of particular traditions and his remarks about distinctive features of form and localization of particular traditions.

As a writer, Ellison was a literary modernist who wrote stylistically advanced fiction deeply infused with folklore, representing African Americans maintaining traditions while experiencing modern life. As a folklorist, he was a modern folklorist, observing and reporting context while recording texts, collecting older traditions maintained by Southern migrants, folklore localized and transformed in the city and emerging urban traditions. Rather than seeing folklore as residual culture, as static relics of a Southern past, Ellison projects a dynamicist view of the children's folklore he collected as emergent in performance. Folklore, and speech in general, are viewed performatively, marked by improvisation and innovation. Folk culture is located within modernity rather than outside it, through folklore collected at the outset of his career as well as in subsequent fiction and essays about African American culture. Tradition and modernity are intertwined throughout the body of Ellison's folklore research and literary production, embodying a view of the traditional and the modern in dynamic interaction rather than as disjunctive forces. While Ellison's brief period collecting folklore occurred early in his career, it represented a highly formative episode that continued to reverberate on many levels.

NOTES

An earlier version of this work was presented at the American Folklore Society's annual meeting in Milwaukee in 2006. Research for this article was carried out while I was a Non-Resident Fellow of the W. E. B. Du Bois Institute for African and African American Research at Harvard University. I am grateful to Roger D. Abrahams, Henry Louis Gates Jr., Felicia McMahon, and John F. Szwed for their encouragement and critical comments about this article.

1. While the manuscript for the proposal for "Children's Rhymes and Games" in the Manuscript Collection of the Library of Congress does not include the author's name, Herbert Halpert refers to it in "Coming into Folklore More Than Fifty Years Ago." He recounted that he was "fired" from the FWP, "mainly because the book I had proposed, on New York City children's lore, was thought to be too large a project—one that would take too long to reach publication" (1992: 451). The proposed book was never published.

2. All of Ellison's transcriptions of children's rhymes and associated field notes are reprinted here as they appear in the reports held in the Manuscript Collection of the Library of Congress without emendation, except for small changes to regularize spelling.

3. During the 1970s, the academic discipline of folklore turned from an emphasis on textual analysis to a performance-centered approach. Viewing folklore as artistic communication in small groups, it focused on how folklore emerges in face-to-face interaction, and on its social and cultural context. Amy Shuman and Charles Briggs write of how "style, content, and context" were "brought under a single theoretical aegis as they were studied in particular, situated acts of communication" (1993: 114).

4. Variants of this rhyme were recited throughout New York City and its suburbs, and in northwestern Connecticut.

5. Halpert notes that this rhyme was also collected at Greenwich House, in Greenwich Village (1946: 172). Greenwich House served a largely immigrant population at the time.

6. This rhyme was also reported from throughout New York City. A variant included in Halpert's "Folk Rhymes of New York City Children" was transcribed (or spelled) differently, as "One, two, three a-lairry, / I spy Mrs. Sarey, / Sitting on a bumble lairry, / Just like a chocolate fairy" (1946: 171). Dorothy G. Mills Howard reported a version from "New York State" as "One, two, three a-larry / I spy sister Sarrie / Sitting on a bumbleberry / Eating Chocolate like a fairy" (1938: 116). Ethel and Oliver Hale indicated that "no one has told us what a bumble-airy or bumble-eery is, so we must assume it is a concocted word, created to fit a rhyme scheme" (1938: 126).

7. Roger Abrahams provides thirty-nine references from throughout the United States of variants and versions of "Charlie Chaplin" as a jump rope rhyme (1969: 26–27). In New York City, Halpert reports that Charlie Chaplin as a counting out rhyme and jump rope rhyme included a variety of last lines: "And turn yourself around," "And turn around to the submarine," "And turn your back to the Kaiser," from Greenwich and Church House, Jones House, and Greenwich House, respectively (1946).

8. Abrahams references sixteen versions of "Miss, miss, little miss, miss: / When she misses she misses like this" from throughout the United States, England, and Scotland, including one from Great Britain that begins, "I know a woman / And her name is Miss" (1969, 123–124).

9. Abrahams lists references to versions and variants found in thirty-one states and Scotland (1969: 102).

WORKS CITED

Abrahams, Roger. 1969. *Jump Rope Rhymes: A Dictionary*. Austin: University of Texas Press.

Botkin, B[enjamin] A. 1958. "We Called It Living Lore." *New York Folklore Quarterly* 14 (3): 189–201.

Byerman, Keith Eldon. 1985. *Fingering the Jagged Grain: Tradition and Form in Recent Black Fiction*. Athens: University of Georgia Press.

Callahan, John F. 1994. "Frequencies of Eloquence: The Performance and Composition of Invisible Man." In *New Essays on Invisible Man*, 55–94. Edited by Robert O'Meally. Cambridge: Cambridge University Press.

Dargan, Amanda, and Steven Zeitlin. 1990. *City Play*. New Brunswick: Rutgers University Press.

Ellison, Ralph. 1939–1940. "Harlem Children's Folklore." New York City Folklore Collections, Work Projects Administration (WPA) Records, Federal Writers' Project: Folklore Project. Manuscript Collection, Box A648. Library of Congress.

———. 1966. "Harlem's America." *New Leader* 26 (September): 22–35.

———. 1972 [1952]. *Invisible Man*. New York: Vintage Books.

———. 1994. "Introduction" [from the 1981 printing; 1952]. *Invisible Man*, xvii–xxxiv. New York: Modern Library.

———. 1995a [1948]. "Harlem Is Nowhere." In *The Collected Essays of Ralph Ellison*, 320–327. Edited by John F. Callahan. New York: Modern Library.

———. 1995b [1958]. "Change the Joke and Slip the Yoke." In *The Collected Essays of Ralph Ellison*, 100–112. Edited by John F. Callahan. New York: Modern Library.

———. 1995c [1963–1964]. "The World and the Jug." In *The Collected Essays of Ralph Ellison*, 155–158. Edited by John F. Callahan. New York: Modern Library.

———. 1995d [1964]. "The Art of Fiction: An Interview." In *The Collected Essays of Ralph Ellison*, 210–224. Edited by John F. Callahan. New York: Modern Library.

———. 1995e [1964]. "Blues People." In *The Collected Essays of Ralph Ellison*, 278–287. Edited by John F. Callahan. New York: Modern Library.

Gaunt, Kyra D. 2006. *The Games Black Girls Play*. New York: New York University Press.

Hale, Ethel, and Oliver Hale. 1938. "From Sidewalk, Gutter and Stoop: Being a Chronicle of Children's Play and Game Activity." Unpublished manuscript. New York Public Library, Special Collections.

[Halpert, Herbert]. n.d. "Children's Rhymes and Games." Unpublished manuscript. Work Projects Administration (WPA) Records, Federal Writers' Project: Folklore Project. Manuscript Collection, Box A647. Library of Congress.

Halpert, Herbert. 1946. "Folk Rhymes of New York City Children." Master's thesis, Columbia University.

_____. 1992. "Coming into Folklore More Than Fifty Years Ago." *Journal of American Folklore* 105 (418): 442–457.

Hirsch, Jerrold. 1988. "Cultural Pluralism and Applied Folklore: The New Deal Precedent." In *The Conservation of Culture: Folklorists and the Public Sector*, 46–67. Edited by Burt Feintuch. Lexington: University Press of Kentucky.

Howard, Dorothy G. Mills. 1938. "Folk Jingles of American Children: A Collection and Study of Rhymes Used by Children Today." Ph.D. dissertation, New York University.

Hymes, Dell. 1981. *"In Vain I Tried to Tell You": Essays in Native American Ethnopoetics*. Philadelphia: University of Pennsylvania Press.

Jorgensen, Marilyn. 1995. "Teases and Pranks." In *Children's Folklore: A Source Book*, 213–224. Edited by Brian Sutton-Smith, Jay Mechling, Thomas W. Johnson, and Felicia McMahon. New York: Garland Publishing.

O'Meally, Robert G. 1980. *The Craft of Ralph Ellison*. Cambridge: Harvard University Press.

Opie, Iona, and Peter Opie. 1959. *The Lore and Language of Schoolchildren*. Oxford: Oxford University Press.

Sanches, Mary, and Barbara Kirshenblatt-Gimblett. 1976. "Children's Traditional Speech Play and Child Language." In *Speech Play*, 65–110. Edited by Barbara Kirshenblatt-Gimblett. Philadelphia: University of Pennsylvania Press.

Shuman, Amy, and Charles Briggs. 1993. "Introduction." Special Issue, "Theorizing Folklore: Toward New Perspectives on the Politics of Culture." *Western Folklore* 48 (2, 3, 4): 109–134.

A longer version of this work was published as "'I Saw Mrs. Saray, Sitting on a Bombalerry': Ralph Ellison Collects Children's Folklore" by the American Folklore Society in *Children's Folklore Review* 32 (2010), and is reprinted here with permission.

CULTIVATING COURAGE THROUGH PLAY

BRIAN SUTTON-SMITH

Analyses have shown that developed forms of play typically include representations of attack, escape, accident, uncleanness, and alienation. Those five contexted perils and their associated emotions—anger, fear, shock, disgust, and sadness, respectively—appear even in the stories of very young children. After studying the stories of six two- and three-year-olds in New York City, we hypothesize that children revel in these stories because of the pervasiveness of distress and peril in their culture and families. In so doing, they create situations of pleasurable mild stress, which they can master through play. Children's early stories are thus an early effort to achieve mental health.

In 1972–1974 my students at Teachers College, Columbia University, and I considered whether the stories children make up are like folk stories. When we first asked children of the Lower East Side (P.S. 3 and a nearby preschool) for their own stories, at first they offered us Cinderella and Little Red Riding Hood. But about the second or third time around, they told stories they had made up by themselves. The 18 students and I sat in the corridors to do our collecting, and some of the better storytellers among the children would attract an audience of youngsters. We took at least one story from each of 350 children between the ages of two and ten; some children gave us more than twenty stories apiece. Our collections and findings are in our book *The Folkstories of Children* (Philadelphia: University of Pennsylvania Press, 1981).

There were many potential analyses (e.g., Propp 1958), but perhaps the most useful for showing that these stories could parallel folktales was the four plot stages used for folktale analyses by Elli Köngäs Miranda and Pierre Miranda (1970):

Stage 1. Usually the story features a subject threatened by a monster or other peril, but there is no response (as in an imaginary game of monsters, typical for five-year-olds).

Stage 2. The subject seeks to escape or be rescued but is not successful (as in a game of chasing, with seven-year-olds).

Stage 3. The central character successfully renders the threat void (comparable to a game of "Mother, May I?" with nine-year-olds).

Stage 4. The danger is removed and there is a complete transformation—there can be no recurrence (as for the victor in any competitive sport, for eleven-year-olds).

But the challenge was to understand why all the folktales and most of the children's stories began with some kind of disequilibrium or "breach element," as Jerome Bruner (1996) would come to call it. Even some stories of children as young as two had these breach elements. Furthermore, studies of preschool children's spontaneous play show that these breaches are central to their own play. One therefore wonders where these disequilibria came from. At the time, I hypothesized that the underlying grammar involved theme and variation (1978). Here's an example from two-year-old Beatrice:

The cat went on the cakies. The cat went on the car. The cookie was in my nose. The cookie went on the fireman's hat. The fireman's hat went on the bucket. The cookie went on the carousel. The cookie went on the puzzle. The cookie went on the doggie.

Here, the vectorial center or theme is "went on," with variations of what went on, or was went on—from cats to cookies to doggies. But where in life did Beatrice get this infringing and surprising "went on" vector? It is easy to suppose that it was inspired by narrative traditions and the way stories are told to young children. Most adults, however, don't like either telling or listening to this kind of childish chaos and proceed to stories that exemplify stages 3 or 4.

In fact, adults are upset by such kinds of play. Good examples come from psychoanalyst Rosalind Gould (1972), whose *Child Studies through Fantasy* is a source of descriptions of what children do when freely at play. The observations were taken in a New York City preschool where the teachers were asked to record play they did not understand. The teachers recorded many examples of death, destruction, and other perils—all "breach" forms—which the teachers selected because they found them shocking. The children were perhaps even encouraged in this when they discovered their teachers' reactions, and thus the examples may not be representative of the total range of play. Nevertheless, here are the first lines of some of the play episodes that so troubled the teachers that they reported them to Gould.

> *Boys:* We are digging for princesses . . . Yeah, ya' don't find them in New York. We're digging our way to find one. Do you know where you could get a real princess? In Ireland or England or something?
>
> *Boy:* This is a skeleton. I am cutting the head off.
>
> *Girl:* I dream about hitting babies when I get big. I talk to my babies but they don't listen. Hitting is the only way.
>
> *Girl:* Let's play another game. No mothers. No babies. Just teenagers.
>
> *Girls:* We're pretending we are witches. It's Halloween night. You can be a ghost or a goblin or a witch. They take children and turn them into gingerbread. They cut them up and put them in jail. I am eating Celeste's head. I'm eating George's arm.
>
> *Boy:* We were going to [pretend] to burn some wood and he would be tied to it. He didn't know we were kidding and he hit Bob so Bob hit him back.
>
> *Girl:* [to the teacher] I'll break your head off and eat it up so you wouldn't be Mrs. F— anymore.
>
> *Boy:* Mrs. C—, I am making a knife to cut those girls over there. Let's get a sharp knife and cut the rope ladders and the people. Just cut off everything.
>
> *Boy:* I am on the track of the choo-choo train and the train's on top of me. Help! My neck came off. Help!
>
> *Girl:* I am a bee [she chases the others]. My finger is the sting. You can have a whole jar of honey. That will last you for your whole life.
>
> *Boy:* We are making a girl-trap to kill some girls again. Girls never fall in, but they might this time.
>
> *Boys:* [in sing song] Lenny, Benny, Fenny. My name is Lenny. Your name is stupid and shit. My Daddy would beat you up. If I had a Daddy, he would get you and get a knife and cut off your head and suck out all your blood.

Themes of physical attack and vulnerability are common, but such breaches are not limited to New York City children of the early 1970s;

somewhat similar catastrophes are found in the free play and free story collections in many other research centers in various states (Sawyer 1996; Fein and Kinney 1994; Corsaro 1985; Bronner 1988; Sutton-Smith et al. 1995) and from Israel (Ariel 2002). And there is no evidence that a few heinous parents are inculcating their children with violent ideas: the same phenomena can be found practiced by children in many parts of the world where children's play and stories have been recorded.

In this study we deal only with the stories of the youngest children in our study—six two- to three-year-olds, three boys and three girls. All told, they produced eighty-five stories in two years. We chose this group because they are generally the very youngest children who can tell stories.

THE HYPOTHESIS

We suggest that these stories have their origins in the pervasiveness of various forms of distress or peril in the macrosociety (the culture) or microsociety (the family) of which the children are members. Like folk and fairy tales, many children's stories feature animals, monsters, or media characters (such as Batman) who are the agents of the breach. We believe that each form of peril has at its center a motivating ancient emotion as well as a specific cultural context. The most pervasive peril in the modern world (and in ancient and tribal worlds as well) is *attack*, as in war, hunting, and other forms of combat and competition seen in media or in reality. The emotion that motivates these varied cultural forms of attack in play is *anger*, which children witness in families as well as in the culture at large. After attack, and often associated with it, are *apprehension and escape* from dangerous, frightening people or monsters, which is represented in play by *fear*. Next are *accidents and disasters*, represented in play by *shock*. Then comes bodily *uncleanness*, which is represented by *disgust*. And finally there are the decontextual *alienations and loneliness* of the modern world, represented by *sadness*.

Those five contexted perils and their associated emotions appeared in the stories of our six young children. Anger is noticeably the largest category, but it is not always easily separable from shock or fear, and in fact, the story categorizations sometimes overlap. We identified breaches in seventy-two of these children's eighty-five stories, with no obvious differences between boys and girls in this admittedly small sample. The many repetitions of the breaches in these stories are not included in the fifty examples provided here:

Anger

The doggie bit the kitten.

The cat ate him all up.

The robber killed the cat.

Mommy was angry.

Grandpa is dead.

Father was angry.

The policeman takes mummy away.

Bill killed the tiger.

A gorilla killed the tiger.

The hunter killed the wolf.

His mommy smack his bum.

Someone bit him in the water.

And him got hit.

People get hurt.

Got mad at the frogs.

Batman crashed his car.

Superman crashed there.

He got bumped and hurt himself.

The robber came and stole the money from the bank.

Batman bumped into a girl.

The man broke a car.

The witch said stick your head in the oven and make sure now it's hot.

Shock

The slide hits the swing.

The bag bumped the fence.

Fall down in sky.

Train fall down in sky.

My Daddy fall off.

A fire burnt the house.

Big flower went boom.

Fire engine broke down.

They crashed the car.

Batman crashed in the fence.

Fear

A monster creeping at the people.

Lost and didn't know way home.

The monkey was afraid.
Batman was lost and can't find him.
A monster came and Robin got scared.

Disgust
It [is] in the worm's mouth.
People stepped on the worm.
She makes pee on the floor.
Charley cat eats dog food.
He ate doo-doo.
The frog ate some fleas.
The fleas ate the people.

Sadness
I fell down and my leg hurt.
Cookie monster hurt his foot.
Cookie monster got bit.
He bumped his lip.
Robbers stole Father's bike.
He went on your head.

Quite often these pieces are parts of longer stories; sometimes they are "vectors" appearing again and again. It is quite possible at this age, however, for children in their play or stories to have fantasies only as long as one of these sentences (as in Gould's examples, above). And yet when seen in the light of the longer if parallel emotional breaches that occur in adult literature, media, entertainment, sports, games, and the arts, these child collections are really not so strange. All human cultures, it seems, create such situations of pleasurable mild stress. "It is, after all, only on stage, or only in a book," one might say. Most of these above child utterances are of the Stage 1 character in the Miranda four-stage scheme outlined above.

We can surmise, along with Freud, that these singular catharses, or "abreactions" in Freud's terminology, are a kind of self-therapy, or put more positively, a form of courage. Maladjusted individuals can seldom make this kind of self-representation and expression for their own curative or life-enlarging purposes, whereas those who are healthy are vividly engaging almost daily, actively or receptively, in forms of play or the arts that carry these mildly stressful pleasures and masteries. Some researchers suggest that such milder forms of stress are more associated with mental and physical health than either too little stress or too much stress (Hall 2003). Cultivating and mastering mild forms of stress through play may be a means for achieving appropriate excitation without the depression or anxiety that comes with either extreme.

Analysis of play has shown that all developed forms of play typically include representations of the ancient emotions of anger, shock, fear, disgust, and sadness (Sutton-Smith 2001, 2002, 2003). In fact, these emotions usually provide the major scenarios for the play. Thus anger is represented through attack in all play contests, fear is represented through physical risk taking, shock is represented in teasing and hazing play forms, disgust manifests itself in gross humor and profanity, and sadness by the inebriation inherent in many festivals. In each of these kinds of play, the theatrically staged primary emotions are contradicted or modulated by the real emotions and masteries within the game itself, such as pride and resilience during hazing, and envy and vigilance in contests.

The duality within the play or the stories—of good and evil, success and failure, emotional positives and negatives—is very similar in its mildly stressful but positive character to many of the classic dualistic techniques that have been used throughout history to maximize personal health. This is done typically by having a subject improvise troublesome and extreme emotions as a way of bringing them under increasing control. These procedures, said to maximize positive over negative emotions, were used centuries ago by Stoics and Buddhists (Hall 2003). It might seem reasonable to suppose that stories with breaches and provocations, which are pursued so early here, even by our two-year-olds, are a primary and even elemental form of early positive emotional health maintenance.

The reason we have not been able to comprehend this elementary fact about play is the everyday hegemony of the work ethic: for several hundred years, play has been considered unreal and essentially a waste of time. Some modern research now suggests that play is an alternative form—not an inferior form—of reality. Other alternative realities that make our lives more bearable, or at least healthier, are found in the arts and in religion, which are no more real (or illusory) than play. They all share similar imaginative ways of making the world—here or beyond—worthy of our belief. Play and religion are strongly connected in most earlier societies and are moving again in a similar direction in some modern thought (Miller 1969; Cox 1969; Goodman 1992).

Children's early stories are thus an early effort to achieve mental health and to join with some luster the world as they experience it. To ban play recesses, depriving children of opportunities to play together and work out their group stories (as is advocated in some work ethic circles), is to sap the mental health that the young need as they struggle to make their world more credible to themselves. Each breach is not only fun, it is an assertion of courage in the face of fantasied disaster.

WORKS CITED

Ariel, S. 2002. *Children's Imaginative Play.* Westport, Conn.: Greenwood Press.

Bronner, S. 1988. *American Children's Folklore.* Little Rock: August House.

Bruner, J. S. 1996. *The Culture of Education.* Cambridge: Harvard University Press.

Corsaro, W. 1985. *Friendship and Peer Culture in Early Years.* Norwood, N.J.: Ablex Publishing.

Cox, H. 1969. *The Feast of Fools.* Cambridge: Harvard University Press.

Fein, G. F., and P. Kinney. 1994. "He's a Nice Alligator: Observations on the Affective Organization of Pretense." In *Children at Play: Clinical and Developmental Studies of Play.* Edited by A. Slade and D. Wolf. New York: Oxford University Press.

Goodman, F. D. 1992. *Ecstasy, Ritual, and Alternate Reality.* Bloomington: Indiana University Press.

Gould, R. 1972. *Child Studies through Fantasy.* New York: Quadrangle Books.

Hall, S. S. 2003. "Is Buddhism Good for your Health?" *New York Times*, September 14, sec. 6, 46–49.

Miranda, E. K., and P. Miranda. 1970. *Structural Models in Folklore and Transformational Essays.* The Hague: Mouton.

Miller, D. L. 1969. *Gods and Games.* New York: World Publishing.

Propp, V. 1958. "The Morphology of the Folktale." *International Journal of American Linguistics* 4 (24): 1–134.

Sawyer, R. K. 1996. *Pretend Play as Improvisation.* Hillsdale, N.J.: Lawrence Erlbaum.

Sutton-Smith, B. 1978. "Initial Education as Caricature." *Keystone Folklore* 7: 521–543.

———. 2001. "Emotional Breaches in Play and Narrative. In *Children in Play, Story, and School.* Edited by A. Göncü and E. L. Klein. New York: Guilford Press.

———. 2002. "Recapitulation Redressed." In *Conceptual, Social-Cognitive, and Contextual Issues in the Fields of Play.* Edited by J. L. Roopnarine. Play and Culture Studies, vol. 4. Westport, Conn.: Ablex Publishing.

———. 2003. "Play as Parody of Emotional Vulnerability." In *Play and Educational Theory and Practice.* Edited by D. Lytle. Play and Culture Studies, vol. 5. Westport, Conn: Praeger.

Sutton-Smith, B., J. Mechling, T. W. Johnson, and F. McMahon, eds. 1995. *Children's Folklore: A Source Book.* Logan: Utah State University Press.

"Cultivating Courage through Play" was first published in *Voices: The Journal of New York Folklore* 30, nos. 1-2 (Spring–Summer 2004): 25–28.

EMERGING TRADITIONS

Dance Performances of the
Sudanese DiDinga in Syracuse

FELICIA McMAHON

AUTHOR'S NOTE

As folklorists know, culture is not static. There have been major changes in the lives of the DiDinga since this article was first published in 2002. The most significant of these changes is that South Sudan separated from Sudan and became an independent nation on July 9, 2011. For all refugees, life is a state of constant flux as their living circumstances change quickly. The Sudanese "lost boys and lost girls" are all in their thirties; they have yet to build a stable community in the United States, and there is no longer an organized DiDinga dance group per se in Syracuse. That could change, but only time will tell. Specifically concerning the DiDinga mentioned in the original article, readers may be interested to know the following:

Of the four DiDinga young women who in 2004 immigrated to Syracuse, one has since moved to California. Two of the women are raising children as single mothers; the remaining two women attended and graduated from American universities.

Dominic Luka graduated from college, married, and is currently living with his wife in Florida.

Joseph Lomong (Lopez Lomong) became an internationally recognized Olympic runner. He was the official U.S. flag bearer for the 2008 Olympic Games in Beijing. Since that time he has also created the Lopez Lomong Foundation, which raises money to bring clean water, education, and health care to people in South Sudan (http://www.lopezlomong.com/lopez -lomong-foundation.html).

Dominic Raimondo moved to Salt Lake City, where he initiated the Sudanese Cow Project at folk arts events in Utah. In 2012, he visited South Sudan, where he is involved in fundraising for his Loudo South Sudan School

*Project (http://www.facebook.com/pages/Loudo-South-Sudan-School
-Project/211850728841906).*

*Lino Ariloka Timan earned a college degree, later starred in Ping
Chong's "Tales of Salt City" at Syracuse Stage, and has returned to South
Sudan, where he is currently involved in nation-building efforts.*

*At this writing, most of the Lost Boys and Lost Girls in Syracuse have
become American citizens.*

Young male Sudanese refugees in Syracuse constantly improvise during
their performances of danced songs. An initial study of their recontextualized traditions seeks to elucidate how group members draw on traditions
in new situations, how the emerging traditions change in form, and, when
form remains the same, what these traditions now mean for the young
men who perform for an American audience unfamiliar with the richness
of DiDinga culture.

My relationship with the DiDinga refugees from Sudan began while I was
teaching a symposium course, "Beauty in Cross-Cultural Contexts," at
Syracuse University. Prior to this project, my goal had been to introduce
my American students to the rich culture of refugees now living in our
city. As a folklorist, I wanted to honor the living traditions of the new-
est residents in the neighborhood surrounding the university by inviting traditional artists from Bosnia, Burma, and Sudan to be a part of the
symposium. After meeting a group of nine young DiDinga men between
the ages of fifteen and twenty-two who were part of the larger Sudanese
group known as "the Lost Boys," I recognized the importance of honoring their group's traditions, which are evolving in a new context—a new
country. Part of my purpose has been to understand the process by which
a group comes to consensus about appropriate and meaningful traditions
performed outside their original cultural context. How is the negotiation
process related to aesthetics and identity, as the DiDinga men select, discard, and recombine traditions learned as children in their tribal villages,
as refugees in camps in Kenya, as students in missionary schools in Nai-
robi, and as residents of Syracuse? It is the kind of question with which I
have been grappling for many years, since I first began ethnographic work
as a folklorist (McMahon 1993).

I found only a handful of studies on this little-known tribe from a remote area in southeastern Sudan. The majority of these publications were

The DiDinga "Lost Boys" performing *ngothi*, the jumping step during the *nyakorot* (DiDinga for the dance proper). Photo courtesy of Felicia McMahon with permission of Charles Lino (group leader).

attempts by linguists to classify the DiDinga language. Faced with a pau-city of published information on the DiDinga culture in general, scholars like myself have to rely on early published accounts written by missionar-ies and by Jack Herbert Driberg, who was the first anthropologist to have worked among the DiDinga, from 1922 to 1935. In 1933, Archibald Tucker had published *Tribal Music and Dancing in the Southern Sudan at Social and Ceremonial Gatherings*, the first documentation of dance songs of other little-known tribes in southern Sudan, but his book is not specifi-cally about the DiDinga. No further work on song traditions in southern Sudan has been published, with the exception of *The Dinka and Their Songs*, Francis Deng's 1973 seminal study on a culturally related tribe.

There is a comprehensive study on DiDinga culture, published in 1972 in German, by Andreas Kronenberg, as well as a 1992 doctoral dissertation by Marilyn Harer Fetterman, who lived among the DiDinga in Sudan dur-ing the 1970s and 1980s. Yet neither was accessible to my students or to the public at large. Using these two publications, I tried to unravel the ways that these young men, wearing the label of refugee, maintained dignity and expressed a viable group identity within an American framework. Although I had many opportunities to observe firsthand the continuity and discontinuity in their traditions as they evolved in Syracuse, my dilemma was how to adequately interpret these traditions performed outside their Sudanese context, which I had never observed.

Because of the civil war in Sudan—a war that began in 1955 and ravaged the country for decades—it was impossible for me for visit these young men's villages. Although DiDinga history remains oral, the collective memory of these young men was vivid and available. It was necessary, therefore, to rely on their descriptions and to note shifts in song performances both synchronically and diachronically since the DiDingas' arrival in the United States. This approach would, by necessity, diverge from the text-centered methodology used by Albert B. Lord and Milman Parry, an analytical approach known as the oral-formulaic theory.

In 1951, Lord copublished with Béla Bartók *Serbo-Croatian Folk Songs*, which presented texts and transcriptions of seventy-five folk songs from the Milman Parry collection and a morphology of Serbo-Croatian folk melodies. This publication laid the groundwork for Lord's magnum opus, *The Singer of Tales*, in which he introduced the theory that was to inspire textual studies of oral literature for decades to come. Since then, recent scholars of oral literature such as Richard Bauman, Dan Ben-Amos, Charles Briggs, Dell Hymes, Dennis Tedlock, and John Miles Foley have shown the relationship of Lord's theory to more developed theories such as performance theory, ethnography of speaking, ethnopoetics, and immanent art. Even a combination of these approaches, however, could not adequately account for the processes I was observing in the DiDinga performances.

Consequently, I began by focusing on improvisation in the emerging traditions of the dance songs of these young DiDinga men, who had lived together for a decade in refugee camps in Africa before arriving in Syracuse in 2001. Capturing the danced songs in text form is not easy. The group's lively and highly repetitive antiphonal music, based on the pentatonic scale, is composed spontaneously and possesses unique musical characteristics such as a frequently changing time signature. The songs in their original village context are tied to specific incidents or specific people and are always in flux. "Generative theory" supports the nature of such mutable songs, described by Bruce A. Rosenberg in his work on black sermons:

Lord ties the creation of new formulas [metrically governed utterances] to the singer's recollection of "the commonest ones." Actually, the singer is freed from such "memory" and such hydraulic reliance. He has at his command not several score or even several hundred formulas which can be altered by a word or phrase substitution but rather a metrical deep structure enabling the generation of an infinite number of sentences or utterances in the meter of his native language. (1990: 147)

The DiDinga singers demonstrated a similar facility with "metrical deep structures," through which a distinct style was apparent. The singers were constantly improvising during their dance performances. Unlike the Murle and other neighboring Surmic-speaking tribes, the DiDinga traditionally do not use a drum. For the most part, their songs are unaccompanied by instruments, except for occasional handheld rattles or bells worn on the forearms and thighs. Percussion is produced by stomping the feet and jumping in rapid sequence. The DiDinga themselves first brought this characteristic to my attention while we were listening to a cassette tape of traditional DiDinga music, which they had brought with them from the refugee camp in Kenya.

"Do you hear that beat?" one young man asked. "The shakers [bells]? We tie them on the legs or we tie them on the waists and some on the wrists."

As in the culturally related Nilo-Hamitic tribes, a favorite dance-song genre among the young men in Syracuse is the *gyrikot*, a mocking and often lewd song whose tempo increases until a culminating insult is made. It is a song type favored by youths both in Sudan and in the United States, and it lends itself to many performance opportunities. As one young DiDinga explained, "*Gyrikot* is all based in love stuff."

But the genre of song held in highest regard is the *olé*, the male bull song. In DiDinga language, *olé* can refer to a bull as well as to a bull song. None of the young men I met had progressed through initiation to warrior status, and thus none wore the black feather indicating the status that gave a man the privilege to sing a fully composed *olé*. Nevertheless, some did recall the beginning stage.

During adolescence, a son is given a bull calf to raise, for which he alone is responsible. This includes composing a song to his animal—the song that will soothe the bull throughout its lifetime, the song that the man will use to call his bull to follow him home after grazing. The importance of the *olé* to a man's identity and the centrality of the bull in DiDinga culture may be difficult for Americans to understand but was elucidated for me and my husband, John, during a lengthy exchange with several of the young men at our home:

Felicia: Do you have one? *Olé?*

Lino: Oh, no, maybe if we would have stayed for some time we would have had one. If I had stayed there, I would have composed one, maybe. But it is not really hard.

Felicia: I heard Andrew and Anthony sing their [Dinka] bull songs once. It sounded very hard.

Lino: Oh, yeah, being creative . . . you have your bull and nobody can touch your bull. If it is dead, it is a matter of life and death. If someone comes, you defend it. Nobody should do anything to it.

Felicia: Is this like your identity?

Lino: Oh, yes, identity . . . very important.

Dominic: Oh, yes, very important.

Felicia: If you went back to the Sudan, after you have had an education—and not everyone has an education—would you still be able to have the bull and sing the bull song?

Lino: Oh, yes! It is our culture! It is our culture. You can't just say no, because it is your culture.

Dominic: I had my bull there. And when I was playing, it was still very very young. I was really in love. So I composed one of the songs to watch it.

John: Do you perform this song? Do you have it in your head?

Dominic: Yes, I created it and when I was with my friends, taking it to grazing, so I was just singing to soothe my young love, my bull. I can sing it . . . That is why, when we were discussing this, in my head, I said, Oh, I am very much happy to hear this and I had it in my heart.

Felicia: Now, how did you other fellows know when to sing [in refrain]? Is this something that you have worked with?

Dominic: No, it is our language.

Lino: He is kind of leading you, you listen to what he says. After several repetitions, you get it.

John: It was very rhythmic. Is this a traditional rhythm or pattern of sound? Much of the Latin and Greek poetry from the ancient world derived from the kind of cultural things that you were just talking about. Pastoral poetry actually started from the songs of shepherds taking care of their sheep. The poems in Latin and Greek are highly developed as written down by poets but they come from the kind of tradition that you were singing, where someone would sing with or to the animals that they were taking care of, as shepherds. Later on the poets developed this tradition into poetry. It is fascinating that you would have engaged with your bull in a poetic way, and the rest of you knew the kinds of traditional response.

Dominic: The song that I sung was about my bull's red head and black sides and that no one will touch until it is gone bigger. That is brief about it.

Dominic L.: He liked the color of the bull, so that is why he sang about the color of the bull.

John: How long did you have this bull when you were young, and how long do people traditionally stay with one particular animal?

Dominic: You know, when I started getting that bull as mine personally, when . . . the mother give birth to it, then it was smooth and heavy and very beautiful and from that point, I was also very involved in taking care of it and taking it home with my friends and milking its mother. Suppose I was still in Sudan, I should love that bull until it's gone bigger and maybe I sell it and get money or maybe I [go to] someone to slaughter or do something in a special way . . . in a different way.

Felicia: So you have a special relationship with this animal?

Dominic: Exactly.

Felicia: Named? Do you have a name for it?

Dominic: Actually, I was supposed to come [sic] with a name for it but because of coming over here, that was the problem. And it was still very young.

Felicia: So you and this animal were kind of bound together?

Dominic: Yeah, because its mother was bought from my uncle, so my uncle brought its mother to the cattle I was taking care of, and from there its mother gave birth, then the young bull just came out very beautiful and I took from there.

Charles: When you make the program, you can put Dominic's bull song at the end? Because the bull songs come at the end.

Because I then expressed an interest in hearing Dominic's bull song, he stood up suddenly, paused, and after making a snorting sound like his bull, he sang:

Oli cani ci marini oo ci homina
Oo! Oli cani ci marini oo ci homina
Locia eet, oli cani ci marini oo ci hamina.
Ci ica aduot ci homina
Lochia eet, oli cani ci marini oo ci hamina
Illale, oli cani ci marini oo ci hamina.
Lochia eet, oli cani ci marini oo ci hamina.

[I love my bull with its red head.
Oh, I love my bull with its red head.
Son of my uncle, I love my bull with its red head
Which no one will stone.
Son of my uncle, I love my bull with its red head
Thank you, I love my bull with its red head.
Son of my uncle, I love my bull with its red head.]

But I learned that songs such as this are not usually performed separately from dance. One young man explained, "Our songs are like proverbs." I interpret this to mean "danced proverbs"—that is, a few words, each pregnant with meaning in a kind of shorthand. Applying Lord's concept of a universal oral formula in Western tradition to fit a non-Western performance was inadequate, so I looked to Robert Farris Thompson (1974) and, more recently, Michael J. C. Echeruo (1994), who suggest that the concept of aesthetics, which originated in the West, be expanded so that it is applicable to non-Western cultures. From this perspective, aesthetics is understood as processual, with the focus on expression or performance of the arts, which Thompson calls art in motion. Both theorists note that unlike premodern Western art, which is representational, African art is performed, nonmimetic, and nonrepresentational: "The term expressionism, commonplace enough in Western art history and theory, may be used here in the sense of a nonmimetic, nonrepresentational fictional statement" (Echeruo 1994: 139). In addition, evaluative responses from perceiving events performed in space or time become an important part of the aesthetic process.

Performing the danced proverbs in an American context suggests a new approach for understanding traditions as emerging. That is, we can validate the dance songs as they emerge and are performed in an expressive manner outside their original context. To do so, we need to discard the view that old and new traditions are definitively opposed. To

Joseph Lomong (left) and Dominic Luka open the *nyakorot* at the Thompson Memorial AME Zion Church in Auburn, New York. Photo courtesy of Felicia McMahon with permission of Charles Lino (group leader).

conceptualize the relation as either-or creates an antagonistic situation in which the dances and songs of these young men would be viewed from rigid categories—as either traditional or invented. From such a perspective, they would be "defective." Instead, I try to honor their dance songs by focusing on the process of the traditions as they emerge in relation to not only the new American context but also the young men's memories of Sudan. And I include in my interpretation the dancers' descriptions and explanations for their choices. I collect these self-critiques in the form of oral commentary, as we review a video of an earlier performance; sometimes I tape conversations like the one included here. For example, during a conversation prior to the first *nyakorot*, the dance proper sponsored on July 21, 2002, by the Schweinfurth Memorial Art Center at the Thompson Memorial AME Church in Auburn, New York, one man explained:

> So these people gather together and prepare everything for us to go there and come and dance for them in their place, so then they also

prepare so when we go [at] the time we are going, as we dance, they dance along. Then we dance our own song, they dance their own song. Now the competition is going! In that process, now they will follow the other people, and then they join in the same thing. It is like uniting. Now when these songs stop, the ladies are in a circle, so it is very funny . . . the ladies are there and the mens [*sic*] are there in a kind of circle [he draws two semicircles]. So the other men, they are clapping their hands . . . they are dancing. So the ladies will come and choose one person. . . . It's funny, like so they come over and they come together like [he claps once] but not together and then [he claps once to indicate bodies coming close and retreating]. After that, when the soloist starts the song, so that these people go and clap their hand [*sic*] and these people go and dance around. So the song is sung twice.

I came to recognize the paradox of DiDinga dance: *nyakorot* is held for the purpose of "uniting," but competition was at the heart of a good performance. It was through this symbolic negotiation process that the best tradition won and then united the people because what was being expressed was the best of a group identity. The paradox of uniting through competition was at the heart of not only the large-scale *nyakorot* but also the danced *gyrikot* and the young man's *olé*, sung to his bull while it was grazing.

In a sense, tradition, like all identity, was constantly changing, however subtly. Much of what is classified as tradition or invention is affected by the rhetoric surrounding the event: "Of course, a song is not really the original or innovative 'composition' of a youth any more than the hymn is really a timeless and authoritative 'tradition.' Songs can be formulaic and derivative and hymns can represent original and individual points of view. The point is that a song rests on as the hymn rests on the rhetoric of timeless traditions" (Meeker 1989: 167). During the process of recontextualization, traditions selected and reformulated by the group for presentation of their group identity allow for affirming and valuing uniqueness and personal history. Like identity, tradition is always in flux—even when an outside expression appears to remain the same. Because times and people change, no tradition, no identity can be truly static. The only static tradition is a dead one.

But who decides which traditions are tied to this community, since issues of identity are at stake here? To recontextualize DiDinga dance, it is necessary to understand how the dance songs relate to these young men's cultural values and the tribal identity that they share with DiDinga in Sudan. Understanding the relationship is important so that anachronisms are not produced. Like language translation, staged public performance involves the process of negotiating meaning from the original context into the new context. Going beyond the classic work on oral literature by Milman Parry and Albert Lord, combined with an "ethnography of speaking," I hope to understand which internal and external forces act on the aesthetics of this tradition—including the role that nostalgia plays in performance. Recording the memories of these dance traditions in which the young men once participated as youth in Sudan as well as the performances in the United States has become an important ongoing project for me as a public folklorist.

At this writing, no DiDinga women have emigrated to Syracuse. There have been outcries from the international community concerning the fate of "the Lost Girls," and some have called refugee policies sexist. However, the young DiDinga men said that parents of girls would not allow them to emigrate alone to the United States: "I think the reason is from the ladies," one said. "They don't want ladies [girls] to go. But boys can go anywhere."

Nevertheless, it is anticipated that some young women will arrive, and when they do, it will be important to note changes in these young men's performances.

WORKS CITED

Deng, Francis M. 1973. *The Dinka and Their Songs*. Oxford: Clarendon Press.
Driberg, Jack H. 1922. "A Preliminary Account of the DiDinga." *Sudan Notes and Records* 5.
Echeruo, Michael J. C. 1994. "Redefining the Ludic: Mimesis, Expression, and the Festival Mode." In *The Play of the Self*, 137–156. Edited by Ronald Bogue and Mihai I. Spariosu. Albany: State University of New York Press.
Fetterman, Marilyn Harer. 1992. "Drought, Cattle Disease, Colonialism, and Lokembe: One Hundred Years of Change among the Pastoralist DiDinga, Eastern Equatoria Province, Sudan." Ph.D. dissertation, Brown University, Department of Anthropology.
Foley, John Miles. 1995. *The Singer of Tales in Performance*. Bloomington: Indiana University Press.
Kronenberg, Andreas. 1972. *Logik und Leben: Kulturelle Relevanz der DiDinga und Longarim, Sudan*. Wiesbaden: Franz Steiner Verlag.
McMahon, Felicia. 1993. "Regional Sports: 'Playing' with Politics in the Adirondacks." *New York Folklore* 19 (3-4): 59–73.

Meeker, Michael E. 1989. *The Pastoral Son and the Spirit of Patriarchy: Religion, Society, and Person among East African Stock Keepers*. Madison: University of Wisconsin Press.

Rosenberg, Bruce A. 1990. "The Message of the American Folk Sermon." In *Oral-Formulaic Theory*, 137–168. Edited by John Miles Foley. New York: Garland Publishing.

Thompson, Robert Farris. 1974. *Art in Motion*. Los Angeles: University of California Press.

Tucker, Archibald N. 1933. *Tribal Music and Dancing in the Southern Sudan (Africa) at Social and Ceremonial Gatherings*. London: New Temple Press.

"Emerging Traditions: Dance Performances of the Sudanese DiDinga in Syracuse" was first published in *Voices: The Journal of New York Folklore* 28, nos. 3-4 (Fall–Winter 2002): 32–36.

FLYIN' HIGH

Kite Flying from the Silk Road to Roosevelt Avenue

ELENA MARTÍNEZ

PHOTOGRAPHS BY MARTHA COOPER

I first went to see the Pakistani kite fliers in the summer of 2000 when many New York City folklorists were conducting fieldwork for the Smithsonian Institution's 2001 Festival of American Folklife. It was fascinating to watch the kite teams "battle" and to speak with the fliers. I went back to watch the fliers once more in 2001, but have not seen them again, since they relocated to a new field after September 11, 2001. The post-9/11 world has brought momentous changes to the Pakistani community. Fearing

Kite flier at Flushing Meadow Park in 2000, displaying kites made in Pakistan. Photo © Martha Cooper.

Fliers bring a kite-shaped bag full of kites, because it is not unusual to go through as many as a dozen in a day's practice. Photo © Martha Cooper.

security detentions, thousands of the city's 120,000 Pakistani residents have left Brooklyn's Little Pakistan and other Pakistani neighborhoods for Canada, Europe, and Pakistan. Fliers nevertheless maintain their kite flying tradition, which has become part of New York City's cultural tapestry.

In September 2001, an article in the *New York Times* reviewed the recent military and political history of Afghanistan, in advance of President Bush's anticipated declaration of war. The piece began, "[Afghanistan] is a nation of warriors, where children glue broken glass to their kite strings to cut down other kites, boys are given rifles at puberty, and old men keep thrushes in wooden cages trained not to sing, but to fight" (Kifner 2001). The attempt to distance the people of Afghanistan was disingenuous—after all, animals are trained to fight and kids use guns in the United States, too—but the article's mention of kite flying is interesting. While kite flying may not be as widespread a recreational activity in this country as, say, basketball, glass-encrusted kite strings are certainly not unique to Afghanistan. Kids in New York City also create kites for competitions and battles. My uncles, who grew up on the "mean streets" of the Bronx, have told me stories about their own glass-string kite fights when they were young:

A *patang* kite. The designs and colors can represent a variety of things. During the International Cup, the New York Meadow Kite Flyers team kites were red, white, and blue, because the group represented the United States. In the big international competitions, kites are stamped with the name of the person who made the kite. The kite maker has to be registered with the World Control Board of Kite Flying. Photo © Martha Cooper.

> We used to take glass bottles to the trolley car tracks and wait for the trolley to come. The trolley would pulverize the glass, and we'd sweep up as much as we could. . . . Or you would break the glass with a hammer, and then put it on a piece of paper with some glue, run the string through it, and you'd have glass string. And then we'd go on the roof, and if there was another kite flying up there, we used to cut theirs down. . . . There were also tails on the kites, and we used to put razor blades on them. (Cooley and Phelan, 2000)

A former resident of East Harlem also remembers:

> We used to fly kites on the roof, and you used that . . . thin wood, from orange crates, put pieces in an X, and got lightweight paper. [The kite] wasn't just to fly, but an element of war. On the edge of the tail you put razor blades, and you had the advantage if you had the wind. You got your kite over [the other guy's kite], and gave it slack. Then your kite would collapse and cut the line. (Dargan and Zeitlin 1990)

Before they are launched into the air, kites are repaired with tape. Photo © Martha Cooper.

Kite battles and competitions are popular throughout Asia, from Afghanistan to Pakistan and India, as well as further east in Japan. I learned about a group of Pakistani kite fliers that regularly met in Flushing Meadow Park and competed using glass string to cut their opponents' kites. In fact, members of the Pakistani, Indian, and Afghani communities all flew kites in the park, but it was the Pakistani fliers who met in teams at the model airplane field to fly kites and practice for international competitions.

In the summer of 2000 I spoke with Sheryar Chaudhry, director of the World Control Board of Kite Flying, United States; Adnan Munawar, chairman of the Kite Flying Association, United States; and Irfan Saleem, captain of the New York Meadow Kite Flyers team. The team has more than one hundred active members who meet on Saturdays and Sundays, weather permitting, from April to October. They began flying kites in Flushing Meadow Park in 1996; in 1998, the team was officially recognized by the World Control Board of Kite Flying and allowed to compete in the kite World Cup. More recently, Flushing Meadow Park's proximity to LaGuardia Airport has forced the kite fliers to move their weekend competitions to Kissena Park in Queens, so that kites will not interfere with air traffic or land on the airport's property.

Americans are generally unfamiliar with this passion for kite flying and professional kite competition, but children in Pakistan fly kites like

To string the kites, the spools are wound with a power drill. Photo © Martha Cooper.

kids in the United States play baseball. Throughout Asia, kite flying is far more than just a children's game—it's a focal point of religious events and competitions. Kite flying is thought to have originated in China more than two thousand years ago, and from there spread to Korea. In both countries it became widely popular. The string was coated with powdered glass, sharp sand, or ground pottery, and at times knife blades were attached. By the sixth century, kite flying had arrived in Japan, where kites were flown mainly for religious purposes, although kite fighting with *rokkaku*, six-sided kites, was also common. In 1921, kite flying was proclaimed the national sport of Thailand. Kite competition in Thailand takes a unique form. Kites are either *chula* (male) or *pakpao* (female), and the object is to capture a kite of the other gender and bring it into your team's territory. In India, the festival of Makar Sankranti, a harvest festival held on January 14, is a traditional day of combative kite flying. In the weeks prior to the festival, lengths of thread that will be used as kite string are stretched between posts so gum and powdered glass can be applied. After the festival, the region appears as a "vision of trees full of strange, bright blooms which are entrapped kites" (Cooper and Gillow 1996: 112).

The Pakistani kite flying tradition comes from India and has its deepest roots and greatest popularity in the province of Punjab, which borders India. Pakistan separated from India in 1947, and in 1972 East Pakistan

Fliers wind their fingers with tape for protection from the razor-sharp kite string. Photo © Martha Cooper.

became Bangladesh. While the three countries share many cultural traits, there are some significant differences, such as religion: Pakistan and Bangladesh are primarily Muslim, while the majority of the Indian population is Hindu. According to Sheryar, the Pakistani style of kite flying originated on the Indian subcontinent about five or six hundred years ago with the creation of the *basant mala*, or festival of kites. This festival was begun by a local king in hopes of uniting Hindus, Muslims, and Sikhs through a national celebration (Chaudhry et al. 2000). Today, this festival is celebrated in Pakistan, India, and Bangladesh. In Pakistan the *basant* is observed in mid-February, and during this time in cities throughout the Punjab such as Lahore, Faisalabad, and Rawalpindi, the skies blaze with the color of thousands of kites soaring from the rooftops.

The New York Meadow Kite Flyers organized their own *basant mala* festivals in 1996, 1998, and 2000. Although inclement weather forced the cancellation of the popular event one year, thousands of people showed up just the same, some from as far away as Washington, D.C., and Boston. As the only event of its kind in the United States, the festival transcends politics and historical animosities, as Indians and Pakistanis gather to fly kites together. The multinational festival also attracts fliers from Bangladesh, Guyana, and the Caribbean.

One doesn't have to attend a *basant mala* to see kite fighting teams in action. Every weekend, kite fliers arrive at the park and split into two teams. Preparation takes about fifteen minutes as the fliers spread out an array of colorful kites on the ground to string them, tape them up, and take some test flights. In addition to readying the kites, fliers have to prepare themselves. They wrap their fingers with duct tape to protect them from the kite lines, or *manjha*, a cotton string with a coating of powdered glass.

The teams use traditional kites shipped from Pakistan. These *patang* kites, made of spliced bamboo and tissue paper, have a hawk-like shape, which makes them easier to control and more maneuverable. To ensure that they flow in the direction of the wind, the kites are flown at great heights, using up to a thousand yards of string, at times making them barely discernable against the blue sky. The goal is to swoop one's kite across an opponent's string and move it up and down in order to cut the string. With the right techniques, and depending on the tautness of the string and the angle at which the kite is flown, it is sometimes possible to cut lines without using glass-powdered strings. In a day's flying (about four to five hours) it is typical for a flier to go through ten or more kites, because cut kites drift away and are seldom recovered. Lucky park visitors may find them in other areas of the park where they have touched down. When the group flew kites at Flushing Meadow Park, a walk through the area around the model airplane field would often reveal trails of kite string that had fallen from the sky.

Immigrants fly kites in part to maintain their heritage, but the popularity of kite flying in the United States also reflects the sport's increasing status back home. With its starring role at festivals like the *basant mala*, professional kite flying in Asia has begun to attract major international sponsors such as Coca-Cola. One year, a Marriott hotel in Pakistan even arranged a *basant mala* on its rooftop. With the promise of monetary success and fame, kite flying is drawing more participants. Players on winning professional teams become celebrities and may be approached to do commercial advertisements.

Kite fighting competitions are popular throughout central Asia. Their broad appeal is reflected in New York City, where Pakistani kite fliers are not the only ones who use the parks for kite battles. In the parking lot near the model airplane field in Flushing Meadow Park, Afghani kite fliers would gather. Instead of powdered glass string they use a material similar to fishing line, and their kites are diamond-shaped and smaller. Kite flying in Afghanistan was a traditional sport for decades until banned in the

Ready, set, go! Photo © Martha Cooper.

mid-1990s under Taliban rule. But since the end of 2001, it has made a comeback; sales in shops along Kabul's "Kite Street" are booming (Peterson 2001). In Afghanistan, kite flying is not a reminder of violent traditions as the *New York Times* article implied, but—in addition to a cultural tradition that goes back centuries—a symbol of freedoms restored.

This year the World Control Board of Kite Flying, United States, received a patent for its *basant mala*. The kite fliers of New York City plan to organize *basant mala* festivals in future years. From the rooftops of the Bronx to the rooftops of Pakistan, from the parks of Queens to the streets of Afghanistan, kite flying competitions will continue to entertain people of all ages.

Note: The title of this article comes from the Silk Road, which was a trade route across Asia to the Mediterranean in active use from approximately 200 BCE to 1200 CE. This route from Nara, Japan, to Venice, Italy, was started by merchants trading goods, but ultimately created places where ideas, music, foods, and religions were exchanged and adapted to new homes. Roosevelt Avenue in Queens is just north of the parks where the kite fliers have their competitions. Due to Queens' ethnic diversity—it is the most ethnically diverse county in the United States—many have likened the borough to a contemporary Silk Road.

WORKS CITED

Chaudhry, Sheryar, Adnan Munawar, and Irfan Saleem. 2000. Interview by Elena Martínez, September 21.

Cooley, Harry, and Richard Phelan. 2000. Interview by Elena Martínez, April 23.

Cooper, Ilay, and John Gillow. 1996. *Arts and Crafts of India*. New York: Thames and Hudson.

Dargan, Amanda, and Steven Zeitlin. 1990. Interview of Ben Swedowsky, 1984. In *City Play*. New Brunswick: Rutgers University Press.

Kifner, John. 2001. "Forget the Past: It's a War Unlike Any Other." *New York Times*, Week in Review, September 23, 8.

Peterson, Scott. 2001. "A Letter from Kabul, Afghanistan." *Christian Science Monitor*, December 3.

"Flyin' High: Kite Flying from the Silk Road to Roosevelt Avenue" was first published in *Voices: The Journal of New York Folklore* 31, nos. 1-2 (Spring–Summer 2005): 22–27.

PETANQUE IN NEW YORK

VALÉRIE FESCHET

First played in New York City in the 1930s (Pilate 2005: 109–110), the bowling game *petanque* has become visible in the public spaces of Manhattan, Brooklyn, and Queens, next to Frisbee, badminton, volleyball, and tai chi. Today, this urban game is practiced by players of French origin (binational and expatriate), French-speaking immigrants of African origin, and, increasingly, English-speaking players. This article uses ethnographic data I collected in 2009 and 2011 to describe petanque play in New York City, including different playing areas, the history of local petanque clubs, important annual competitions and events, ordinary practice, and the personal journeys and motivations of the players.

THE HISTORY OF PETANQUE

Since the eighteenth and nineteenth centuries, outdoor bowling has been extremely popular in France, as in the other countries of western Europe. There were and still are many regional variations of the game. In Provence, the traditional game was called *la longue provençale*, or simply *la jeu provençale*, and was similar to the Italian game of bocce. *La longue provençale* was very popular, but very difficult. Players needed to be agile and muscular, with a good sense of balance. Over time, certain players of the "long game" began playing the "small game"—as one said, taking no notice of the contempt in which they were held.

Petanque was thus invented at the beginning of the twentieth century in the south of France by players who revolted against the difficulty and elitism of *la longue provençale* and decided to play *ped tanco* ("feet fixed" in Provençal). The new game was called *piedtanque*, which finally became *pétanque*. The "round," the circle from which the players have to throw

Alfred Levitt playing petanque in Central Park, ca. 1970s. Photo: Private collection (photographer unknown).

their balls, became sacred. Touching it, or moving out of it, became a serious offense. The playing distance was reduced. The rules were simplified—in short, a revolution! The game of bowling, played only by fit men, became accessible to everyone, including women, children, and the aged.

Although the first competition was held in 1910 in La Ciotat, a little town near Marseille, it took almost fifty years for petanque to be officially accepted. The Fédération Française de Pétanque et de Jeu Provençal (FFPJP) was born in July 1945; the international federation, Fédération Internationale de Pétanque et Jeu Provençal (FIPJP), was founded in 1958. Fifty years later, more than eighty-eight countries and more than a half a million individuals are members of the international federation. In France and in many others countries, there are countless recreational players.

The introduction of petanque to the United States as a competitive sport has been slow. In 2009, there were only 1,456 registered players in the whole of the United States, compared with 313,985 federation members in France and 29,787 in Spain. Nevertheless, my observations in New York show that petanque is becoming increasingly popular in this country.

THE GAME AND THE RULES

Several American web sites focus on petanque. They all teach the pronunciation of the game's name, point out the simplicity of play, and outline the rules:

> Petanque, pronounced "pay-tonk," [is] one of Europe's most popular outdoor games. . . . The aim is to toss or roll a number of hollow steel balls ("boules") as close as possible to a small wooden target ball, called the "but" or "cochonnet" (French for "piglet"). Players take turns, and the team that ends up nearest to the target ball when all balls are played wins. Petanque can be played on most outdoor surfaces, without any set-up. Nothing is decided until the last player plays the very last boule. (www.petanqueamerica.com)

The rules are posted in front of the courts in Bryant Park, Manhattan, in the following form:

> The game is played by teams of one, two, or three players on any small area of bare ground or crushed stone gravel, but never on grass or pavement. A coin toss determines the first team to play. A player on the first team selects a starting place and draws a circle 14–20 inches in diameter on the ground. A player on the first team then tosses the jack a distance of 20–33 feet. The player's feet must remain within the circle until the ball touches the ground. Standing in the circle, a player on the first team then throws a ball to place it as close as possible to the jack. The opposing team then throws its balls, attempting to get closer to the jack than the opponent.
>
> A team continues to throw until one of its balls is closer to the jack. Should the jack be hit, the game is played from the new location of the jack. . . . The winning team [in each round] is the one with the closest ball to the jack. . . . A team receives one point for each ball nearer to the jack than the opponent's closest ball. The game continues until one team reaches 13 points.

It is still impossible to find petanque balls in New York stores. Players have to buy them online—but new players still manage to show up with their own equipment before long. Experienced players sometimes offer their old balls to newer players.

Passersby in American parks often confuse petanque with the Italian game of bocce, which was popular in New York before petanque appeared on the scene. While the games share a common ancestor, they differ considerably. Bocce balls are large and made of colored wood, while petanque balls are smaller and made of metal. Bocce players throw their balls after a three-step run, while petanque is played with feet fixed. Bocce courts are smooth, sandy, and groomed, but petanque courts are stony and ungroomed.

Most New Yorkers still know next to nothing about petanque. Curious and intrigued, they will often ask players for information when they come across a game. They are quite surprised to discover that this game, which seems only recreational, is actually an international competitive sport. The exchanges between players and the New York audience are always warm and lighthearted. Some players even have fans. One Wednesday afternoon in April 2009, a group of young people stopped around the Bryant Park courts to watch some games. They didn't hesitate to cheer and comment on the players' feats from the sidelines. I have never had so much support aiming for the cochonnet! Petanque play in New York is far more open, cool, and shared than it is in France these days, where petanque courts are often inaccessible to casual visitors, and the games are serious and solemn.

BASTILLE DAY PETANQUE TOURNAMENTS

The remarkable spread of petanque in New York in the last thirty years is certainly linked to the success of popular contests organized to celebrate Bastille Day on July 14. These annual competitions existed by the 1960s but took place outside the city, in New Jersey, during picnics hosted by New York's Breton community. Later, during the 1980s, a Bastille Day tournament was organized by a Manhattan restaurant called Provence. It took place on McDougall Street in SoHo and was sponsored by Veuve Cliquot champagne. But according to petanque players, the competition wasn't serious enough, and it eventually ran out of steam. In 2001, the annual competition moved to Smith Street in Brooklyn and is now organized by the Bar Tabac and Robin des Bois restaurants. It has become a festive event anticipated by players and fans. Encouraged by the success of the Smith Street event, Cercle Rouge restaurant on West Broadway in Tribeca held its own Bastille Day competition in 2009.

Lucien Rakotojaona in the semifinals of the Cercle Rouge Bastille Day tournament, July 14, 2009. Photo: Valérie Feschet.

These events require considerable preparation. Tons of sand are poured; the streets are blocked, traffic stopped—and a French village on a feast day emerges. The exuberant clothing and behavior recall Pagnolesque scenes. More than ten thousand people often attend the Brooklyn competition, despite the heat. A guillotine sits in the middle of the street. Some people snap photos of friends with their heads under the blade. Others don't seem to understand what the object means; the link between the fall of the Bastille and petanque isn't clear.

The French themselves simply know that there can't be a July 14 without a game of petanque. Petanque appropriates the moment, the history.

BRYANT PARK

The Bastille Day competition is an annual event that has become an enormous success. Petanque is also played on a daily basis, however, within the urban space of the city. Since 1992, Bryant Park has become the principal spot. Situated just behind the New York Public Library at 42nd Street

Pierre Le Goff (right) plays with a friend on the petanque courts at Bryant Park, April 2009. Photo: Valérie Feschet.

between 5th and 6th Avenues, one could say that Bryant Park is the heart of the town. Jerome Barth, vice president of business affairs for the Bryant Park Corporation (BPC), granted me an interview that proved instructive for understanding the evolution of petanque in New York City. During the 1970s, the park was a symbol of the city's decline: a "no-go zone," it was called Needle Park by locals because of the heroin dealers who congregated there. In 1980, Dan Biederman, a town planner working for the city, founded the Bryant Park Corporation. Its aim was to improve this public space with the help of private funds. Work began in 1988, and the park was closed to the public for four years. When it reopened in 1992, petanque was among the free activities made available to the public. The BPC took inspiration from French villages, where the *place* (central square) plays an important role in town life. The BPC wished to adapt this model while keeping the natural aspect of a park, with a large grassy space open to all, as Americans like.

Petanque was a prudent choice. The urban planners of the BPC wanted popular, convivial outdoor games that are relatively easy to set up. Petanque boasts an international federation, with millions of players throughout the world; the game can be played anywhere and doesn't require complex or expensive equipment. Two petanque playing areas were built at the northwest angle of the park. New York's oldest petanque club, La Boule New Yorkaise, was invited to use the petanque courts. In exchange, the BPC asked the club to welcome amateurs, giving free lessons and lending equipment. The instructors are now paid by the corporation, but for seven years they took turns working for nothing and progressively increased the number of club members.

The ambience of the Bryant Park playing areas is extraordinary. There are a lot of players, especially between midday and two o'clock. A more surprising discovery is the "Old" Bretons—*les anciens*, as they are called. Most of these Breton petanque players immigrated in the 1950s and 1960s. Working mainly in the restaurant business, they still form a tight-knit community, with many living relatively close to the park. Some of these players came from Ariège and the vicinity of Nice. For all of them, petanque is an opportunity for sociability, getting out to meet and spend time with compatriots, which is very similar to the way petanque is played in France.

CENTRAL PARK

Before Bryant Park reopened, many Bretons and other French played in Central Park. I believe they already played there in the 1930s. Some players practiced petanque in France before coming to the United States, but many of them discovered the game during the 1960s in New York—in the pathways of Central Park, where games went on every weekday, or during Le Stade Breton's annual picnics. Some Breton restaurants on the West Side, like Tout Va Bien and Sans Culottes Sports, were actually dedicated to petanque (and soccer).

There is no specific area for petanque in Central Park, but players are generally tolerated by the authorities. They play on free ground, as petanque enthusiasts love to do. Sometimes they have to move to a new place. According to Pierre Le Goff, a player born in New York of Breton parents, players used to gather in the 1960s and 1970s near 106th Street on the West Side, where in 1974 the first big La Boule New Yorkaise contest was held, attracting ninety players from Quebec (*New York Times* 1974). Over the intervening decades, the games migrated to at least three other locations in the park, before settling at the current location on the horse-riding alley just behind Tavern on the Green. This area in the southwest of Central Park is close to a former French residential neighborhood. Before the 1990s, many in the French community (particularly Breton) lived on the West Side. Most of the French restaurants were situated there as well, although the restaurants have now moved to Brooklyn or SoHo, Tribeca, and the East Village.

The practice of petanque in Central Park, however, does not belong exclusively to the French. There is also a playing area behind Bow Bridge, one of the park's seven original cast-iron bridges, which is a meeting place for players from the East Side.

THE OLD WASHINGTON SQUARE COURTS

Some other petanque players met in Washington Square Park (about fifty blocks south of Central Park). Washington Square Park is a crucial area in the history of petanque in New York City. Joe Bettro remembers the site's early history. Joe was born in 1927 in Calabria, Italy. He arrived in New York at the age of nine. As a child, he lived in Brooklyn, before moving to the West Village in Manhattan, not far from Washington Square Park. Although he is Italian, Joe had never played bocce, which is not a traditional game in Calabria. He never saw a game of petanque until the 1970s, when he met a multinational group of petanque players practicing near the Washington Arch at the bottom of 5th Avenue. Joe was quickly invited to join them, and he hasn't stopped playing ever since. During my research in 2009, he was enjoying his retirement by visiting all of the petanque areas of Manhattan daily, beginning with Central Park around midday, then Bryant Park, and finishing the afternoon in Washington Square.

I learned from Joe and his friends Hans Jepson and James Barr that Alfred Levitt, the founder of La Boule New Yorkaise, started the magnificent petanque areas in Washington Square Park in 1983. The story of the old courts of Washington Square shows how motivated the early players were to practice their favorite game in the best conditions. When New York University expanded in Greenwich Village in the 1970s and 1980s, the Italian quarter that surrounded Washington Square was destroyed. Alfred Levitt took the opportunity to convince the park commissioner to build a petanque court in Washington Square. Levitt and his friends used to play near the triumphal arch but dreamed about a real *boulodrome*, like in Provençal villages: well demarcated, with fine earth and gravel, and above all for players only, undisturbed by passersby. Levitt finally obtained two courts for the exclusive use of members of La Boule New Yorkaise on Saturdays and Sundays.

Unfortunately, the petanque area was destroyed in 2009 when the park was renovated—a sad day! But two new areas have been promised by the municipality and will soon be ready for play. No doubt the history of petanque at this place and the Bryant Park model helped to convince the urban planners.

PETANQUE ONLINE

http://labouleny.com
http://newyorkpetanque.com/NewYorkPetanque/Our_Club.html
http://brooklyn-boule.blogspot.com
http://www.petanqueamerica.com
http://www.usapetanque.org

FRANCOPHONE PLAYERS OF AFRICAN ORIGIN

Let's head back to Bryant Park, where French-speaking players of African origin—a group becoming more important both in numbers and in sporting performance—often gather. Some of these players arrived in New York about twenty years ago, such as Lucien Rakotojaona, originally from Madagascar. When through an invitation from another Madagascan he discovered members of La Boule New Yorkaise playing in Washington Square Park, he was so happy that he went there every evening after work. Thiam Amadou is from Senegal. He is in charge of the technical team at Bryant Park and became a member of La Boule New Yorkaise in 1999. Like Lucien, he also plays regularly in Flushing Meadow Park, with the Bretons and Madagascans who live in Queens. They play there all year round—under a bridge if it rains.

Others arrived in New York more recently and were already very good players. Keita Bangali, from Guinea-Conakry, has lived in Manhattan for five years. He returned to his old passion for petanque and now plays every day. Youssef Hass comes from Morocco. After playing while visiting his family two years ago, he wondered if there was anywhere he could play in New York and discovered the Boule New Yorkaise web site. Emile

Boujeke just arrived in New York in 2009. He learned petanque in 1999 in Bafoussam, Cameroon, and worked as an instructor and referee before arriving in this country. In New York, he searched online for information on petanque and came across the Boule New Yorkaise site. I also learned that Wolof players from Senegal used to meet in a park between the New School library and Columbia University.

The symbolic usages of petanque for these French-speaking players are specific to the former French colonies. Africans could not participate in competitions organized by the federation until quite recently. The African countries have now appropriated petanque. Through it, they can affirm a national—or sometimes an ethnic or communal—identity. Their collective and individual histories are distinct, and their social and cultural references are different, but petanque gives these players a common bond and an opportunity to express themselves in the urban space and meet one another.

BINATIONAL PLAYERS

With one foot in France and one foot in the United States, petanque is for binational players an expression of their double nationality. Those I met have taken up petanque with great enthusiasm. Thierry Julliard is a young French man whose mother is American. He grew up in Saint-Rémy-de-Provence and completed his studies in London and New York. Thierry discovered petanque when he was a child. For his tenth birthday, his mother gave him his first set of recreational balls, then later an old man offered him "real brand new balls," usable in competition. He began playing in local contests in his village. He would practice each Wednesday evening with his friends, and after coming home and putting his bag down, he would head out again to play with older players. In New York in 2008, after long years without petanque, he discovered the courts in Washington Square. It was a big surprise and a great joy.

Christophe Chambers, head of a design agency in Manhattan, is also a passionate player. His mother was French, from Poitiers. His taste for petanque comes from his childhood, although his family did not practice the game. He played during his adolescence and became a member of La Boule New Yorkaise in 1994 when he discovered the players at Washington Square Park. At present he moves between homes in New York and Austin, Texas, where he just founded a new petanque club.

Robert Dunn doesn't live in New York City, but in Syracuse. His mother was also French. He grew up in France in Saint-Benoît-la-Forêt near Poitiers, which is where he learned to play petanque, and came to United States in 1984 at the age of twenty-four. He had played petanque as a child in France with his mother's family and his friends, but when, in April 2009, he discovered by chance La Boule New Yorkaise members playing in Bryant Park, he had not practiced for a long time. Nevertheless, his comeback to the courts was so serious that, after only a few months of regular play, he won the Cercle Rouge Bastille Day Tournament in July 2009. He visits the city once or twice a month to play petanque—a four-hour drive.

ENGLISH-SPEAKING PLAYERS

Petanque by no means appeals only to French, binationals, or French-speaking Africans. Not at all—there are also plenty of English-speaking players from all parts of the world. Yngve Biltsted, an architect, was born in Denmark in 1943. While traveling by Volkswagen van through France in 1974, he saw a petanque game for the first time in a little village. "I fell in love immediately," he said. He started playing petanque in Copenhagen in 1984, before settling in New York in 1986. During a walk in Washington Square, he found himself face-to-face with petanque players Joe Bettro and Hans Jepson. "What the hell! They're playing here!" he thought. He became a member of La Boule New Yorkaise in 1988, then vice president, and served as president from 1992 to 2005. He has regularly competed at the local, national, and international levels.

Ernesto Santos works in information technology. He was born in Cuba of a Cuban father and Chinese mother. He arrived in New York at the age of eleven and began playing petanque in 2003. He had never heard anything about the game before that. He says he likes "the calm of petanque games, the concentration the sport requires, and the tactical creativity of the game." He takes part in all the competitions he can. He has been president of La Boule New Yorkaise since 2007.

Richard Meas has been playing petanque for twenty years. He lives in Westchester County, thirty minutes by train from Manhattan, where he works. Nicknamed Te, Richard had to leave Cambodia in the late 1970s because of the Khmer Rouge. After living briefly in Thailand, Indonesia, and France—where he learned petanque—he arrived in New York in 1983. He found the Manhattan petanque courts during his walks in the town.

Lorissa Rinehart plays at Bryant Park, April 2009. Photo: Valérie Feschet.

He practices twice a week. An excellent player, very motivated and competitive, he has participated in many national and international competitions and often wins the tournaments he attends.

Generally, the members of La Boule New Yorkaise live or work close to Washington Square Park or Bryant Park. They discovered petanque during their daily routine—generally during a lunch break or in the evening after work. Such was the case for Chris Artis, a native New Yorker and the current vice president of the club, who was working at a Manhattan publisher located near Bryant Park when he came across the petanque players by chance. The same goes for Lorissa Rinehart, who was doing research in the public library when she saw the players for the first time. She lives in Brooklyn and, like Chris, practices two or three times a week in Bryant Park and occasionally on the edge of the baseball pitches in Prospect Park.

These English-speaking players appreciate the fraternal, relaxed atmosphere of petanque, but generally see the game as a serious, competitive sport like golf or tennis. Alec Stone Sweet spends several months a year practicing in France and competes each year at major international competitions such as La Marseillaise à Pétanque and Mondial de Millau. Hans Jepson's approach is also essentially competitive. His first contact with petanque was in Washington Square Park, where he saw players practicing. Fascinated, he returned the following weekend, and the players invited him to join them. He says he is now "retired" from petanque, but between 1985 and 2007, he took part in seven world championships and won numerous U.S. tournaments. He also helped to unify the Federation of Petanque USA (FPUSA), the official governing body of petanque in the United States, of which he was the first president. Hans stopped playing a few years ago, when he decided to devote more time to his wife and to practicing his religion. He felt that he had played at his best in the 2007 world championship and wanted to go out "on top."

PROSPECT PARK AND THE NEW YORK PETANQUE CLUB

Until 2009, a group of excellent players from Provence played in Bryant Park and Washington Square Park. These Marseillais, as the southern French are called, immigrated more recently than the Bretons—mostly in the 1980s. Many of them work in restaurants, but others are computer specialists or work in import-export, perfumery, or other businesses. They were already confirmed players before coming to New York, playing top-level petanque in numerous international championships. Jean-Pierre Subrenat (the New York Petanque Club's president), along with Eric Bertin, Xavier Thibaud, and Americans Joe Martin and Steve Ginsberg, represented the United States during the 2010 petanque world championship in Izmir, Turkey. They competed against players from forty-eight nations and five continents. The U.S. team finished eighteenth, a very respectable showing considering the level of competition and the absence of a widespread petanque culture in the United States. The French team carried the day, in a victory over the Malagasy.

When these players discovered that petanque existed in New York, during Provence restaurant's Bastille Day tournaments in 1997 and 1998, they enthusiastically joined La Boule New Yorkaise. The playing courts available in Manhattan did not prove adequate for competitive petanque, so they joined several American players in 2009 to create another club, develop a more energetic competition policy, and build their own petanque court. The New York Petanque Club's web site explains that, "for unconditional love of the game," they obtained a concession at the parade ground in Brooklyn's Prospect Park. The club has laid out petanque courts, which allow members to train and organize important competitions without being at the mercy of the public activity program at Bryant Park.

Since the New York Petanque Club's founding, the New York petanque scene is split into two camps that now confront each other in competitions under different banners. On one side is La Boule New Yorkaise, founded by a Ukrainian and more recently run by English-speaking players with no direct links with France. Paradoxically, the logo of the club is composed of French symbols: the Washington Arch and the Statue of Liberty. And on the other side is the New York Petanque Club, founded at the initiative of French players. The new club has an English name and an American symbol: the Brooklyn Bridge.

McCARREN PARK AND BROOKLYN BOULE

Despite this competitive approach, some Americans do view petanque through a romantic and aesthetic lens. (These are compatible—not competing—visions of the game, in my opinion.) Peaceful, democratic, unselfish representations are sometimes at the heart of players' motivations, as is the case for Bruce Janovski, who reached the final of the Smith Street Bastille Day tournament in 2010. Bruce was born in Brooklyn. He has never been to France, but he read Peter Mayle's 1993 book *A Year in Provence*, which mentions the importance of petanque in the region. Bruce liked what he read and was immediately won over when he saw the Bryant Park players.

This ideological aspect, represented by literature and film as well as objects, attracted Tristram Drew, an artist living in Brooklyn in the Williamsburg area. Several years ago, Tristram set up an informal club called Brooklyn Boule so that fans of petanque can meet in the shade of the very old oak trees in McCarren Park.

The club's web site offers a creative, fresh vision of petanque. Tristram creates photomontages highlighting petanque in the Brooklyn area. The montages superimpose different dimensions and fantasies: for example, there is a petanque ball next to Pikachu in the Brooklyn Parade and the logo of his club superimposed on a rooftop water reservoir. This is a playful view of petanque, freed from popular French and Provençal folklore.

PIT STOP AND THE FRENCH RESTAURANTS

Until the summer of 2009, Brooklyn players also had another place to meet: the Pit Stop restaurant on Columbia Street. This small and charming restaurant opened in 2004, but finally went out of business. From April to October, the restaurant maintained two small petanque playing areas in the rear courtyard. The manager aimed to create a relaxed atmosphere, using an aesthetic based on reclaimed urban objects (signposts, tires, metal bars) and incorporating many allusions to petanque in France.

New York has a whole network of French restaurants linked by professional or friendly ties. The "petanque connection" structures bonds of friendship based on shared memories. A former manager of Pit Stop explained, "Monday evening, it's an aperitif at Bernard's place [Robin des Bois on Smith Street in Brooklyn]; Wednesday, it's at Pit Stop; Friday, at Harween and Gilles's place, Flea Market [in the East Village]." These restaurants, to which should be added the Bar Tabac in Brooklyn and the Cercle Rouge in Manhattan, all display objects belonging to French popular culture—the sporting and social universe of petanque.

MEN, WOMEN, AND YOUNG PEOPLE

Traditionally, petanque has been played by men—but women's petanque is currently taking off all around the world. For a little more than a decade, women have been allowed to participate in specific competitions, and they have their own competitions at major international championships. On recent visits, I saw a number of women playing on different fields in New York, and dozens of women players participate in Bastille Day tournaments. Among the licensed players in France, 15 percent are now women; my impression is that the proportion is similar in the United States, although I am still gathering data on that question.

Young players are very rare in New York. I have observed only two young players in Bryant Park and at competitions, both playing with their fathers. This is probably linked to the changing uses of urban space in the town center. Children and teenagers spent their free time playing in the street in the 1970s and 1980s (Dargan and Zeitlin 1990), but young people today are much less visible. Children instead play sports and active games, including football, soccer, baseball, and skateboarding, in equipped and fenced squares or in larger natural spaces, away from the urban space itself. But given the interest of young people as they pass the grounds in Bryant Park with their parents or teachers, I expect that there will soon be municipal youth petanque or high school clubs, as already exist in Oregon.

PETANQUE FOR ALL

The playing areas in New York are now numerous, located in public parks, at petanque clubs and restaurant courtyards, and on private grounds (some players who live in New Jersey and Long Island have petanque areas on their properties). Players come from many different places and backgrounds. Some players are CEOs of big companies, managers, entrepreneurs, or foremen. Other players work in restaurants or are students, teachers, writers, shopkeepers, craftspeople, or artists, while others sell bus tickets or even fruit. Each player projects specific values onto petanque. For some, petanque is a way of retaining the best of what they have lost, especially a certain masculine sociability. For others, it is a sort of historical reappropriation, a new competitive space to conquer, or a new space for social reverie.

Alfred Levitt once said that "this French game *piedtanque* [petanque] is freedom, imagination, fraternity, and even health" (Pilate 2005: 111). The New York players generally appreciate the democratic character of the game and the fact that this sport is directly in touch with urban spaces. To play in the heart of Manhattan, in the middle of the urban tumult, isn't seen as a handicap but as a use of space and time that symbolizes productivity, speed, and reactivity. In New York—perhaps more than elsewhere— petanque is a sort of sport counterculture. Everyone can compete, which is not the case for other sports. Players don't need to be young or athletic. Men and women, the young and the old, can play together. In most games, there's no money at stake, no mediation. For an hour or two at lunchtime or in the evening after work, the only aim is to get as close as possible to the little cochonnet.

WORKS CITED

Dargan, Amanda, and Steven Zeitlin. 1990. *City Play*. New Brunswick: Rutgers University Press.
New York Times. 1974. "90 from Quebec Come Here to Compete in Petanque." September 23.
Pilate, Martine. 2005. *La véritable histoire de la Pétanque: La légende des frères Pitiot*. Morières, France: Cardère.

"Petanque in New York" was first published in *Voices: The Journal of New York Folklore* 37, nos. 1-2 (Spring–Summer 2011): 12–23.

WORK

MEDIATING BETWEEN TWO WORLDS

The Sonideros *of Mexican Youth Dances*

CATHY RAGLAND

The New York metropolitan area's young Mexican immigrants are a community living in transition, continually shifting between their memory of Mexico and the reality of life here in the United States. Their weekend social events, called *bailes*, feature light shows, sound manipulations, and loud *cumbia* dance music played by deejays known as *sonideros*. The theme of being transported to another place runs through the evening, and in fact, in reading the poetic dedications and salutations composed by the young dancers, the *sonidero* takes them from Queens to Oaxaca, from Puebla to Paterson. Through the *sonidero* they maintain connections to Mexico and to relatives and friends in other parts of the United States. *The sonidero* is one of them, and with him as their mediator, they can revisit their place of origin and share the displacement and the ambiguity of the bicultural immigrant experience.

The Mexican population has become one of the fastest-growing immigrant communities in the New York–New Jersey area. Mexicans work in city restaurants, delis, bars, hotels, factories, and construction sites and as day laborers on the streets. Unlike their counterparts in the West and Southwest, these new immigrants are marginalized and have little political power or social impact. That isolation, and their concentration in service-industry jobs, has created an intensely unified community. The metropolitan area's Mexicans are in constant communication with the home country, and many residents send money to maintain family-owned businesses, remain involved in family decisions, and even help organize community events in Mexico (Smith 1999).

In the New York area, more than half of the Mexican immigrant population is male and between thirteen and twenty-two years old. Their median duration of stay on their first trip (without returning home to visit) is approximately thirty-four months. Conversations with many of these youths and other community members have revealed that a large majority of the young men have actually been sent to the United States to work. Depending on the economic status of his family, the young Mexican man sends more than half his earnings home. In many cases, he is also responsible for helping other family members come to the city, including his parents, aunts, uncles, younger siblings, and cousins. One young man who had been living in New York for eight years described his coming to the United States as a right of passage:

> Where I am from, when you turn sixteen you are ready to go to the U.S. to work. At this age you are considered an adult and you are obligated to work and send money back home. You must do what you can to help your family.

The majority of the Mexican immigrants in New York and New Jersey, more than 60 percent, are from the Mixteca region of Mexico, which includes the states of Puebla, Oaxaca, and Guerrero. In recent years, New York and New Jersey have seen an increase of immigrants from Mexico City, particularly a suburb on the road to Puebla called Ciudad Nezahualcóyotl, nicknamed Atlíxco because of its transformation from shantytown to sprawling suburb, largely funded by Mexican workers in New York. Most of the immigrants are from rural parts of Puebla, such as Tehuacán and Atlíxco, although many report having lived in Mexico City.

Because these young men have come here without their primary family members, the Catholic Church plays an important role in offering them support and social services. But it does not fully serve the need for social relationships with other young Mexicans. In Mexico, friendships would traditionally develop at neighborhood and family gatherings, such as weddings, birthday parties, baptisms, and *quinceañeras* (the coming-out ceremonies and parties for fifteen-year-old girls). In New York and New Jersey, the most popular and youth-specific events are weekend dances, or *bailes*, held in clubs, restaurants, community centers, and bingo halls, primarily in Queens, New York, and Paterson, New Jersey.

Weekend *bailes* are promoted to these young men. Young women are also present, although the male to female ratio is roughly 3 to 1. The focus of the dances is the *sonido*, or "sound system," and there can be six or more systems set up at any given dance. At the bingo hall in Paterson, the *sonidos* are arranged in a circle around the immense dance floor. The hall

Fausto Salazar, a.k.a. Potencia Latina, works with a crew of five and owns an elaborate, fully digitized sound system featuring sixteen channels. Photo: Cathy Ragland.

is decorated as for a wedding reception, with balloons tied to the tables and backs of chairs and streamers dangling from light fixtures. Booths sell tamales, tacos, bottled water, and, for those of drinking age, cold Corona beer. Dances in New York City are at smaller clubs, generally the Casablanca or Town Hall in Jackson Heights, or sometimes in restaurants. There are even fewer women at these dances.

The *sonideros* are responsible not only for the music but also for other aspects of the *baile.* They may organize and promote the dance, and they own the elaborate and colorful lighting systems and smoke machines. A large *baile* usually includes a guest *sonidero* from Mexico, usually Puebla. The *sonideros* are always male and at least ten years older than most of the dancers. They are recognized for their voice "personality," which they manipulate by sound effects (delays, reverb, echoes), processed tape loops, and samples. Mostly it is over-the-top distortion with lots of reverb, but the desired effect is always the same: big, loud, and superhuman.

A *sonidero* takes great pride in his technology and ability to transport his audience. He has a stage name, like El Condor ("The Condor") or Potencia Latina ("Latin Power"). Each *sonidero* also has a logo and a boastful tagline to market himself as a personality, such as *la maxima autoridad del sonido* ("the maximum authority of the sound system") or *el destructor de leyendas* ("the destroyer of legends"). Some of the more popular *sonideros* are Conga, Orgullosito ("Little Pride"), Mágia ("Magic"), Candela ("Flame"), and Fantasma ("Ghost"). Nearly all the logos—seen on business cards, vans, jackets, and T-shirts—use the green, yellow, red, and white of the Mexican flag; several include the Stars and Stripes or other American iconic symbols.

One popular Queens-based *sonidero* is Arturo "El Condor" Escalante, who attributes a *sonidero's* success and popularity to charisma as well as technical know-how:

> Some *sonideros* have lots of great equipment and many people like all the effects and lights and such, it creates an ambiance, but [the *sonideros*] have to project a personality and have good ideas about how to use the music, their voice, and the equipment that they have.

Escalante can be seen on the streets of Jackson Heights, transporting his sound system in a converted taco truck decorated with his logo—the American flag and the Statue of Liberty's crown emblazoned with the word "Condor" in the colors of the Mexican flag. Underneath the logo are the words *El Gigante de Nueva York*, "the Giant of New York."

AT THE DANCE

At the *baile,* the *sonidero* creates what anthropologist Robert Rouse has defined as a "socio-spatial environment" (1991) with the sheer power of his voice and acts as the voice of a displaced community. The *sonidero* is also a virtual navigator of the sound experience at the *baile* as well as the authoritative voice of a distinct genre of music, created and recorded exclusively for these *bailes.*

Each *sonidero* begins his set with a largely taped introduction lasting five minutes or longer. The sound collage comprises samples from radio advertisements and announcements, in English and in Spanish, and musical excerpts, many of which are English-language popular songs. There is always a countdown to "liftoff," with space-travel sounds and talk of being transported to some other place via the *disco mobile,* which is always "ready for travel." The *sonidero* repeats his stage name often and touts his powerful system—*el señal más potente* ("the most powerful signal"). The introduction continues with boasts about the authenticity of the coming musical selection—*música electronica inteligente* ("intelligent electronic music")—but the *sonidero* also extends greetings to the other deejays in the hall.

During the introduction, most dancers are standing, focused on the *sonidero*, although they do not actually see him, since he always positions himself behind his stacked sound system and out of view. Always visible, however, is the *sonidero*'s crew, generally four or five younger men. As the introduction proceeds, smoke from the smoke machine envelops the dance floor in a giant cloud. The feeling is very much of being "transported" to another place that is part fantasy, part irony, and very much in perpetual motion. The introduction ends with the sound of a spaceship landing and the *swoosh* of doors sliding open.

After the landing, the *sonidero*'s voice is more intelligible, with minimal effects. Instead of American dance genres such as house, hip hop, or rap that dominated the liftoff portion, we now hear Latin music styles like salsa, *bachata*, or merengue, but not the *cumbias* people came to dance to—not yet anyway. The *sonidero* speaks directly to the audience and welcomes the dancers to the Bingo Hall. Seconds later they are also welcomed to Mexico: *Bienvenidos a Mexico, bienvenidos a New York.*

PERFORMING THE DEDICATIONS

Now the dance takes a different course. In this portion of the set, the dancers, primarily the young men, become active participants in the *sonidero*'s show by writing his script.

The *sonidero* now plays cutting-edge *cumbia* dance hits like those by Los Angeles de Charley ("Charlie's Angels"), Los Angeles Azules ("the Blue Angels"), and Los Socios del Ritmo ("the Partners of Rhythm"). The *cumbia* dances are not the same as those made popular by the norteño and Tejano bands—Selena, Bronco, and Los Bukis, for example—that dominated the Mexican and Mexican-American *cumbia* scene in the 1980s and early 1990s. The *cumbias* of the *sonidero bailes* here and in Mexico are largely instrumental and feature a *vallenato*-style accordion, usually accompanied by an Afro-Colombian percussion instrument called the *guacharaca*, which is a wooden scraper; the vocals are mixed much deeper in the song's overall sound. These *cumbia* recordings are longer than the

The Mexican deejays, or *sonideros*, employ images of strength, power, and force in their business cards and cassette tape covers. They freely mix the Stars and Stripes with the yellow, green, white, and red of the Mexican national flag. Photos: Cathy Ragland.

more commercial variety, generally six minutes. Although this *cumbia* style makes references to the genre's Colombian (particularly Costeña) origins, recordings are almost exclusively Mexican.

Once the *sonidero* starts the dance with the first *cumbia*, he continues to speak through the microphone, boasting about the power and force of his *sonido*, repeating his stage name often, welcoming the other *sonideros* on the evening's bill, and recognizing the local promoters of the show and audience members with whom he is acquainted. He will also comment on a song's title or lyrics or note that the dance is in honor of a special event.

However, his most important job is reading the dedications and saluta-tions given to him by the young dancers. And as more of these come in, there is less improvised banter. While the *sonidero* is changing compact discs, setting up tapes, and manipulating effects and lights, he must read from a steady stream of hundreds of salutations and dedications written on napkins and scraps of paper and handed to him by his crew. At this moment, the *sonidero* is a mediator, a ventriloquist of sorts, who speaks what is on the minds and in the hearts of his community.

A popular *sonidero* living in Passaic, New Jersey, Angel "Orgullosito" Lezama, offers this interpretation of his role at the *bailes*:

> As a *sonidero*, you must capture the sentiment of the dedication and who it is being sent to. You are helping that person create an imagination, an image, something very special that will be sent to a family member, a friend who is living somewhere else, or someone at the dance with you—someone that he wants to get to know.

Lest that description of the *sonidero*'s role at the *baile* sound more functional than creative, Lezama adds that style and performance are essential to delivery of the salutation:

> You must speak clearly and follow the rhythm of the song and you must talk and think at the same time. By doing that you create your personality and use the effects. But you must keep things moving and read all of the salutations and dedications. You don't want to completely block out the song, but you want to be part of it, too.

At thirty-six years of age, Fausto "Potencia Latina" Salazar is one of the oldest and most respected *sonideros*. He has been a *sonidero* in New York for more than sixteen years and is considered a stylistic innovator and mentor. "I am the grandfather of the all of the *sonideros* here," Salazar said to me one night at a *baile* in the Paterson bingo hall. He also offered his insight into creating a unique *sonidero* style:

> It is important that the people can recognize my style, without even hearing my name. I am very in tune to the music and by pausing, even for a brief moment, I can connect with where I am going with the performance, and I am sure to express better the idea behind the dedications. Some of them are really quite beautiful and some are just silly. But I respect what they have to say.

Even to my outsider's ears, Salazar was clearly the best of the six *sonideros* at the bingo hall that evening. And although his voice was as loud and distorted as the others, his presentation style and delivery of dedications had a flow and creative character that set him apart. He would extend a vowel or add syllables to emphasize a word, or sound out a person's name or nickname. Although he never changed the wording of a dedication or salutation, his voice explored an array of personalities and expressions that revealed the deep cultural meaning or significance of what was being read. Through his style he created a complex role for the *sonidero*—interpreter and mediator as well as messenger for his community.

Many of the salutations and dedications are written in a loosely poetic style with varying degrees of rhyme and imagery. Songs are dedicated to girlfriends, friends, gang members, neighbors, relatives, parents, even the *sonidero* himself. Other dancers simply acknowledge their own presence at the dance, often naming the *sonidero* who is mixing the music and stating that they are *presente* ("there") with the *sonidero cien porciento* ("100 percent"). There is usually mention of the individual's current home borough or town as well as his home state and town in Mexico. Sometimes these locales are mixed up: Puebla, New York, or Brooklyn, Mexico. Dancers may also mention other cities in the United States where friends and relatives are living and working.

At the end of the set, a compact disc duplicating machine is brought out, and those whose salutations and dedications were just read by the *sonidero* queue up to purchase recordings for five dollars each. The CDs consist of the entire set—three or four *cumbias*, lasting about thirty minutes—plus the liftoff introduction. These CDs are mailed to the friends and relatives named in the salutations and dedications, and also to anyone whom the dancer wants to bring into the experience. The sales are completed quickly, since the next *sonidero* will have already started his set and the dancers want to engage him with more dedications.

Examples of dedications and salutations were collected at a bingo hall dance in Paterson on December 11, 1999. Note the references to location and to maguey (a variety of cactus) and mesquite, both powerful symbols of Mexico. The dance styles named in the first dedication—*cumbia*, salsa, and danzón—have their origins in other Latin American countries (Colombia, Puerto Rico and New York, and Cuba, respectively), but all have been adopted as Mexican popular music styles, particularly danzón and *cumbia*. Unlike other dances in the local Latino community, whose attendees are from various Caribbean and Latin American countries, the *sonidero* dances are exclusively Mexican.

DEDICATIONS AND SALUTATIONS

Example 1

Cumbia, Salsa y Danzón,	*Cumbia, Salsa y* [and?] *Danzón,*
Lizbet te quiero Lisbeth	*I love you*
con todo mi corazón	*with all my heart*
Hasta Los Angeles, California	*All the way to Los Angeles, California*
De parte de Victor	*from Victor*
Cien porciento Fantasma	*100 percent with the Ghost (sonidero)*

Example 2

Espinas de Mesquite	*Thorns of the Mesquite*
espinas de Maguey	*Thorns of the Maguey*
Potencia Latina	*Latin Power (sonidero)*
la pura ley	*the absolute law*
Att: El Flaco y el amor	*Att: "the Skinny" and the love*
de su vida, Martha	*of his life, Martha*

Example 3

Entre calaveras y esqueletos	*Between skulls and skeletons*
cuando llegan los primos	*when the cousins (friends) arrive*
e inquitos todos	*and everything is a mess*
se quedan vien (bien) quitos	*they will make it all right again*
diavolicos (diabolicos) sienporsieto	*diabolical 100 percent*
(cien porciento)	
Primos: El Cholo, El Malaber,	*Cousins: The Halfbreed, The Juggler,*
El Ardilla, El Catrin, El Gato	*The Squirrel, The Dude, The Cat*

Example 4

Puebla, Neuva York	*Puebla, New York*
yo estoy con el mejor	*I am here with the best*
el más chingon	*the most badass*
chabelo toño sagrado	*the guy with the sacred tone*
Fausto nacho polo	*Fausto nacho polo (sonidero)*
Puebla, Chalchiupan	*Puebla, Chalchiupan*
Puebla de los ángeles	*Town of the angels*

THE MAXIMUM AUTHORITY

The *sonidero* dances are opportunities for young, predominantly male Mexican immigrants and U.S.-born Mexican Americans to develop a social network. Through the *sonidero* they maintain connections to their home country and to those relatives and friends living the immigrant, bi-cultural experience in other parts of the United States. While creating a life here, they can recall their place of origin and, as young people with varying degrees of actual memories of Mexico, develop a history that is imagined and based on both Mexican and American myths, both their own experiences and those of others.

The *bailes* allow for such a simultaneous existence. Through the *sonide-ro*, dancers invoke friends and relatives and imagine their presence. They can speak to them and bring them into the local space, while also speaking to those present at the dance. The foreground and background of the experience shifts from New York to Mexico throughout the evening, much like movable or expandable borders—the new space of the migratory experience. As a result, the young authors of the dedications and salutations as well as those overhearing their poems at the dances are able to travel from New York to Los Angeles to Mexico to Puebla and back again, retracing the migration route many of them actually took to get here. As mediators of this experience, the *sonideros* use technology to assert their claim to *la maxima autoridad*, "the maximum authority." Their electronically treated and manipulated voices are painfully loud, sometimes garbled, and distorted. They call attention to themselves and the power they can assert, similar to the border-blaster deejays on the Mexican side of the Texas border, who during the early days of radio would overpower American radio stations and penetrate as far north as Yakima, Washington.

In *Club Cultures*, Sarah Thornton describes how a deejay can authenticate a music form by rendering it essential or integral to the community (1996). In the *baile*, the *cumbia* is used as a backdrop to the dedications and the *sonidero*'s own sonic manipulations. Although he talks while the music plays, the *sonidero* respects it by pausing appropriately and picking up its rhythm. He respects the salutations and dedications as well and never elaborates on them or interjects his own words or comments. This deep level of respect for both elements and their purpose in the sound environment authenticates the *cumbia*. It is not commercial radio and record sales that have made this genre of *cumbia* popular among Mexican youth; rather, it is the power of the *sonidero* and the social context of its use for the community.

LIVING LIFE AFTER "THE GREAT ADVENTURE"

"For me, *la gran aventura* began when I turned sixteen," recalls Angel Lezama, now twenty-eight. "I left Mexico with two friends, and it was a very dangerous and hard journey. But we always believed that we would go back to Mexico one day."

"The great adventure" is how Lezama and other young Mexican men in New York refer to their journey from Mexico. Lezama, also known as Orgullosito ("Little Pride"), is a popular *sonidero* with six years on the dancehall scene.

When Lezama and his friends left Mexico City, they traveled first to Tijuana. "In Tijuana we tried to find work on the U.S. side, but it was really a hard life there," he said. "We were always worried about being deported and we didn't know what would happen to us. Crossing the border is like that—you never know what will happen."

Friends of Lezama's were living and working in New York, and so he decided to try life in the city. He began by working in restaurants as a busboy and then a prep cook. "I met a lot of other guys from Puebla, even from my own town. I saw that I could make something here and help my family."

Lezama's journey parallels that of many Mexican immigrants now living in New York City. Based on a 1999 report in *La Vitrina Cultural Affairs*, published by the Mexican Cultural Institute of New York, most immigrants living here initially traveled from rural towns in Puebla, Guerrero, and Oaxaca to work in Mexico City. The lack of jobs and low pay in that economically depressed city pushed them to border towns like Tijuana, and then on to cities like New York, Las Vegas, and Chicago, where the demand for service-industry workers is high. Teenagers and young men form a majority of the metropolitan area's Mexican population, and most are responsible for sending a large portion of their earnings back home to their families.

Lezama now lives in Passaic, New Jersey, with his mother and siblings, whom he petitioned to bring to the United States from Puebla, and owns a small Mexican restaurant. "I work every day, and I have my *sonido* every weekend and Thursday nights," Lezama says. "I've been back to Mexico twice in the last four years. But it took about that long before I was able to go back the first time. For now, this is my home."

The *sonideros* can be trusted because, like the dancers, they have experienced the displacement and the ambiguity of the immigrant existence. Many of the personal stories of *la aventura* ("travel") told by these young adults are familiar to the *sonideros* themselves. This is the real-life experience of a community that is divided among various cities and cultures—New York, Los Angeles, Chicago, Texas, Tijuana, Mexico City, and Puebla—and between two countries with complex political relations. The *sonidero*'s role in the *baile* allows these Mexican youths to "come to Mexico," as one *sonidero* described it.

The *baile* is a place of negotiation, a place to resolve the conflict that many Mexican immigrants have about leaving their country, with its tradition of family-owned businesses, to work as low-rung laborers in the service industry, and about maintaining two distinct lifestyles. The *sonidero* offers them an opportunity to be heard and to share that exchange with others, both present and distant. At these dances the young men can express a shared identity as Mexican-Americans while they experience an entertainment form that is new, exciting, and completely modern.

WORKS CITED

Binford, Leigh, and Edgar Lezama. 1999. "Immigration: Poblanos in New York." *La Vitrina Cultural Affairs*. New York: Mexican Cultural Institute.

Central Intelligence Agency. 1999. *World Factbook*. Washington, D.C.: Central Intelligence Agency.

Kaplan, Caren. 1996. *Questions of Travel: Postmodern Discourses of Displacement*. Durham: Duke University Press.

Maciel, David R., and Maria Herrera-Sobek. 1998. Introduction to *Culture across Borders: Mexican Immigration and Popular Culture*. Tucson: University of Arizona Press.

Paredes, Américo. 1993. *Folklore and Culture on the Texas-Mexican Border*. Edited by Richard Bauman. Austin: University of Texas, Center for Mexican American Studies.

Rouse, Roger. 1991. "Mexican Migration and the Social Space of Postmodernism." *Diaspora* (Spring): 8–21.

Smith, Robert. 1999. "Immigration: Dimensions of Mexican Migration to New York." *La Vitrina Cultural Affairs*. New York: Mexican Cultural Institute.

Thornton, Sarah. 1996. *Club Cultures: Music, Media, and Subcultural Capital*. Hanover, N.H.: Wesleyan University Press.

"Mediating between Two Worlds: The *Sonideros* of Mexican Youth Dances" was first published in *Voices: The Journal of New York Folklore* 26, nos. 1-2 (Fall–Winter 2000): 8–14.

IN THE MIDST OF A MONASTERY

Filming the Making of a Buddhist Sand Mandala

PUJA SAHNEY

In June 2005, I was selected by the New York Folklore Society to serve as a summer graduate intern at the Dutchess County Arts Council in Poughkeepsie. My first project was to assist folklorist Eileen Condon and a crew of fieldworkers in filming and photographing the Buddhist cultural festivities celebrated at the Kagyu Thubten Choling (KTC) monastery in Wappingers Falls, New York. I had been in the United States for one year at the time. As a Hindu from India, I am not altogether a stranger to Buddhism. As Eileen described the monastery's stupa on the bank of the Hudson River, I pictured Hindu temples along several rivers I know in India.

Lama Chopal finishing the outer ring of a Buddhist sand mandala. Photo: Puja Sahney.

Lama Chopal pours sand meditatively on the outer rings of the mandala. Photo: Eileen Condon.

When she spoke of documenting their fire puja, I pictured the *havans* (fire rituals) that my family held in our house.

Located on the riverbank in Wappingers Falls, the Kagyu Thubten Choling monastery seems hidden among trees. The monastery was founded in 1978 as a one-story building on seven acres of land. The monastery is now a retreat for serious students of the Kagyu branch of Tibetan Buddhism. On the day after my arrival in Wappingers Falls, I accompanied Eileen to the monastery to meet the crew that had volunteered to assist in making the documentary. The first thing that caught my eye on arriving at the monastery was the stupa by the river. It is a white building, with beautiful golden ornamentation on the roof and walls. Stupas were the first form of Tibetan architecture—originally "simple mound-shaped" structures of brick and mud to cover the ashes and relics of the Buddha—but over the centuries they have become more elaborate (Wangu 1993: 86). Ani Yeshe Palmo, a nun at the KTC monastery, explained that a stupa is also a "representation of the Buddha's mind and is one of the things that an authentic monastery is supposed to have" (Palmo 2005). Ani Yeshe is a former folklorist. She had met with Eileen earlier in the year, introducing the monastery's cultural activities and engaging the Dutchess County Arts

Council's interest in capturing its cultural art. Ani Yeshe told me that the KTC stupa was built for America. Buddhists believe that building a stupa helps to protect the environment and the country and to pacify aggression, terrorism, and negativity (Palmo 2005).

As I got out of the car at the monastery, still gazing at the stupa, I saw monks and nuns walking from it to the main monastery building. They had just finished chanting. Many of the monks were also busy getting tents ready for the KTC Olympics, which were to be held in ten days. The KTC Olympics—an annual event—allows members of different branches of the monastery to get together for discussion and training. The 2005 KTC Olympics would include a *wang*, in which a learned practitioner gives students empowerment or permission to undertake certain meditation practices. The sand mandala that we planned to photograph and film would be part of the empowerment ceremony. In a tent close by, several monks were getting *tsa tsas* ready for the stupa. Tsa tsa literally means "representation"; they are little stupas made of clay, each with a small mantra roll inside with thousands of mantras written on it. The tsa tsas are put inside the stupa. According to Ani Yeshe, the tsa tsas are so filled with blessings that they help the stupa to magnetize and radiate energy (Palmo 2005). When we headed to the dining hall of the main building, I saw monks and nuns busy with dinner preparations. In spite of all the activity, there was a sense of quietness all around. Everyone was circulating in a peaceful way that made me almost self-conscious of my steps. Friendly smiles greeted us everywhere. Karen Michel and Brian Farmer, who would assist us in filming and photographing the festivities, had already arrived at the main building. Ani Yeshe arrived after a few minutes. As we got down to dividing up the work, Eileen voiced her preference to film the making of the mandala for the Dutchess County Arts Council's folklore archive, while Brian and Karen decided to document the festive activities of Olympics weekend.

THE SIGNIFICANCE OF THE MANDALA

The sand mandala's creation was the most elaborate Buddhist ritual that that our group recorded. The mandala's religious and symbolic significance is more complex than film can capture, but its patterns and colors are a folklorist's delight. When I first heard of the sand mandala, I couldn't quite imagine how the finished object would look. Although similar to the

Indian art of *rangoli*, Tibetan sand mandalas have more intricate patterns with secret meanings. They can also be made from paint or can be three-dimensional constructions—but they cannot be made up. All mandala designs come from the deity himself and have to look exactly as the written teaching says they should (Palmo 2005). The mandala we witnessed was made of colorful sand. It was the mandala of Khorlo Demchok, an extremely complex deity encompassing qualities of wisdom, compassion, and all things of merit.

The word *mandal* is the Sanskrit word for circle. Sand mandalas are symbolic of the circle of life and death. Although they are made painstakingly, they are destroyed after the ceremony, reflecting the Buddhist doctrine that nothing is permanent. Most often, the completed sand mandala is thrown into a river, where its sand is believed to bless all the land the water touches. Mandalas are made when a need is felt to heal the environment and other living creatures. There are other motivations as well:

> Making . . . the mandala is also a Tibetan meditative practice; sound, sight, and motion are not treated as distraction but as means to channel physical energies into currents that carry the spirit forward instead of derailing it. Mandalas are treated as the current of sight and with their colors and holy patterns they treat the eyes to icons whose holy beauty draws the beholder in their direction. (Smith and Novak 2003: 108–109)

MAKING THE MANDALA

On the day that work on the sand mandala was scheduled to begin, Eileen and I headed to the stupa an hour early to set up our cameras. We figured that a mandala would require major preparations, but when we reached the stupa, we were met with only a blank blue board, five feet square, on an easel at the entrance. The monks and students who were to make the mandala were still at breakfast.

The heat of the day had already begun, so we decided to enter the stupa. It had not yet been fitted with a lock, but once the door was bolted, it could only be opened through the delicate intricacies of a metal rod waiting at the entrance. At our previous meeting, Ani Yeshe had demonstrated the whole process to us. One had to insert the rod carefully between the two doors and give it a slight push. After a few tries each we finally were able to push it open. The stupa is extremely small and tight inside, but peaceful, with the sounds from outside shut out. A man was meditating on the carpet in front of the stupa's huge bronze statue of the Buddha. The lights were dim, adding to the majesty of the statue. After we brought in all our equipment and loaded the cameras with new tapes, we sat down in front of the Buddha, and I gazed at it. The Buddha is sitting in the pose of Enlightenment, with legs folded in the lotus position and hands held loosely on his lap (Wangu 1993: 85–86). The peaceful smile, erect back, and hands in the lap looked so relaxed that before I knew it, I was holding the same posture. I looked over and saw Eileen sitting the same way. I have no idea how long we sat there or when the man who was meditating left. I opened my eyes with a start when I heard someone walk into the room. The crew that was to make the mandala had finally arrived.

When I first noticed Lama Chopal, he was already bending over the blue board and putting it on a stand. He is a gifted craftsman, trained in traditional Tibetan art. I quickly glanced at Eileen to see if we were to begin filming. She was already getting out the digital camera. Lama Chopal didn't bring the board inside the stupa. He left it at the entrance. He was measuring the board with his fingers and a piece of paper. He then took a long string from a roll and placed it horizontally on the blue board. A student standing next to him, as though instructed, then pulled at the thread, and it left a chalk line across the blue board. He repeated the same process vertically. Someone leaned over and whispered that the point where the lines cross is the exact center of the board and that there cannot be any mistake.

The two lines are called the Brahman lines. Barry Bryant explains, "The radius of the mandala is then divided along the Brahman lines into thirteen equal parts. The divisions are not done mathematically but by trial and error, folding a strip of paper until it has thirteen equal parts totaling the length of the radius" (1992: 183). For about four hours Lama Chopal continued to draw lines in the same fashion across the board; only once in a while would he use a compass to draw a circle or a ruler to take measurements. Mostly he used paper, folding or cutting it to different sizes as he measured.

As he did so, there were students or other monks pulling at the string, and by noon the entire board was covered by zigzagging lines. The chalked string is a traditional and ancient way of laying out the mandala, developed before rulers and other instruments of measure. The geometric figure of a mandala is usually a "circle inside a square and is regarded as the

Metal cones traditionally tapped to release sand, alongside Buddhist prayer beads. Photo: Puja Sahney.

dwelling place of the gods," according to Madhu B. Wangu. While creating the two-dimensional sand mandala, the monks are visualizing the palace of the deity: a form of meditation. In the center of the mandala is a "figure of the Buddha or some other divinity, while surrounding it are fantastically intricate symbols and depictions of other gods and religious scenes" (Wangu 1993: 94).

While Lama Chopal and two students worked on making the outline of the mandala at the entrance, Ani Karma Chotso—a nun visiting from Florida, who was in charge of the sand mandala project—began to open small packets of color and set them out in bowls. These would be the colors used in the mandala, she said. The color would be laid between the outlines, which would make the mandala like a colorful painting of sand. Mandalas are made from the colors black, white, red, blue, yellow, and green. There are three shades each of red, blue, yellow, and green, making a total of fourteen colors. While in ancient times the sand of colored stone would be grated, "these days white stones are ground and dyed with opaque water colors to produce the bright tones found in the sand paintings" (Bryant 1992: 177–178). Ani Karma had ordered the best sand available on the Internet. The sight of the small colored packets drew almost all those around the stupa inside, making the small space quite stifling for a moment.

While Lama Chopal was still busy making the outlines, Ani Karma let the assembled students begin practicing laying the colors on old newspapers. Sand mandalas are made on thick wooden boards with objects called *chak-pur*s. A chak-pur is a cone-shaped funnel that is perforated on the narrow end. One scrapes a flat, metal rod against the cone, and the vibration allows the sand to flow like colored water through the perforations. The rubbing of the rod and the cone is believed to be symbolic of the union between compassion and wisdom (Bryant 1992: 195). While the sand trickling out of the chak-pur is indeed a beautiful sight, the vibration between the chak-pur and the rod creates a feeling of spirituality in itself. It is a sound of manual labor, but more meditative and soothing. Bryant explains, "The monks interpret the sound of the hollow metal chak-purs being rubbed together as an expression of the Buddhist concept of emptiness or the interdependence of the phenomenon" (1992: 195).

While the sound of the chak-purs filled the stupa, Lama Chopal continued to work diligently on completing the outline. He had now begun the inner patterns of the mandala, using a black pen to draw the intricate designs. It took Lama Chopal, assisted by a few students, a day and a half to complete making the entire outline of the mandala. The following day, Lama Chopal and the rest of the crew got down to work laying the color carefully on the mandala. He would begin on the outline and then carefully fill the remaining areas. Sometimes he would painstakingly shade the areas using different light, medium, and dark tones.

After two days filming the making of the mandala, Eileen felt confident to leave me alone with the camera. Each day as the lunch hour approached, Lama Chopal asked the crew to take a break and have some lunch, and each day he invited me to join them. Many monks and nuns recognized me and would greet me in the dining hall or on the campus. By the third day of work on the sand mandala, I had begun to feel at home in the monastery. After lunch, the crew would head back to the stupa, and the afternoon session would get underway. Lamas, other monks, and nuns constantly dropped in to admire the mandala and encourage the crew making it. Often, a Buddhist would chant mantras in a corner while the crew worked, adding to the meditative atmosphere inside the stupa. The biggest treat for everyone would be when someone from the monastery kitchen would bring in a big steel vessel of Indian chai.

By the fourth day, the mandala was nearing completion. I had seen all the stages of its making and had by now become familiar with the sounds of the chak-purs and the way that the workers' hands moved. During the afternoon session, Ani Karma came up to me while I was filming and suggested that I try my hand at the chak-pur. I was a bit surprised but also flattered that she had asked me. Usually only monks make a sand mandala. The KTC crew was mostly Buddhist, but most of the workers were not monks or nuns. The Kagyu Thubten Choling monastery wants to encourage the mandala tradition in America and does not see the benefit of limiting participation. I had been hesitant to ask Lama Chopal if I could color a section, but by then I should have known better than to fear that a monk would refuse anything to anyone. So later on, while he was working alone on the mandala, I asked him if I could give it a try. I was glad that he was delighted by my request.

The feeling of holding the chak-pur in my hands was overwhelming because it held so much history and tradition. I didn't dare to start on an intricate design; I instead chose to color a broad quadrant. I moved my hands, and the color just fell like magic from the narrow end. As I knew from observation, "The flow of the sand is controlled by the speed and pressure used in rasping. Slow, soft rasping causes the sand to trickle out, even just a few grains at a time, while harder, faster rasping causes it to pour out in a steady stream" (Bryant 1992: 195). I bent a bit closer to the board in order not to spill anything outside the line. By then the rest of the crew trickled in and smiled to see me at work. At first my hands moved quickly. But after twenty minutes of sitting on the ground, my bent back and crossed legs began to tire. My hands, too, started to ache. I looked around and saw the others working diligently and felt ashamed of feeling tired so soon. It was only after I had been at it myself that I began to admire the stamina and dedication of the people around me. Coloring the mandala was an exhausting task that required immense concentration, physical stamina, and a steady hand. After I got back to filming the process, I would sympathize with people when they turned around, stretched their legs, massaged them a bit, and then got back to work.

At the end of the fifth day, work on the mandala was finally ending. People from the monastery came down to watch. Many of the monks and the nuns began chanting mantras, while Lama Chopal gave the mandala a few final touches. It was finished. In the corner of the stupa, the mandala held within itself the positive force that all the strength and goodwill of the crew had given it.

DISMANTLING THE MANDALA

After five days of labor on the mandala, its ultimate fate was to be thrown into the river at the end of the KTC Olympics. Although I was inclined to use the word "destroy," Buddhists see it as a form of blessing on all the land where the water flows and also on any aquatic life in the water. For them it is a great sharing, instead of destruction.

The sand mandala was taken with due reverence to the water in a blue truck, in which all the crew who had made the mandala also rode. I was surprised that everyone sat quite merrily in the open truck with the mandala. I had assumed that they would be nostalgic to see their labor swept away, but once again I was misinterpreting the Buddhist doctrine of impermanence. "The dismantling of the sand mandala may be interpreted as a lesson in nonattachment, a letting go of the self-mind," Bryant notes (1992: 230). Several monks and nuns tilted the board, allowing the sand to slip into the river. While most of the sand went into the water, some of it was saved for future blessings. I asked Ani Yeshe Palmo what became of the blue board on which the mandala had been made. She said that it was carefully placed in the woodshed until the next time they make a mandala.

I was surprised at how happy I was on the way home that last day. The Buddhist doctrine that everything is impermanent had become a reality for me, too. I was simply glad that I had been part of the mandala's journey this once. Buddhists believe that even looking at a mandala is a blessing, and after a week at the monastery, I did feel truly blessed.

WORKS CITED

Bryant, Barry. 1992. *The Wheel of Time Sand Mandala: Visual Scripture of Tibetan Buddhism.* New York: HarperCollins.
Palmo, Ani Yeshe. 2005. Interview by Puja Sahney, July 25. Tape recording.
Smith, Huston, and Philip Novak. 2003. *Buddhism: A Concise Introduction.* New York: HarperCollins.
Wangu, Madhu B. 1993. *Buddhism.* New York: Brown Publishing.

"In the Midst of a Monastery: Filming the Making of a Buddhist Sand Mandala" was first published in *Voices: The Journal of New York Folklore* 32, nos. 1-2 (Spring–Summer 2006): 19–23.

SET IN STONE

The Art of Stonework and Wall Building in Westchester County

TOM van BUREN

Stonework must surely rank as one of the oldest of folk arts, if only for the longevity of the material used—hence its presence in the historical record. While an immense but finite supply of wood drew Europeans to the shores of North America, once they had exhausted local forest stands through clearing, burning, ship building, and construction, stone became the material of choice. The ensuing works in stone have been the longest lasting remnants of vernacular architecture. In few places is this story more apparent than in the southeastern corner of New York State, where the Dutch first settled some four centuries ago and the English soon followed. Like most of the coastal regions close to urban and industrial

Dulio Prado's crew assembles a wall in Bedford, New York. Photo: Tom van Buren.

New old-style dry stone wall in Salem, New York, built by Kevin Towle. Photo: Tom van Buren.

development, the pace of forest depletion was accelerated, leading to increased use of stone.

As any visitor to that part of New York can tell you, Westchester is covered not only with geological formations of excellent building stone but also with glacial stones. Since the earliest Dutch settlements in the region, generations of wall builders and masons made immediate use of the readily available resource and left their mark on the landscape. A tour around the county reveals a patchwork of projects, from colonial-era buildings and farm stone walls (often referred to as "stone fences" in contemporary accounts), to the nineteenth-century mansions of robber barons, to the twentieth-century reservoirs and Robert Moses's parkways with their famous bridges. This nearly four-century-long orgy of stone building drew professional as well as accidental masons from every corner of the world, from the days of slavery, to the waves of Irish and Italian immigrants who built the dams and bridges of the county, to the current Guatemalan and Ecuadorian masons who now uphold the trade.

The purposes to which stone is put, the techniques masons have used, and the builders themselves have all changed over the years. This evolution reflects changes in the availability of materials; technologies of quarrying, stone splitting, chipping, and carving; and the use of stone structures. Just as significant have been the evolving immigrant populations

Everett Cantamessa (left) with a student in the BOCES stone shop. Photo: Tom van Buren.

and ethnicities of stone masons themselves and the cultures of stonework that they have brought with them.

In the winter of 2008, the Folk Arts Program of ArtsWestchester (formerly the Westchester Arts Council) presented a mixed media exhibit on stonework as an occupational folk art. Mounted in the council's gallery in downtown White Plains, the exhibit—featuring images and examples of stone carving and setting and stone wall building—was titled "Set in Stone." The project began in 1996, when folklorist Amanda Dargan began research for the Westchester Arts Council. At that time, second and third generations of Italian stoneworkers were still active. Their fathers and grandfathers had come to Westchester from Italy to build New Croton Dam, the Kensico Dam, and the many arched bridges of the parkways. Hundreds of institutional buildings, from churches to the county courthouse, benefited from this pool of skilled labor. The postwar period also saw a massive housing boom in towns like Eastchester, Yonkers, and Tuckahoe, with many new homes built with veneer stone and massive chimneys.

More recently, a fashionable revival of the farm wall—which Katonah-based journalist and author Susan Allport calls "walls of affluence" in her

Mason Manuel Inga Lazo
standing in an archway he
built in Mahopac, New York.
Photo: Tom van Buren.

1990 book *Sermons in Stone*—has drawn hundreds of Latin American stoneworkers, who can often trace their ancestry to the epic wall builders of the Andes. The housing boom of the past decade has prompted a renewal of the trade, with a major influx of masons from Ecuador and Guatemala.

The "Set in Stone" exhibit was divided spatially according to three distinct themes. Around the gallery's perimeter, the historical context of stone building—from regional geology to the quarries to the generations of projects and styles—was presented in text panels and documentary photographs. In the center, text and photographs recording the lives and work of six masons were exhibited, with actual stone structures erected in the gallery. Finally, on another floor of the gallery, members of the Westchester Photographic Society presented stunning photographs of stone structures great and small from around the county.

Featured master mason Everett Cantamessa is a living exemplar of this occupational legacy. Born in Mount Vernon to a family of quarrymen and masons from Bergamo, Italy, he grew up in the trade, working through the postwar housing boom and on major institutional projects such as the buildings of West Point. He taught his son Eric, who is now the head teacher at the BOCES stone shop in Yorktown Heights. The family's history and documentation about the shop formed a central part of the exhibit.

Another key mason featured in the exhibit is Manuel Inga Lazo, born outside the colonial-era city of Cuenca, Ecuador. One of the original featured masons in Amanda Dargan's 2006 research, he has since expanded his contracting company to include four brothers and has built projects all over Westchester County. Since immigrating to the United States in the 1980s, he has returned to Ecuador many times to document archeological sites where his ancestors built massive structures of stone without any mortar. Other featured masons included Brazilian Dulio Prado and his mostly Guatemalan crew, who have the distinction of being some of the fastest drywall builders in the region, and Kevin Towle, who designs and builds spectacular landscaping projects in the Salem area of Westchester.

These are but a few of the masons whose lives and works were featured in the exhibit. The photographs that accompany this essay are a small part of the exhibit.

"Set in Stone: The Art of Stonework and Wall Building in Westchester County" was first published in *Voices: The Journal of New York Folklore* 35, nos. 1-2 (Spring–Summer 2009): 12–17.

AN ETHNOGRAPHY OF
THE SARATOGA RACETRACK

ELLEN McHALE

The backstretch of the thoroughbred racetrack at Saratoga Springs, New York, is an "intentional" community, a voluntary community forged through a common occupation—the care of the racehorse. Here the assistant trainers, exercise riders, jockeys, and others tend to the horses that are a locus for wealthy owners and high-society spectators and bettors. This backside community creates its own identity through naming practices, speech, and the use of language. It is a community that views itself as generous, open, and regular yet is marked by secrecy and control and ruled by chance. Because the workers' future is never certain, allegiances are tenuous and identities are constructed.

From the second week in July through Labor Day, Saratoga Springs experiences the carnival known as the Racing Season. During this six-week period, thousands upon thousands of spectators throng into a city of sixty thousand, swelling its population. The subject of interest, the thoroughbred racetrack, employs thousands of people: betting clerks, waitstaff, custodians, parking lot attendants, food service workers, groundskeepers, tip sheet hawkers, security guards—all of whom take temporary employment during the racing season.

Besides the workers of the "frontside" are the thousands of workers in the "backside." This underclass of track workers comprises temporary residents of Saratoga Springs who are permanent employees in the business of racing. They are the people whose lives are inextricably linked to the horses: the grooms, "hot walkers," trainers, assistant trainers, and exercise riders.

Since 1996, I have been documenting the traditional arts and culture of the backstretch. My survey has taken me through the hierarchy of racetrack officials and workers, from the placing judges who determine the races' winners to the grooms who muck out the stalls and the hot walkers who cool the horses down. This is a work in progress with substantial fieldwork still to be undertaken.

THE TRACK AND ITS WORKERS

Saratoga has a long and distinguished history as a first-class racetrack. Already a resort in the mid-nineteenth century because of its mineral springs, Saratoga Springs had an early reputation for an interest in fast horses. This interest was confined to wealthy residents and resort-goers until an Irish-born boxer and gambler, John Morrissey, returned to upstate New York from New York City in 1863. Placing an advertisement in a racing newspaper, the *Spirit of the Times*, Morrissey proclaimed that there would be three days of racing at Saratoga, with two races each day. Attendance warranted more racing, and the meet was extended to a fourth day. The grandstand, still in operation today, was built for the meet in 1864. The newly constructed racecourse was considered the best racecourse in the country, an opinion still expressed by many. From these beginnings, Saratoga has become a world-class thoroughbred racetrack that supports a six-week season with ten races each day.

A unique world of work revolves around the racetrack, with specialized roles and tasks, specific language and vocabulary, rituals, and a shared knowledge and history among the people who make the races occur. Because of their common experience, those who work at the racetrack make up a distinct occupational folk group, with shared experiences, a specialized language, specific tools and techniques, and unique customs and beliefs. Their occupational world is dictated by the horse. Each day has a routine, a ritualized series of activities that constitute an attempt to control the unpredictable and make a racehorse run to its full potential. One groom explained:

> I come in about four-thirty. Feed breakfast. Most people have watchers [who observe a horse to make sure it is eating well and shows no signs of illness] when they feed breakfast. We don't because the stable's not that big. But I come in about four-thirty. Feed. Muck out my stalls. Then about five-thirty [to] six we start training. You know, we pack them up and send them to the track. They come back, we bathe them. But that lasts until ten or ten-thirty. Then we do them

The "backside" community at the Saratoga Racetrack has its own folkways and occupational lore. Photo: Dorothy Ours, courtesy of the National Museum of Racing and Hall of Fame.

up. We put all kinds of liniments and poultices on them and put bandages on them. We feed about eleven a.m. Then we come back about three-thirty. Muck out the stalls again and feed them about five. And then we're done.

It's a long day. We do get a little bit of time off but you can't do a lot. Not really. We're usually gone by twelve and you have to clean up, so about twelve to three, what can you really do? You can't go shopping. What we do, we get every other afternoon off.

We both come in every morning. I rub three and Jerry rubs three and the hot walker, he's rubbing the pony. That's good . . . we come back every other afternoon. Because the mornings, that would be too tough to do for one person. But it's not bad, every other afternoon. And sometimes we swap afternoons or I pay him to come back for me. Something like that.

By six or six-thirty a.m., the exercise riders have begun the horses' daily workouts. It is the exercise riders' job to advise the trainer about the mood and fitness of the horse. He or she will let the trainer know if the horse is "off," an indication that there might be a hidden physical ailment. The workouts continue for the next few hours, as each horse is run through its paces. Untried horses—two-year-olds that have not yet raced—are schooled during this period. If they are entered in an upcoming race, they will be taken to the practice starting gates. The horses are then led to the shedrow between the barns and walked until their body temperature cools. They will be bathed, rubbed down, and returned to their stalls. Other service people begin to appear—the salespeople for feed, shoes, and medicines are arriving—as do the farriers who will fit each horse entered in the day's races with new aluminum shoes.

If a horse is entered in that day's race, the trainer has the groom remain with the horse and accompany it to the track. Many grooms are proud of the part they play in the success of their horses, but they are frustrated as well, for the grooms are the most invisible people at the track. Although they, the exercise riders, and the hot walkers have been involved with the horse on a daily basis and are present at the race, in the winner's circle it is the owner, trainer, and jockey—who arrives only minutes before the race to take his mount—who receive the accolades.

> The jockeys get 10 percent [of the purse]. It's too much for them. I've spent more time with this horse in the morning time than with my wife. You know what I'm saying? I'm feeling like the groom should be getting more than what they're getting. How much time do *they* spend with them? Two minutes? They're on them maybe two minutes. They come out and work them sometime and that's it. You could put a monkey on a horse and it could win. They should at least recognize the groom and the hot walker.

The racetrack world is a stratified society and the hot walkers are at the bottom. It is in this low-skill position where many people begin their racing careers. A former jockey who is now the wife of a trainer began by "walking on the hots." From that position, one can move up to groom and become involved with the horses' training regimen and care. From there, one can become an assistant trainer or, if one is an aspiring rider, begin to gallop the horses. Both of these positions can be a springboard to the more prestigious posts of trainer or jockey—provided one enjoys the mentoring and intervention of a sympathetic owner or trainer.

To move up the ladder, one has to fall in with "the right people." Many workers remain at the level of groom or rider, waiting for an opportunity to move up. As one woman groom said,

I got a training permit over a year ago but it's so tough for women. So tough. I've talked to a couple of people and they say, Yes, yes, I'd love to have you train a couple, but they never say when. Come on, give me a break.

Those born or married into the world of the racetrack often find a niche. One woman began making racing silks—the jackets worn by jockeys—after she married a jockey. One of their children is now a jockey in Europe, the other is a sales representative for a large horse auction house.

CHANCE AND RITUAL

Just as with other sporting activities, horseracing involves elements of chance, but as sociologist Carole Case points out, activities in the backstretch to prepare the horses are ritualized to minimize the risk. Techniques that appear efficacious will be repeated in an attempt to duplicate the favorable outcome. One trainer routinely shares his best Scotch with a certain horse, believing that it makes the horse run faster. Other trainers use magnetic blankets, deep tissue massage, or specially mixed salves for sore legs and feet. Trainers are not allowed to practice veterinary medicine, and any infractions of the strict rules governing accepted treatments can lead to censure or loss of one's training license. However, salves and liniments are often concocted from secret recipes.

I had a filly that had bad feet and [my father would] tell me some kind of stuff to use. It was a combination of a medicated mud, a poultice with bran, Epsom salt, and a black drawing salve which is a combination of all of that stuff. You use that as a drawing to get the heat out. That was pretty good.

The old-timers, they made their own medications. Now they buy everything. I don't think that's so good. Like when my father trained, he'd use like cucumbers, stuff like that for cracked heels. Now they've got all those salves and stuff. I mean, it does the trick but it takes so long to do it. With the cucumbers and whatever stuff he'd use, in two or three days it was gone.

Just as with other routine activities, there is a proper way to groom a horse, to wrap its legs, to walk it. Walking is always done clockwise in the

Ted Baxter, a veterinarian's assistant, practices horse dentistry at the 2001 Fiesta of Racetrack Traditions. Photo: Dorothy Ours, courtesy of the National Museum of Racing and Hall of Fame.

shedrow, at a certain pace with the horse at a certain distance from the walker. The ground around the stables is raked into smooth concentric circles at the conclusion of each day's grooming, but not just for neatness: uneven ground could cause a horse to stumble or twist a joint. Carole Case points to the efficacy of these rituals as a way to mitigate the uncertainty of life at the track. A groom cites an example of how suddenly a reversal of fortune can strike:

> You can see it's not the easiest. All that horse wants to do is bite at that guy. And anything can set them off. They just feel good and want to play. All of that stuff.
>
> [They can take off on you] easily. Yeah, so easy. We had a filly not too long ago. She was getting a bath and she'd just come over from England so they're not used to having the shank over their nose. That's how we had it across her nose. And something spooked her. She went straight up and flipped and broke her shoulders. She broke both withers. But she's O.K. now. She had a lot to come off and she came back and she's won in races. Thank God.

The element of chance that is experienced in the backstretch of the racetrack can negate weeks of training. A pebble is kicked up, a horse-shoe is thrown, a saddle slips. Any of these seemingly minor events may cause a chain reaction in which a horse is injured, and those who work with the horses are reminded that their occupation is highly dangerous. One exercise rider was thrown from his horse during a morning gallop; his broken ribs left him unemployable for the remainder of the year. A groom is stepped on by a horse, his foot breaks, and he is temporarily out of work. Unemployment can be devastating in this world of contractual employment.

Despite all the rituals and efforts to mitigate risk, the race, I was told, is determined in large part by the excellence of the horse. The "jock" plays only a small part in the outcome. Dave Erb, a former jockey and trainer, said,

> There's no limit to what you can do if you're lucky and get a good horse. There's an old saying "Riders don't make horses but horses make riders." You only have to get on one or two good horses and then you're in demand. I've seen a lot of riders, real good riders who could compete with anyone, just never got that break. Just never got a good horse to ride.

In addition, it is commonly believed in the backstretch that ultimately, the trainer's care has little effect on the horse:

> You know, there's one old-time trainer says, Any dumb son of a gun can train a horse but the guy that can keep the horse at the races, that's the good horseman. Which I believe is about the truth. If you just use common ordinary sense, you can get a horse fit and ready to run.

IDENTITY MARKERS

In his edited volume *Usable Pasts*, Tad Tuleja draws attention to the variety of stylistic resources people use to manipulate their identities: any cultural trait can denote group membership. In the backstretch, one's identity is often a constructed identity. Personal and family identities take second place to one's job position, employer, or ethnic group. Nicknames abound, and surnames are virtually nonexistent among grooms, hot walkers, and gallopers. To locate someone in the backside, one must know who that person works for and what number barn he or she is in. Some positions change during the day. One's location might be described as, "He rubs for Sciacca in the morning and then he gallops for Lukas. You can find him in the receiving barn. That's where he hangs out." There are no addresses.

Those who work in the low-skilled positions of hot walker and groom are wholly at the mercy of the trainer—and the horses in their care. If a horse is not performing well at one racetrack, it can be shipped without a

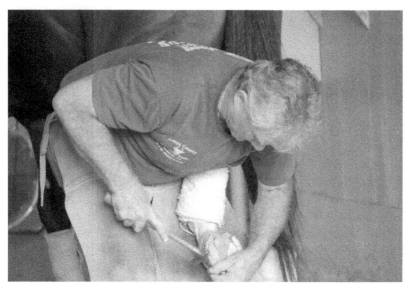

Farrier Tim Shortell shoeing a horse at the Belmont Racetrack, Elmont, New York. Photo: Ellen McHale.

moment's notice, and the groom and the hot walker ride with the horse in the trailer to the new racetrack or perhaps back to the home barn in Kentucky or Florida. Because of the migratory nature of this work, allegiances are tenuous and identities are constructed.

Nicknames reflect one's constructed identity. They may connote physical characteristics—"Red" for a red-headed groom, or "Chicaleen" for a walker who is short and baby-faced. "Cowboy" comes from Michoacán, Mexico, known for its horses and cattle. "Cookie" and "Bon Bom" have other, perhaps more personal origins.

One marker used at the racetrack is the specialized vocabulary that denotes membership in the life of the backside. Wisdom and lore are imparted through proverbial expressions. "Riders don't make horses but horses make riders" acknowledges the horse as the determinant of a jockey's fate: jockeys need to win races before they can be hired to ride winning mounts. Another proverb that speaks to the uncertainty of life at the racetrack is, "Chickens today, feathers tomorrow": one's fortunes can change within moments.

As with other occupational groups, a specialized argot serves as a marker for group membership. A groom "rubs" a horse. A horse that wins his first race "breaks his maiden," as does a jockey who wins her first race. When a horse "spits the bit out," he has been running well and then all of a sudden falters. An exercise rider "gallops" horses. The horse who isn't being worked hard but is being ridden for daily exercise and to keep in shape is said to "cruise." This specialized language is important in maintaining a boundary between those who inhabit the horse world and those who are merely spectators on the frontside.

MATERIAL CULTURE

Jules Prown, in his work on material culture, defines material culture as "the study through artifacts of the beliefs—values, ideas, attitudes, and assumptions—of a particular community or society at a given time" (1982: 1). Material culture in the backstretch serves as another indicator of identity. Racing silks, the jackets and caps worn by the jockeys during a race, are identity markers. Each owner registers his colors and silk design with the Racing Association, and from then on they identify his horses, jockeys, and barns. Trainers use color-coordinated feed tubs, and initialed and color-coordinated stable gates. A Jewish trainer incorporates the Star of David into his stable designs, and an Irish trainer colors all his stall decorations and accoutrements in the orange, green, and white of the Irish flag.

Even the plantings around the barn are color-coordinated to match the owner's silks. The planting of flowers is one of the first activities in the week before the meet begins. As trainers arrive with their horses and workers to set up the barn, flowers are planted in color schemes that mark territory for the six weeks of the meet.

Outriders, employed by the New York Racing Association to serve as assistants and troubleshooters within the race course fences, own their own horses and also use colors on their tack as well as in mane and tail decorations. When seen from afar, the rider may be unidentifiable, but the horse's decorations will be seen, indicating identity.

Those who work in the backstretch experience risk within their daily work and have little sense of control over circumstances. Consistency is described as "What have you done in the last few minutes?" and the concept of luck peppers everyday speech: "It's one business where you can go from nothing to having great wealth—*if* the luck is with you." Within this bounded world ritual persists, on the chance that it might affect outcomes and contain the chaos that lies just underneath a thin veneer of order. In this intentional community, identities in the backstretch are forged through one's relationship with the horse. In a world where the horse is king, it is truly "Chickens today, feathers tomorrow."

WORKS CITED

Abrahams, Roger. 1982. "Play and Games." *Motif: International Newsletter of Research in Folklore and Literature* 3 (June).

Case, Carole. 1991. *Down the Backstretch: Racing and the American Dream*. Philadelphia: Temple University Press.

Harrah-Conforth, Jeanne. 1992. "The Landscape of Possibility: An Ethnography of the Kentucky Derby." Ph.D. dissertation, Indiana University.

Hotaling, Edward. 1995. *They're Off: Horse Racing at Saratoga*. Syracuse: Syracuse University Press.

Jones, Michael Owen. 1997. "How Can We Apply Event Analysis to 'Material Behavior,' and Why Should We?" *Western Folklore* (Summer–Fall): 199–214.

Prown, Jules. 1982. "Mind in Matter: An Introduction to Material Culture Theory and Method." *Winterthur Portfolio* 17, no. 1 (Spring): 1–19.

Thomas, Jeannie B. 1995. "Pickup Trucks, Horses, Women, and Foreplay: The Fluidity of Folklore." *Western Folklore* (Summer–Fall): 213–228.

Tuleja, Tad. 1997. *Usable Pasts: Traditions and Group Expression in North America*. Logan: Utah State University Press.

"An Ethnography of the Saratoga Racetrack" was first published in *Voices: The Journal of New York Folklore* 29, nos. 1-2 (Spring–Summer 2003): 7–11.

STAND CLEAR OF THE CLOSING DOORS!

Occupational Folklore of New York City Subway Workers

RYN GARGULINSKI

Studies of occupational lore vary widely, their subjects ranging from factory workers, librarians, college professors, and hospital workers to window washers and lawyers. Some dangerous occupations that have been examined include police officers, air force pilots-in-training, miners, and firefighters. In the transportation category, researchers have looked at New York City taxicab drivers, porters, and flight attendants. In almost all such studies, the emphasis is on logocentrism—the spoken over the written word. "Let the people speak for themselves," as folklorist Jack Santino (1988) put it.

Subway tales can be found in Sally Charnow and Steven Zeitlin's folklore and oral history of transit, *I've Been Working on the Subway* (in which workers term a number of narratives "war stories"), Robert Snyder's collection entitled *Transit Talk*, Marion Swerdlow's book *Underground Woman*, and columnist Jim Dwyer's book *Subway Lives*. With those sources as background, I decided to hear for myself what New York City subway workers had to say.

My fieldwork began in July 1998, when I approached a token booth clerk and said I was doing a thesis project on the New York City subway system. First he asked, "Why?" Then he held his nose in the universal gesture that says, "It stinks." It has been a long road ever since. I have interviewed at least fifty New York City Transit employees—conductors, train operators, token booth clerks, office employees, track workers, subway managers, even the transit chaplain—wherever I could find someone willing to talk. This meant catching workers between shifts at the Stillwell Avenue terminal in Coney Island, talking to conductors on the job while riding the train, and frequenting subway stations. Only two subjects allowed me to tape their interviews. Some even looked wary when I produced pen and paper, and I had to commit my finds to memory until the informants were out of sight. All exchanges were in the manner of a formal interview rather than a "natural" setting where the stories would normally be exchanged.

After collecting a number of subway stories, I categorized them, analyzed them, and examined their functions. I also examined their themes and variations—which are what make them folklore. How does the transmission of these stories illustrate formulation and dissemination of folklore? Who tells them and why?

I realized that accident and cautionary narratives were the most common. They would be my topic. I then took a fresh approach in my interviews, searching only for that type of subway story. I chose the accident and cautionary stories that came up most frequently, struck me as the most interesting (or gruesome), or contained examples of the types of details I wished to discuss.

What I found amid all the debris, rats, and grime in the subways was a community of close-knit workers who share, besides their jobs in the bowels of the most diverse city on the planet, a number of stories that bind them. Many of these binding tales fall into the accident and cautionary genre and can be broken down into five major categories: accounts of death; near-death (and close-call) stories; tales highlighting the unstable environment; hero narratives; and tales that deal with humor, pranks, and the absurd. For this article, I focus on a single category: tales of death.

EXAMPLES

Dismemberment. Severed heads and dismemberment are a major theme found again and again in the subway tales. Ask any subway worker about a corpse (or parts of it) and he or she will be sure to come up with at least one story. Take, for instance, the homeless guy who got his head smashed by an incoming train. When he fell, head gushing blood, a woman on the platform took off her shirt to use as a tourniquet on his skull.

Then there was the conductor who had worked the subway for more than forty years. One day he was concerned about some rowdy kids in the rear cars. He stuck his head out the window to investigate—only to have his skull shattered by a protruding signal. "He was in a million pieces," said my informants.

That narrative is similar to the story of the conductor found dead in his cab:

The city's Transit Authority workers tell and retell stories that entertain, instruct, and horrify. The use of insider jargon in their occupational folklore functions like a password to signal their membership in the group. Photo © Martha Cooper.

A conductor pulled out of the station with no problems—no one was stuck between the doors—and the train pulled safely into the next station. But after it reached the station, the doors didn't open. The train operator radioed his conductor to ask him what the problem was. There was no answer. He radioed again. No answer. He tried a third time to no avail. When the operator finally left his post and walked back to the conductor's booth, he found the conductor dead, still standing, with half his head shorn off. He must have left his head out too long and been partially decapitated by one of the signs jutting out from the tunnel walls.

Also in the decapitation category is the story told by a conductor about kids jumping up and down on the roadbed adjacent to the tracks where his train was pulling into the station. A young passenger had apparently been goofing off between cars and fallen under the train. The cops had cut power to the tracks where the kids had congregated and their dead friend lay. The conductor was one of the first workers on the scene to see the lifeless body of the child on the tracks. "A chunk the size of a softball was cut out of his head . . . his brains were spilling out of his head." One employee in yet another incident said that he would never forget a decapitated head he had seen smoldering on the third rail: "It was a gruesome sight. The skin was turning gray and there was steam coming out of its nose."

There is also the tale of the passenger who was waiting for the train at the edge of the platform. This story came from an instructor who tells it in his safety classes at the Transit Authority:

> I was off duty and my wife had something to exchange in Gimbel's. It was still the rush hour, and I'm waiting for her toward the middle of the platform near the down stairs from the mezzanine. And you see, they always have a habit, the local will pull in the station, and the express is already three quarters at the receiving end of the station. Well, the local, as soon as he pulls into the station, he'll open his doors, let people out, and right away close the doors before the express train comes to a full stop. Meanwhile, this man's running down the stairs, and I hear, "Hold it! Hold the train! Hold the doors! Hold the doors!" And I look, and there's another guy at the edge of the platform reading the newspaper—this is a true story. The man running nudged him accidentally because he jumped down the last few stairs and lost his balance. He nudged him far enough for the express train coming in to hit his head. Boom! It hit his head, it cracked, blood splattered. And the other man made the local just before the doors closed up. He didn't even realize he'd killed a man. That man was a DOA. On the platform, dead. (Charnow and Zeitlin n.d.: 32)

Suicides. Suicides are another theme in accident and cautionary narratives. "It's the worst around holidays," one worker informed me, relating a story of a young mother on the platform, holding her child's hand, who jumped in front of an oncoming train on the Fourth of July. And a newly trained conductor talked about the eighteen-year-old who jumped to his death in front of a train the week before Christmas.

"I refuse to drive my car under the el-line," began one transit worker. "Let me tell you why." He then related the tale of a motorman on the overhead line who had the misfortune of blasting into someone jumping in front of the train—a "jumper." Although chunks and arms and legs were found on the track under the train, there was no head. Not to worry. It turned up the following day in the back seat of some guy's convertible. Evidently it had fallen from the overhead line to the street below, not to be noticed by the driver until the next day.

Another tale involves a jumper who hit the front of the train with such a force that he smashed through the train's front window, breaking the train operator's arm.

"I've never seen a suicide, thank God," one worker said. A fellow worker was not so lucky. A man jumped in front of the train a week before the train operator was about to retire. "Now he has to live with that image the rest of his life."

ANALYSIS

The first issue that must be addressed is what, exactly, makes these subway narratives folklore. Writes Jan Harold Brunvand in *The Vanishing Hitchhiker*: "All true folklore ultimately depends upon continued oral dissemination, usually within fairly homogeneous 'folk groups,' and upon the retention through time of internal patterns and motifs that become traditional in the oral exchanges" (1981: 3). Certain internal motifs—the five major themes of death, close calls, the unstable environment, heroes, and humor—run throughout the subway accident and cautionary narratives.

The scariness inherent in the accident and cautionary subway stories can be found in tales presented by the Brothers Grimm: "Little Red Riding Hood," "Hansel and Gretel," and "Cinderella." They all contain a dark shadow of foreboding, warning listeners to act in a safe manner. Of course, accident and cautionary stories are, by their very nature, gloomy and full of gruesome humor.

Another factor that makes the subway tales occupational lore is their manner of transmission: these stories are told, reshaped, and told yet again—sometimes with slight variations. In one tale I heard several times, a story about a man pinned between the subway car and the platform, the victim is sometimes found between the car and the tunnel wall. Always a male, he is either a homeless man on the tracks or a passenger who was pushed, was careless, or was attempting suicide. In some cases he dies the second the train pulls out of the station; in others, the emergency team lifts the train from the tracks with air bags and transports him to the hospital before he perishes. He is sometimes granted his last request: a cigarette or a beer, or both. This story is so popular that it became an episode of television's *Homicide: Life on the Street*; in turn, a show was then aired about the making of this particular episode. Some transit workers may not even be aware that they are participating in what we know as "narrative folklore"—the passing down of wisdom through their stories. Explains Brunvand:

> When we follow the ancient practice of informally transmitting "lore" . . . by word of mouth and customary example from person to person, we do not concentrate on the form or content of our folk-lore; instead, we simply listen to information that others tell us and then pass it on—more or less accurately—to other listeners. (1981: 1)

For example, a subway worker asking a fellow employee whether he has heard about the young track worker who was "smeared by a train in this very spot" is doing much more than relaying information. He is participating in a tradition.

That tradition is played out among a homogeneous folk group—in this particular case, the subway employees. They are all working for the same boss, New York City, under the same hazardous conditions. They also work very closely with one another. Subway work by its very nature is social. Subway employees are regularly assigned to work together. The train operator–conductor relation is similar to that of police partners: one becomes the other's right-hand man. Track workers are always assigned to work in groups. On the job or on breaks or in locker rooms, transit workers have ample opportunity to talk to one other.

As in any occupation, subway workers use jargon to signal their standing within an elite, privileged group. Their terms include "roadbed," "jumper," "tube," and "indication." They also use nicknames to differentiate the subway lines. For instance, the B line is Bravo (formerly Boy), the Q train is Quincy, and the No. 2 train is the Deuce. The use of this specialized language, like knowledge of the decapitation stories, proves that the speaker has "earned his stripes" in the profession—and also keeps the outsiders out.

More importantly, it is the telling and retelling of certain subway narratives that *creates* the community of folklore. In many instances, the transit workers would have nothing else in common besides the bond they share through their work environment. The stories act as a glue that reinforces the bond and brings the community together. Besides being part of the occupational community, through their storytelling they distinguish themselves as members within that community: "the guy who tells the story about . . . ," "those who have heard the story about . . ."

Another element common to the accident and cautionary tales is their function. They all serve to encourage safety by reinforcing the importance of remaining alert and careful. In toto, they can be taken as a big list of "don'ts." Don't let your guard down; don't feel safe and comfortable; don't forget to use caution; don't underestimate the power of a roaring train; don't become distracted.

In some of the narratives, the workers themselves explain the purpose of the story. For instance, after relating the tale of the dead-on-arrival on the platform in the Gimbel's story, the safety instructor commented, "I tell that story to [emphasize] safety with the workers. Never stay too close to the edge of those platforms; workers have a habit of doing that. You never know who's running for a train or who may get a dizzy spell and fall against you. Always maintain safety: stay away from the edge of platform levels" (Charnow and Zeitlin n.d.: 32).

The death tales warn workers about the dangers of their work and re- mind them that they are reckoning with forces mightier than they. The third rail is a force beyond their control. Trains are brutal and fatal. Work- ers must always be on guard against mechanical failure as well as human error. People can be cruel—and sometimes just as dangerous as anything else workers find in the subways. Token booth clerks have been torched to death, and workers should be scared.

And they are also warned to expect the unexpected. Nowhere is safe, as exemplified by the tale of the worker who left the lighting department after many years. He finally had the chance to get off the tracks and trans- fer to the telephone department. One day he and his partner were crossing the tracks between platforms and *boom*—he stepped right into the path of a roaring train. The narrators of the tales themselves at times concluded their stories with cautions: "This is a very, very dangerous job" (Snyder 1997: 53). Some of the warnings could perhaps be prefaced with the line, "Oh, the things that you'll see!" Suicides. Severed heads. Smoldering corpses.

In addition to the many tales about worker fatalities, there are other stories in which workers have had a brush with death. Being cautious and being prepared are lessons to be learned—so are being alert and knowing limitations. Tales remind workers not to rush or try to "make up time" by speeding through dangerous curves. Postings in the subway stations even warn, "Most accidents happen when people are in a rush." Workers who are tired, anxious, or drunk or on drugs are also hazards.

The tale of the fatal Malbone Street train crash (Cudahy 1999) continues to be told precisely for the benefit of such workers. This crash, which killed 93 (some sources say 102) in 1918, had the fatal element: a fatigued and poorly trained operator. The tale continues to serve as a warning and is circulated among current workers as well as found in almost every book on the New York City subway.

Another lesson is community. Subway employees *must* work together to ensure the safety of all involved. "Out of such shared dangers and work routines emerges a sense of camaraderie" (Snyder 1997: 90). The working relationship is not just a partnership—it could be a matter of life and death.

"People of all ages love a good scare," writes Brunvand (1981: 47). Some narratives are, indeed, meant to horrify listeners, but not without an underlying lesson. Subway accident and cautionary narratives are *not* told for the sole purpose of enjoyment. Every tale of death and destruction is closely followed with a message of caution. Some of the gory stories encourage the listener to let his imagination run: "What if I had slipped *just one inch* to the right and fallen on the third rail?" "What if I didn't happen to look the other way and see the train racing toward me from the opposite direction?" In this category is the tale of the track maintenance supervisor who took the day off, only to hear that the man filling in for him was fried while cutting a cable on the tracks: "He went up in a ball of flames" and spent more than six months in a burn unit. The supervisor lives with the thought, "What if I had gone to work that day? That could have been *me*."

CONCLUSION

Occupational accident and cautionary narratives are alive, well, and circulating in today's workplace. They reflect the dangers and concerns of workers in hazardous jobs. They serve a variety of purposes and, as part of occupational lore as a whole, constitute a major part of oral tradition. They also give workers "at least a measure of personal control over [their] working lives" (McCarl 1988: 35). The narratives reveal "a variety of strategies used by workers to insure informal control of work safety. The seriousness of the fatality account resulting in a new safety procedure and the catharsis of the near-miss narrative underscore the way verbal accounts of work techniques provide insiders with necessary information in a compelling form" (McCarl 1988: 40–41). This measure of control is extremely important, especially in unstable environments like the New York City subway system. The tales tell workers what to look out for, how to avoid potential disasters, and how to do things differently from a fellow worker who was not so cautious—and paid the price.

Two aspects common to all occupational accident and cautionary narratives stand out: they are simultaneously specialized and universal. Although their phrasing and jargon may be unique to a particular field, the tales share the language of everyday life. They have a universal application that transcends the boundaries of a particular occupation and can be appreciated by everyone, regardless of his or her job. Everyone loves a good story, and almost everyone should be able to relate to the subway narratives. Their primary purpose—to teach and warn—has universal appeal.

The subway itself is universal. It is an important part of the life of all New Yorkers—the millions of passengers and fifty-five thousand transit employees alike. The subway is a microcosm of this diverse city. Although the subway train itself is forever in motion, its territory remains constant, stable. The stories travel through the vast array of tunnels—656 (some sources say 714) miles of track—to the hundreds of token booths in which workers sit, to the B line, the N line, constantly on the go.

This study shows that a simple exchange between subway employees can be more than it seems. A final case in point is the conversation between two subway workers that I overheard while riding a train. "What a jackass," one said, referring to a young worker who showed up drunk on his first day of training and was instantly fired. The kid's father, a subway bigwig, had gotten him a plum assignment, but as the other worker said, "He didn't know how good he had it." An exchange that brief (and seemingly inconsequential) between subway employees in reality does a lot more. As in the subway accident stories, the workers are weaving their on-the-job knowledge into communal subway worker knowledge, venting their emotions, providing a warning for other employees not to follow suit, and, most importantly, shaping their own occupational lives.

WORKS CITED

Brunvand, J. H. 1981. *The Vanishing Hitchhiker*. New York: W. W. Norton.
Charnow, S., and S. Zeitlin. n.d. *I've Been Working on the Subway*. New York: New York Transit Museum.
Cudahy, B. 1999. *The Malbone Street Wreck*. New York: Fordham University Press.

Dwyer, J. 1991. *Subway Lives: 24 Hours in the Life of the New York City Subway*. New York: Crown Publishers.

McCarl, R. S. 1998. "Accident Narratives: Self Protection in the Workplace." *New York Folklore* 14 (1-2).

Santino, J. 1988. "Occupational Folklore: Overview and Afterword." *New York Folklore* 14 (1-2): 105.

Snyder, R. W. 1997. *Transit Talk: New York's Bus and Subway Workers Tell Their Stories*. New York: New York Transit Museum; New Brunswick: Rutgers University Press.

Swerdlow, M. *Underground Woman: My Four Years as a New York City Subway Conductor*. Philadelphia: Temple University Press, 1998.

"Stand Clear of the Closing Doors! Occupational Folklore of New York City Subway Workers" was first published in *Voices: The Journal of New York Folklore* 27, nos. 1–2 (Spring-Summer 2001): 28–31.

RESISTANCE

TWO SPIRITED PEOPLE

Understanding Who We Are as Creation

CURTIS HARRIS AND LEOTA LONE DOG

INTERVIEWED BY DEBORAH BLINCOE

EDITOR'S NOTE: Curtis Harris is on staff at the American Indian Community House (AICH) in New York City. Leota Lone Dog serves on the AICH Board of Directors.

Deborah: Would you like to start by telling me something about the significance of the name of your organization?

Curtis: Well, we came up with the two names out of a book I think that many of us had read, called *Living the Spirit*, and there were two people, two characters or ancestors, who were written about in the book. And part of the original scope of what we were trying to do was not only to raise the visibility of gay and lesbian people in the Native community but also give some focus to the fact that we had a historical tradition in the communities, and that it wasn't something that we were just thinking about or something that came about because it was new and exciting. It was something that we just wanted people to remember, and so we thought of using two characters or two ancestors from history. Just as gay and lesbian people use Eleanor Roosevelt or Gertrude Stein or any of those people as historical markers for the general community, we use WeWah and BarCheeAmpe as markers for our community.

Deborah: Would you like to say a little about who WeWah and BarChee-Ampe were?

Leota: Well, WeWah was a Zuni, I guess you would call him a cross dresser, and his role in his nation was that of a woman. He carried on the functions that a woman normally would carry on. And when found by the anthropologists they just assumed that this was a woman who just happened to be very big and had male features and physique. And he traveled to Washington as a representative of his tribe. In his tribe he had been the go-between between anthropologists and his nation. He was a very intelligent person. It wasn't until he passed away that it was discovered that this was actually a man. I guess his role in Washington, in that society, was that he had access to the women that were there and the men who treated him as a woman. In any case, he was an esteemed member of his nation.

BarCheeAmpe, on the other hand, was a woman warrior. According to legend, she led the life of a warrior, and hunted and had I think it was four wives. In using these two, as Curtis said, that was to do something about the visibility of Native Americans in this country and the history that has been submerged, consistently submerged. It's difficult for people outside of our community to remember the names. We didn't want to go by some acronym and develop some kind of name so that it would be easy to remember, because it's important that our traditions and our cultures be remembered as they are and not assimilated. And I think of the book *Sappho Was a Right On Woman*. Using Sappho, it makes people want to find out, "Well, who was Sappho?" So I guess part of our intention was, "Who were these people?" Thus we revere our history through the names.

Deborah: BarCheeAmpe was a mythic figure in what community?

Leota: Crow.

Deborah: Maybe now is the time to go on and talk about the term Native Two Spirits.

Curtis: I'll start the discussion by saying that it's a term that is relatively new, in the sense that most indigenous people had in their own languages references to people whose sexuality or whose gender made up other parts of the Circle of that community. Often they were names that were used in reverence or in honor. In some cases the roles were very, very clearly defined in terms of your sexuality or your gender. Sometimes they were not—they were defined in terms of being just a part of the community. But in many cases, Two Spirited people or people whose sexuality or gender were maybe the third, were seen as the carriers of medicine, were seen as people who could mediate because of the balance that they were known to have in terms of the balance between male and female.

So in looking at these traditions, Native people—Leota knows a little bit more about this in terms of historical contents because she's been a leader in the Two Spirit community for a little bit longer than I have—a lot longer. The name Two Spirited came from a group of people in the Midwest who had heard that term used in some of the communities in that part of the country. We've adopted it because it does encompass more traditions than any of the other terms that we've come across, and it also is a fairly accurate reflection in terms of how most of our communities see us. Also, we as gay and lesbian people have been real involved in our communities and have struggled to hold onto our positions in our community under the influence of the colonizers.

So "Two Spirit" is a relatively new term, but it's an ancient tradition. It's one that is recognized by many traditional Indian people, and that's another whole issue—tradition and nontradition. Many people in our communities who have traded in their Indian spirituality for Christian spirituality often don't recognize it. So our role has been to increase the visibility not only of our presence in the community, whatever our sexualities are and whatever our genders, but also to increase the visibility of our histories as participants and parts of the Circle in our communities. So that's where that term comes into play.

And then the obvious flip side to that is that early on, and I know Leota can tell you stories about this, is that in struggling to maintain our identities in the larger gay and lesbian community we were often asked to make a choice because of the nature of the adolescence of the gay and lesbian community. In terms of who we are and what our identities are, it was a choice between being gay and lesbian and being American Indian or Native American. For many of us, that was a choice that we couldn't make. We were Indian and we happened to be gay or lesbian or bisexual or heterosexual or Two Spirit. And we can't make those decisions. Those decisions are made for us by the Creator. So we started to use this term because we didn't feel comfortable in many cases in simply defining ourselves by the colonizers' culture which said that you were now going to be either gay or lesbian or bisexual.

The idea of the Kinsey scale from 0 to 6, 0 being completely heterosexual and 6 being completely homosexual, it seems to be part of the definition of being gay or lesbian or bisexual. You're at one point on that line. Well, in our communities, many of our communities, the tradition of sexuality is that you're at one point on a Circle, and that all the points are connected, and you can be at any point on that Circle at any one period in your life, and you don't necessarily have to be at one end of the line. And I think that's a major difference between many of our cultures and the cultures of the colonizers, is that it is a circular and a connected sense of tradition as opposed to a linear, with really no options and no way for the ends of the spectrum to ever be connected. So I think all of that is a part of what Two Spirited is—that's my take on it. Leota?

Leota: Well, I think also it reflects the balance within our communities that we wanted to continue on. Just being gay or lesbian and using those terms already sets up a division and becomes in some ways adversarial. You have the gay struggle or the lesbian struggle, when it's all really one struggle.

One point at which we came up against a lot of opposition was when we were struggling to lead the gay and lesbian march here in New York City in 1991, and explaining our position as indigenous people here in North America and what our position was on marching together and leading the march when traditionally the march had been led by women. As indigenous people here in this hemisphere it was important for us to maintain the balance as an organization and maintain that as an organization that was going to march. And that opposition was the women's struggle, the feminist movement and the struggle that had gone on for many years to get in the position of the march. You know, I recognized that struggle; I had been a part of it. But also, once I left the larger gay and lesbian community to come and work in my own community, it was important for us to put that across. I guess a lot of people didn't understand the impact of colonialism and what we were trying to do, and thought it in opposition to the gay and lesbian struggle.

I find my work here is not just as a woman, as a lesbian, as a mother, it's all one struggle. It's the politics of domination and the struggle against that domination. So I find that I can incorporate all of who I am, and what Two Spirited means to me is part of that incorporation of who I am as an individual.

Deborah: May I ask both of you, do you have particular community ties? What communities within the Native community do you have ancestral ties with?

Leota: I'm Lakota, Mohawk, and Delaware, more closely affined with Lakota. I'm on their rolls, and I take part in more of the traditional rituals of that nation. Most of my family that I know of is in South Dakota, so most of my ties are with the Lakota nation.

Curtis: I'm Apache, and I come from a reservation in Arizona.

Deborah: We were discussing about how traditionally in many of the Native communities, the role of people who were ambiguous in terms of sexuality or gender, or who had achieved a balance or crossover, that that was traditionally a revered position. And then you mentioned the contrast between traditional Native Americans and nontraditional, those who have adopted Christianity, and that there's a difference in attitude there. But

I wonder whether the position of Two Spirited people is still in any way recognized traditionally as sacred or special, whether it's still a revered role or position.

Curtis: Well, you know, it's pretty hard to shake some of the things that you've been raised with. One of the jokes 1 made with a friend of mine was he kept referring to God as a woman. And I said, "You're so 80s. God is a gay male." And it sort of struck him funny and then he realized what I was saying was that the Creator is everything that we are. It's not just one identity. And if you look at many of the traditions in North America, the Creation stories often make reference—and sometimes even in particular the Navajo stories of Creation—to people who are not of either gender that we would recognize, male or female; they were third, sometimes fourth gender people. And so if you're brought up with that tradition, then it's not so hard to make the leap, or even the step to understanding who we are as Creation, as different gender beings, as different sexual beings.

So there are traditional people who look at sexuality and gender in a much different way than people who have really and probably still are living under the influence—what is it, DUI, driving under the influence of Christianity. It is very hard for them to understand the traditional notions of sexuality unless they're willing to let go of some of those Judeo-Christian thoughts of there being an Adam and an Eve, Adam coming first of course, and Eve being just a part of Adam. What I'm saying is that tradition can vary among people depending upon where they are in terms of their own recognition of their own traditions.

Now those of us who've worked in our own community in New York City, and certainly Leota and I, have talked with many, many people across the hemisphere in terms of who we are as sexual beings and sexual identities. When we have had some common discussions, I think my learning has come from meeting other people from around the hemisphere who have had to share with me their traditions and their stories. In my particular people's histories, there were no references to beings with sexual identities in terms of Two Spiritedness. But we were also a people who never kissed and didn't discuss sex. So just because they're not written down doesn't mean they didn't exist. And just because they're not talked about by many of our elders doesn't mean it didn't exist, because many of our elders went through that colonization process as well. And only now are we beginning to uncover some of those stories, and sometimes it's because other peoples can remember. In many cases, the Pueblo people in New Mexico know the stories of my people, the Apache—stories that we've forgotten, or have let go. But the Pueblo people knew us throughout history, and they can remember the stories for us.

The idea of tradition and nontradition as it plays out in our urban community is also a really different dynamic, and Leota as someone who grew up in an urban community is someone who has dealt, tried to reach a balance, with that and continued to really hold onto her identity as an urban Indian. I don't know, Leota, is that fair?

Leota: Yeah, well, growing up in New York City, for the longest time I thought I was the only Indian in New York—the only Indian child, at least. But of course as I've gotten older and found the community, which was a very—it's like a secret. It's like a secret that there are Native Americans in New York City. It's a secret that there's a Community House. And one of the goals that I wanted to achieve was to have our organization become more visible.

I think what's happened is that indigenous people in this hemisphere are in recovery, and in that recovery we're defining and redefining who we are. And we have to go back to learning our traditions, but also there are ways that we have to create new traditions in order to survive in this world as it is now, today. Even our ceremonies are revised in order to adapt to the people who are taking part in them now. It's just not the same. I guess I find that a lot of people want to think that if they don't see you in beads and feathers, you're not Indian enough. I had that feeling for a long time, and I know the feeling when I first came out was, "Well, I guess I'm not Indian," because I'd never heard of any of my ancestors and what their roles were. And I guess it's just a process we all have to go through to uncover who we were, who we are now, and what our position will be for the future, and for seven generations from now.

I remember talking to my mother at one point, and somebody was asking her, "What about God the Father?" and "They call him this," and "They call him that." And she said, "Well whoever said it was a man?" Well, that's right, whoever said God the Father was a man? Even though they had the name "Father," that didn't mean that that was a man. In any case, I guess that this year, 1992, has put a lot of pressure on a lot of Indian people to go back and just for our own selves heal within our own community, talking back and forth and defining who we are. And with all the misrepresentation that's been out there for so long, we ourselves have to find out what was the truth, and what will be the truth. It's a very long and involved process.

Even with our organization, and with finding out how much we are influenced by the sexism that's out in the larger community, and homophobia that's in the larger community, it's a struggle all the time. One of the reasons that I am very much committed to keeping this organization alive, and making sure that people know about us, and speaking about it, and writing about it, it's for people who were like me—isolated. And there are many of us who are still isolated, even within the city.

It took the longest time for me to find out that the Community House was here, and then I had trepidations about coming because I was a lesbian. And fears about coming here because how Indian is Indian—what did that mean? I was raised on the Lone Ranger and Tonto, and Rin Tin Tin, so of course we were the enemy. And my own self-hatred at some points was, "Well, I don't want to be Indian." I always was. But I didn't know what that meant. So it's a very exciting time for our organization, for other organizations that have caught that, since 1987 when we had our first gathering in Minneapolis. So the impetus is all throughout the country to keep our identities alive and the connections. We're more than just a local community. We're local in the fact that we work with a lot of Indian people who come to the city, but our community is national and international. It's not as confined as a lot of gay and lesbian organizations are here in the city. For our survival we have to maintain our connections throughout the nation.

Curtis: The whole notion of organization—you know, the gay and lesbian community get real frustrated with us, because we don't even pretend to follow *Robert's Rules of Order*, we don't do procedural stuff that normal organizations are seen to do in that community. We meet when we need to meet. We talk when we need to talk. And because most of us communicate through the Community House, because we are part of a larger community, and we've made it very clear that the gathering of Two Spirited people would never be defined outside of the larger community, it's real hard for people to understand. Because we've made a commitment as Two Spirited people to come together to work in our community, in the general Native community in the city. And for many people who are not willing to do that, it's not easy for them to continue to be involved in WeWah, or even be involved with some of the folks—because we're so wrapped up. Leota's on the board here. I'm a staff person here. And most people who are involved or have been involved in WeWah have in some way also been connected to the Community House.

It's real hard for an organization to be seen as successful in the gay and lesbian community if we don't follow the same time clock. And the other thing is that people want us to meet every Saturday at 7:00 in the same room. And it's like we have a different time clock than other people, and what is urgent for you may not be that urgent for our community. Because urgency is defined by your experience here in North America as non-Indian people. Urgency for us is the protection of Mother Earth, for example, but it's going to take a long time for us to heal what has been done to her. So if anything I've learned from some of the people here at the Community House that there is a time to move quickly, but there is also a time to move slowly. And, believe me, when they say slowly, if you want to translate that into European time, it's *very* slow. But that's just how we are. And we are successful, I think, being able to survive because of the way we look at how we run our organizations. The Community House has been the most successful urban organization in the country, because it has moved to the beat of Indian time, as opposed to some of the other time clocks that tend to run you down very quickly.

So my last suggestion to people who are interested, after reading this article or after hearing us or whatever, is that patience often will pay off in working with Indian people. A lot of times I read mail that says, "I want the newsletter *now*," "I want to talk with you *now*." But I have commitments, and there is a time to talk to you, but it has to be on my time. Because you're one of 249 million people that are non-Indian in this country, and I'm one of 1.9 million that happen to be Indian. So we have to move very carefully and very slowly in how we work with other communities, and we would hope that that's recognized.

Leota: I just wanted to say one thing. Curtis works on the HIV/AIDS project here at the Community House. And when he's talking about what is urgent or what is important for us, one of the most important things is to disseminate the information on the threat of HIV to our communities. Just as diseases ravaged our communities when the Europeans first came, this is a significant threat to our population. One of the outcomes of this effort is opening up discussion on sexuality. And opening up with the young people and the elders within our community is also, I think, one way of addressing the Two Spirited people within our community, and the acknowledgement, and also informing about the traditions that were in our various nations. I just wanted to give Curtis a pat on the back, because he's worked very hard in this area.

Curtis: I appreciate it. Thank you, Leota. You've raised a very good point in that for the first time, because of this disease, we have actually been able to acknowledge publicly the people in our community who have been leaders, who have passed on because of AIDS, and who have been able to acknowledge their sexuality. We talk about what has AIDS done to our communities. Well, one of the things it has done to Indian peoples is it has helped them in many cases to reawaken to issues of sexuality. So, I appreciate that word of confidence, but it is really our community, I think, that has opened itself up to a better understanding of what's going on. I'm not saying that AIDS phobia doesn't exist, and that there isn't homophobia in our community, but it's certainly less, I believe, in our community than it is in others.

Deborah: Do you want to say anything more about what kinds of things your organization does?

Curtis: Well, WeWah as an organization primarily gets people involved in the larger community. It was formed because we were walking around the American Indian Community House sort of looking at each other, going, "Well, I know she's queer, and I know I'm queer . . ." But we never thought, "Well what happens to people who come in here, not knowing anyone else . . . ?" So we're sort of the welcome wagon. We encourage people—sometimes push people—into roles of responsibility in the community. And we represent our community.

I was asked to represent our community as an openly gay Indian man. And because of the incredible leadership here at the Community House, which is primarily heterosexual, they have been so supportive that that's probably one of the reasons that our organization has been able to exist side by side, because we've had the support of the community. We've never had any attack, no one's criticized us. And I think also it's the fact that we are a group that doesn't participate in functions that are associated with alcohol or drugs or anything like that. It keeps everyone sort of mindful of what are some of the issues in our community.

We participate in events in the community. We support events in the community. We have our own events. In the larger gay and lesbian community, we've marched in the gay and lesbian parade—we've marched for three years in a row now. We hosted a conference for Two Spirited people here at the Community House. Each of us represents the organization at a lot of different functions, and so our organization participates in that way. We're represented in some of the larger gatherings in the gay and lesbian community. We have people on different councils in the Native community. So we're here just as a reminder, I think.

Leota: Right, I think our organization exists because of homophobia within our community and the larger community. I don't know if we would be this entire separate entity if that were not so. The line is very blurred as far as "This is WeWah and BarCheeAmpe and this is the American Indian Community House." We're just as much a part of the Circle as the gallery and artists, or the theatre department, or whatever it is. We're all working toward one goal. It's not a separate goal. The main impetus is that we maintain our identities as Indian people. We've struggled, and we resist the colonization that continues and the genocide that continues. It's really hard to say that "I'm Two Spirited," or "I'm Native American," because I'm really all these things. Tomorrow it may be one thing, today it may be another thing. There's no separation when I'm working with WeWah within the Community House.

Deborah: I have one final question that might help us to wrap things up. It's clear from everything that you've said to me that the Two Spirited community has a lot to offer in terms of ways of thinking about the world, and ways of thinking about sexuality, and just ways of thinking about being. The Two Spirited community and the Native community has a tremendous amount to offer if other communities, the communities of the colonizers, as you say, would listen. I'm wondering what you have experienced as you travel out into the larger gay and lesbian community or the larger community, in talking about gay and lesbian issues—have you come across that sense of enlightenment, or a feeling that there is another way of looking at things?

Leota: Well, I think that has happened, although I think a lot of people are more open to that particularly when it comes to the balances with the earth, and what's happening to the earth, and what's happening to people in general. I find that there is a receptiveness when we talk, to what we're espousing at any lecture that we might give. There's still a lot of ignorance that goes on. People just still don't know who we are, still have no idea what happened to the Indian people here, still have their stereotypes.

I just had a friend not too long ago say, "Well, on the reservation, are they still living in teepees?" It's incredible to think that somebody would ask this, a grown person. Because, what would they be doing in teepees? This is still what we come up against, as people who are in our own country and who are here. That's how submerged our history has been and how submerged we are still as Indian people. So when we go out to speak, this is something that people just don't know, they have no idea. They don't know what we're about. Unfortunately, a lot of times the people who do come are the ones who are very interested and want to know and may have done some reading. So there's still a whole population out there that doesn't want to know and couldn't care less.

Deborah: I thank both of you for taking the time to talk. I don't know whether either of you has anything else that I haven't asked about that seems important that needs to be said.

Curtis: Well, I would like to say that when you asked about visibility and how do you get the word across, it's people like you who do representative articles on our struggles. It's important for us to be heard in as many ways as possible. Because we don't all want to be defined in one particular stereotype—not that we want to be defined at all in stereotypes. But we do have a diversity, and it's important for that to be seen.

"Two Spirited People: Understanding Who We Are as Creation" was first published in *New York Folklore* 19, nos. 1–2 (1993): 155–164.

CAMP WOODLAND

DALE W. JOHNSON

Progressive Education and Folklore in the Catskill Mountains of New York

A summer camp once sought to help children understand the democratic roots of their country by exposing them to the traditions and tradition bearers of the Catskills. The camp grew out of New Deal programs that provided work for artists. Under the direction of Norman Studer, with the help of Herbert Haufrecht and Norman Cazden, youngsters collected folk songs and stories, learned traditional crafts, and documented the disappearing traditions of the region's people. The camp's integrated population and celebration of local tradition bearers seemed subversive to some, however, and with its director under pressure, it closed in 1962. But its legacy lives on in the former campers who were inspired to make their life's work in folklore.

Camp Woodland was a summer camp for children, located at the head of the Woodland Valley, near Phoenicia, New York, in the heart of the Catskill Mountains. It operated as a nonprofit educational institution from 1939 to 1962. Under the direction of Norman Studer, it followed the philosophy of progressive education, inspired by the theories of John Dewey. At the time of the camp's beginning, the U.S. government was finding work for artists and professionals through the Works Progress Administration (WPA) and other New Deal programs. This gave an opportunity for folklorist Ben Botkin and others to encourage an interest in collecting and examining American culture. Norman Studer called this "the culture of democracy" (Studer and Levine 1987). Believing that children could find their democratic roots through their heritage and the heritage of other Americans, he developed a system of collecting local folklore and history as a way to link young campers to their country's culture:

> We came to believe that all children must know their roots, and develop a pride in their backgrounds. Education must teach the

democratic American tradition in a way that would make it come alive. (Studer and Levine 1987)

Contact with the local residents in the Catskill region and their oral traditions was essential for children to develop a true sense of democracy, Studer believed. He and camp counselors established links with communities in the region and introduced children to local tradition bearers. In a way, it was an attempt to recapture the sense of community life that was rapidly disappearing in the region, as well as creating the sense of what philosopher John Dewey termed "self-realization"—the ability to achieve happiness within the world in which one finds oneself (Menand 2001: 237).

So besides the usual summer camp activities such as sports, swimming, hiking, arts and crafts, and singing around the campfire, Norman Studer also instituted a hands-on folklore collecting approach. Field trips to meet tradition bearers throughout the region were an important component of the camp experience, and in later years, after relationships had been formed, local residents would come to the camp and demonstrate traditional skills in logging, bark stripping, blacksmithing, hoop shaving, shingle splitting, square dance calling, and other activities. They would recount to Studer and the children the stories of their lives, the tall tales and songs from the region. Many of these tradition bearers became regulars at the camp and came every summer. Older campers were involved in building projects and helped assemble a folk museum that included material items of the Catskills, including tools.

Another unique feature of the camp was its integration of African American children into its activities. In the introduction to his book *A Catskill Woodsman: Mike Todd's Story*, Studer states, "The camp was interracial, at a time when most Americans were being taught that interracial living was positively subversive." During peak years at the camp, there were some two hundred campers of all ethnic groups, typically aged eight to sixteen years old.

Many summer camps at the time held what was called "color wars," with campers divided into two factions for competition. Studer considered this a very destructive practice that would cause rancor among the youngsters. In contrast, to promote harmony at Camp Woodland, he held "Olympics" in which the various "bunks" would represent different countries. Each "country" would learn a representative song, game, and sport, which they would take turns presenting each evening. This included foodways of the country they represented. Taken very seriously was the

Square dancing at the Catskill Folk Festival, ca. 1944. The festival was the highlight of the summer camp session. Photo: Courtesy of the estate of Herbert Haufrecht.

tradition of flag raising each morning during the Olympics. Another tradition was the Sunday morning gathering, which was basically secular in nature but had a spiritual feeling for the campers.

As music director, Herbert Haufrecht helped initiate serious folk song collecting at the camp in 1941, and this work was taken up a few years later by his successor, Norman Cazden, who maintained a long friendship and collaboration with Haufrecht. Cazden continued at Camp Woodland until 1960.

The result was a collection of 178 songs, which later became the monumental two-volume *Folk Songs of the Catskills*. Representing some forty years of collecting by Cazden, Haufrecht, and Studer, the collection offers more than a hundred songs from singer George Edwards. A meticulous work, it includes notes about the practitioners and the region as well as descriptions of the process by which the songs were documented. The collection was still in draft form when Cazden died in 1980; it was finished by Haufrecht and published by the State University of New York Press in 1982, with a preface by Pete Seeger and an introduction by Norman Studer.

Lacking today's practical devices for recording, Haufrecht and Cazden enlisted the assistance of Camp Woodland's children in their fieldwork. They organized the campers into teams, each of which was assigned to learn one stanza of a song. Haufrecht and Cazden would notate the music of the song while it was sung, and later they could assemble the lyrics from the transcribing done by campers. In some cases, traditional singers stayed at the camp for a week or even a month, which offered a leisurely opportunity for documenting songs. Studer eventually assembled more than 250 reel-to-reel tapes of interviews and folk songs that are now in the Camp Woodland Collection at the University at Albany. This collection also includes many photographs related to the camp, as well as the *Neighbors* magazine published by campers, and other papers.

NORMAN STUDER

Norman Studer (1902–1978), educator, folk enthusiast, poet, and humanist, was the founder and, for all of its twenty-four years, educational director of Camp Woodland. Inspired by the ideals of progressive education, the camp was unique for introducing young people to local Catskills culture through folklore and for its integration of African American youngsters. Born on a farm in Ohio, Studer came east as a young man spurred by his desire for knowledge and curiosity about varied cultures. At Columbia University, he studied with educational philosopher John Dewey. In 1933 he became a teacher at the "Little Red Schoolhouse" in Manhattan, and went on to become director of the Downtown Community School. Norman Studer's philosophy of education and humanitarian values made an indelible imprint on countless educators, students, and campers.

Studer was the author of many articles on the tradition bearers of the Catskills, which he researched with Herbert Haufrecht, Norman Cazden, and scores of counselors and young campers from 1939 to 1962. Some of Studer's articles appeared in the *New York Folklore Quarterly*, and some later reappeared in the book *I Walk the Road Again: Great Stories from the Catskill Region*, edited by Janis Benincasa and published by Purple Mountain Press. He was a coauthor of *Folk Songs of the Catskills.* He also wrote *A Catskill Woodsman: Mike Todd's Story*, and a narrative poem about Mike Todd called *All My Homespun Days*, which was released by Smithsonian Folkways Records.

Camp Woodland's musical traditions included a weekly square dance called by Catskill resident George Van Kleek, who was always accompanied by his wife Clara and sometimes by the youngsters themselves. Singing and performances of plays based on folk themes were regular events. Both Haufrecht and Cazden were known for composing musical works based on folk themes and local history, and these were performed by campers for local audiences. Robert DeCormier, a music counselor at the camp in later years, wrote for the campers a cantata about Sojourner Truth.

By far the most important event at the camp was the annual Catskill Folk Festival. Held in August, it brought square dance callers, storytellers, dancers, artisans, and musicians from the region together with campers and visitors to celebrate the heritage of the Catskills. Saturdays were usually the highlight of the festival and included singers, jig dancers, fiddlers, and storytellers on the Simpson ski slope near the camp. The festival then continued indoors with an evening session of impromptu jam sessions and storytelling. The evening would end with a square dance, with calling and music provided by local musicians and the campers themselves. As the introduction to *Folk Songs of the Catskills* states,

> These annual festivals became very important events to their local participants. Through their contributions, they gained dignity through renewing and reconstructing their own neglected and almost forgotten past.... Thus the festivals reaffirmed and reasserted the creative potential of do-it-yourself culture, and they helped re-establish that creativity as a viable mode within young people. (Cazden, Haufrecht, and Studer 1982: 5)

The end of the summer season was usually marked by a banquet presided over by Norman Studer, which was at times an emotional farewell. One year Studer had been called to testify about his work in front of the New York State Un-American Activities Committee and missed the end-of-summer banquet. When he returned later that night, the staff sat up with him while he related his experiences before the committee. According to Cazden's former wife, Courtney Cazden, before they retired for the evening they sang together "Friends and Neighbors," a song collected from the area that is documented in *Folk Songs of the Catskills*.

The song took on new meaning in the context of Studer's experience earlier that day. "Friends and neighbors," the song begins, "I'm going to leave you . . . neither have I done any wrong." That Studer had been questioned by the state Un-American Activities Committee had no effect on the local community's relationship with the camp, however, and his daughter, Joan Studer Levine, recalls that local people knew the Studers to be staunch defenders of democratic ideals. The communist witch hunters of the 1940s and 1950s also persecuted Norman Cazden, and he was blacklisted from academia for more than sixteen years.

Camp Woodland finally closed in 1962. Three of the trustees who had founded the camp in 1939 used a poorly worded severance agreement to reassume authority after years of following a hands-off approach. Although they had always managed the camp themselves, sometimes with very few resources beyond their own, Norman and Hannah Studer were defeated by these disagreements and finally resigned. Norman Studer died in 1978.

The work of Norman Studer, Herbert Haufrecht, and Norman Cazden was recognized by Benjamin A. Botkin, Charles Seeger, Herbert Halpert, Louis C. Jones, and Harold Thompson of the New York Folklore Society, and countless others. In the very first volume of the *New York Folklore Quarterly* in 1945, Norman Studer announced an upcoming winter folklore conference in New York City, to be sponsored by Camp Woodland; the program reads like a Who's Who of midcentury folklorists:

> Session I: Benjamin A. Botkin on "What is Folklore."
> Session II: Harold W. Thompson, President of the New York Folklore Society, on "Folklore Resources of New York State."
> Session III: George Herzog on "Contributions of National Groups to our Folk Culture."
> Session IV: Dr. Charles Seeger on "Folklore in Community Living."
> Afternoon Roundtable session to be presided over by Louis C. Jones, editor of the *New York Folklore Quarterly*, on the topic, "The Utilization of Folklore in a Democracy." Among the participants in this round table, in addition to the speakers of the morning sessions, will be Elaine Lambert Lewis, who conducts a weekly folklore program on radio station WNYC. Evening concert organized by young composer Herbert Haufrecht.

Studer's continuing interest in folklore led him to organize a folklore conference in 1946 called "Folklore and the Metropolis" at the Elizabeth Irwin High School. Another folklore conference was sponsored by Studer in 1954 at the Downtown Community School in Manhattan, where he was director, entitled "City Folklore and Its Uses" (Botkin 1954: 153–155). A year later, at the East 14th Street Labor Temple in Manhattan, Studer organized an all-day conference with educators, social workers, and folklorists called "Puerto Rican Folkways: Pathways to Understanding" (Botkin 1955: 73–74).

NORMAN CAZDEN

Norman Cazden was born on September 23, 1914, to Russian immigrants. He went to Julliard and City College in New York City before arriving at Harvard in 1944. During his Julliard years, Cazden was active in the intellectual life of the city—playing for Blitzstein shows, composing for modern dance companies, and writing serious compositions, including a symphony. After studying musicology with Charles Seeger and becoming friends with Herbert Haufrecht and Aaron Copland, he came eventually to the study of folk song. Along with Haufrecht and Copland, Cazden composed significant works based on folk themes.

He was introduced to Camp Woodland around 1941 by its musical director, Herbert Haufrecht, whom Cazden succeeded in that position in 1945. He remained as musical director until 1960, and with camp director Norman Studer and Herbert Haufrecht collected the material for *Folk Songs of the Catskills*.

While at Harvard, he studied composition and wrote his Ph.D. dissertation on whether musical preferences are innate and universal or culturally based. He taught at Vassar, the Peabody Institute, and the University of Michigan before taking a position at the University of Illinois in 1950. In 1953, he was denied a chance at tenure because of FBI investigations for the House Un-American Activities Committee, and he was fired from his job at the university. He testified in Washington, was blacklisted, and was denied academic positions for the next sixteen years.

He taught piano privately during these years and worked on folk song analysis. The Cazden family's last summer at Camp Woodland was in 1960, and in 1961 they moved to Lexington, Massachusetts, while Norman's wife Courtney went back to school and subsequently took a teaching position. In 1969, Norman and Courtney parted ways, and he took a position at the University of Maine. Besides *Folk Songs of the Catskills*, his works include *Dances from Woodland*, *The Abelard Folksong Book*, *Three Catskill Ballads for Orchestra*, *A Book of Nonsense Songs*, *American Folk Songs for Children*, and *A Catskill Songbook*.

HERBERT HAUFRECHT

Herbert Haufrecht was born in New York City on November 3, 1909. He began his musical studies with his mother Dora in 1916 and continued at the Institute of Music in Cleveland. In 1930, he received a fellowship in composition at the Julliard Graduate School. While working as a field representative of the Resettlement Administration for the Department of Agriculture in West Virginia, he was exposed to traditional music and began a lifetime of folk song collecting. He published *Folk Songs in Settings by Master Composers* and coauthored the two-volume *Folk Songs of the Catskills*, published in 1982. Through his lifetime, Haufrecht was a staff composer for the Federal Theater Project of the Works Progress Administration and wrote the scores for many musical plays, including *We've Come from the City, Boney Quillin*, and *The Story of Ferdinand the Bull*. He worked as a musician with Burl Ives, the Weavers, Pete Seeger, and Judy Collins, for whom he wrote the *Judy Collins Songbook* in 1969. From 1941 to 1945, he was music director at Camp Woodland, where he began his long collaboration with camp director Norman Studer and musicologist Norman Cazden.

After World War II, Haufrecht was an editor and arranger for Mills Music, Associated Music Publishers, Ricordi Publishers, and others. He was the national music director of Young Audiences, Inc., which brought innovative music programming into the schools of New York City. He also composed many significant pieces of music, including *Symphony for Brass and Tympani, Suite for String Orchestra, Blues and Fugue for Viola and Piano, Etudes in Blues for Piano*, a one-act opera *A Pot of Broth*, and numerous songs. His final composition, *A War Prayer*, was performed in Kingston, New York, in 1995. His wife of fifty-seven years, Betty Haufrecht, described him as "a man of enormous creative gifts, who was loved and respected by all who knew him."

The influence of the Camp Woodland experience on the folklore world is striking, and many former campers are now involved in cultural activities in some way. Just a few examples follow. Former counselor Karl Finger leads cultural tours to places in eastern Europe and elsewhere. Richard Bauman went on to become one of the "Young Turks" of folklore and in 1976 wrote the influential work *Verbal Art as Performance*; he continues a distinguished teaching career at Indiana University. Eric Weissberg is a noted musician from the Woodstock, New York, area who performs and records with internationally known recording artists. Janis Ian became one of the most respected songwriters of all time. Kara Yeargans works for the New York State Council on the Arts in the Arts in Education Program. Pete Seeger visited the camp each summer for more than twenty years and learned the song "Guantanamera" there. Joseph Hickerson, camp counselor in 1959 and 1960, became the head of the Archive of Folk Culture at the Library of Congress, where he served for thirty-five years before retiring in 1998.

The children of the camp directors have also made their mark. Joan Studer Levine, husband Norman, and their son, composer Eric Levine, worked for years to preserve materials from the camp and eventually saw the collection safely archived at the University at Albany. Joanna Cazden was prominent in the folk song revival of the 1960s, and with her mother and sister placed Norman Cazden's papers at Ohio University.

On October 4–5, 1997, former camper Karl Finger and scholar Neil Larsen joined Joan Studer Levine to invite Camp Woodlanders to New Paltz, New York, for a reunion. A list of 182 alumni and alumnae was eventually assembled. Former camper Eric Weissberg of Woodstock brought one of the old signs from the camp for display. Gathering at the student union building at the SUNY–New Paltz campus, campers reminisced and shared photographs and memorabilia. A panel moderated by Greg Finger with Joan Studer Levine, Bob Steuding, author Paul Mischler, Herb Haufrecht, and others discussed Camp Woodland's legacy. Events included square dancing with traditional Catskill musicians Hilton and Stella Kelly, and an evening concert that featured Jay and Molly Unger, Micky Vandow, Karl and Greg Finger, Laura Cooper Stein, Eric Weissberg, Joanna Cazden, Eric Levine, and a chorus of children from Kingston, New York, singing excerpts from Herb Haufrecht's "We've Come from the City." The next day, former campers carpooled to the site of the Catskill Folk Festivals in Phoenicia and were joined by Pete Seeger, who led a lengthy sing-along. Attendees then made the pilgrimage to the camp itself.

Camp Woodland was part of the explosion of interest in the 1930s and 1940s in New York State and the country concerning our democratic heritage and ideals and the search for an American identity. Numerous publications including the *Tennessee Folklore Society Bulletin, Southern Folklore Quarterly, California Folklore Quarterly*, and the *New York Folklore Quarterly* all appeared within a decade of one other (Hand 1975). That interest spawned a generation of New York folklorists and enthusiasts such as Benjamin A. Botkin, Norman Studer, Norman Cazden, Herbert Haufrecht, Edith Cutting, Louis C. Jones, Herbert Halpert, Elaine Lambert

Lewis, Harold W. Thompson, Allen Walker Read, Marjorie L. Porter, and Emelyn Gardner among many others. New York folklorists were at the forefront of the applied folklore movement and believed in the notion that by returning folklore to the people, one promoted understanding between diverse groups. As Louis Jones said, "[folklore] like money and manure needed to be spread around" (Jones 1982: xviii).

On the editor's page of the first *New York Folklore Quarterly* (1945), Jones wrote, "Thus we have our part in building this nation's knowledge of itself, a task that seems to us to be as important for a whole people as for an individual." He was speaking of the New York Folklore Society and the *New York Folklore Quarterly*, but his observation relates to Camp Woodland equally well. Long before the Foxfire project and other programs that introduced young people to folklore collecting, Norman Studer, Norman Cazden, and Herbert Haufrecht with other New Yorkers helped us as a nation to come to know ourselves, and the legacy of Camp Woodland is reflected in the creative spirit and vibrant personalities of its many former counselors and campers.

ACKNOWLEDGMENTS

I was greatly assisted by the following people who allowed themselves to be interviewed and who corresponded at length with me: Joan Studer Levine, Norman Levine, Eric Levine, Betty Haufrecht, Joanna Cazden, Courtney Cazden, Betsy Cazden, Neil Larsen, Karl Finger, Joseph Hickerson, Geoff Kaufman, Janis Benincasa, Dr. Harry Stoneback, Pete Seeger, Eric Weissberg, Jim Corsaro, and many other campers, counselors, and researchers. I am also indebted to the many writings of Norman Studer about Camp Woodland and the Catskill Folk Festival. At the University at Albany I would like to thank historian Gerald Zahavi and archivist Brian Keough for their continued interest in sharing the Camp Woodland story, and their commitment to preserving Camp Woodland materials for future generations. Special thanks to Dr. Ellen McHale of the New York Folklore Society for her interest and advice.

WORKS CITED

Botkin, Benjamin A. 1954. "Upstate, Downstate." *New York Folklore Quarterly* 10 (2): 153–155.

———. 1955. "Upstate, Downstate." *New York Folklore Quarterly* 10 (1): 73–74.

Bresnan, Debra. 2000. "Living Legacy." *Woodstock (N.Y.) Times*, April 6.

Cazden, Norman, Herbert Haufrecht, and Norman Studer. 1982. *Folk Songs of the Catskills*. Albany: State University of New York Press.

Corsaro, James. 2001a. *Report on the Norman Studer Collection*. Schenectady: New York Folklore Society.

———. 2001b. *Report on the Herbert Haufrecht Collection*. Schenectady: New York Folklore Society.

Hand, Wayland. 1975. "Louis C. Jones and the Study of Folk Belief, Witchcraft, and Popular Medicine in America." In *New York Folklore, Somewhere West of Albany: A Festschrift in Honor of Louis C. Jones*, 7–14. Schenectady: New York Folklore Society.

Jones, Louis C. 1982. *Three Eyes on the Past: Exploring New York Folklife*. Syracuse: Syracuse University Press.

Haufrecht, Herbert, and Norman Cazden. 1948. "Music of the Catskills." *New York Folklore Quarterly* 4 (1): 32–46.

Menand, Louis. 2001. *The Metaphysical Club*. New York: Farrar, Straus and Giroux.

Studer, Norman. 1940s. "The Story of Camp Woodland." Camp promotional materials.

———. 1945a. "Winter Folklore Conference." *New York Folklore Quarterly* 1: 59–60.

———. 1945b. "Catskill Folk Festival." *New York Folklore Quarterly* 1 (3): 161–166.

———. 1960. "Folk Festival of the Catskills." *New York Folklore Quarterly* 16 (1): 6–10.

———. 1962. "The Place of Folklore in Education." *New York Folklore Quarterly* (Spring): 3–12.

———. 1988a. *A Catskill Woodsman: Mike Todd's Story*. Fleischmanns, N.Y.: Purple Mountain Press.

———. 1988b. "Yarns of a Catskill Woodsman." *New York Folklore Quarterly* 11 (3): 183–192.

Studer, Norman, and Joan Studer Levine. 1987. *The Woodland Sampler*. Notes to the recording. New York: Self-published.

"Camp Woodland: Progressive Education and Folklore in the Catskill Mountains of New York" was first published in *Voices: The Journal of New York Folklore* 28, nos. 1–2 (Spring–Summer 2002): 6–12.

EMPLOYING MUSIC IN THE CAUSE OF SOCIAL JUSTICE

Ruth Crawford Seeger and Zilphia Horton

JULIA SCHMIDT-PIRRO AND KAREN M. McCURDY

Communicating political principles through music was the strategy of two musicians of the mid-twentieth century. In New York City, early in her career, Ruth Crawford Seeger composed avant-garde classical pieces with a political message. Later, in Washington, D.C., she turned to transcribing folk songs as a means of moving political ideas across American social classes. Zilphia Horton, working in rural Appalachia, used music as direct action on the picket lines of the labor movement and later in the civil rights movement. Through the leadership programs at the Highlander Folk School, Horton taught folk music to many civil rights leaders. Each woman worked independently of the other in musical traditions usually thought antithetical, yet they were equally committed to social justice. They successfully employed music to further progressive politics in the twenty years preceding their premature deaths in the early 1950s, while leaving a legacy of effective musical strategies that would be adapted by leaders in later social movements.

Particular pieces of music stand out in American popular culture as auditory shorthand for social movements they've come to represent. Musicians themselves have similarly been associated with the politics of various eras. Ruth Crawford Seeger (1901–1953) and Zilphia Horton (1910–1956), who mobilized music for political purposes in the interwar years, were two such musicians. Both were classically trained and politically progressive—Crawford Seeger (hereafter Crawford) as a pianist and composer and Horton as a pianist and singer—and they deployed music in their political and social activism for social justice. Zilphia Horton directed the music and arts programs at the Highlander Folk School in the impover-ished Appalachian region of rural eastern Tennessee. She worked in a di-rect-action style, first in the labor movement and later in the nascent civil rights movement. Meanwhile, in New York City, Ruth Crawford was en-gaging musically in politics more indirectly, early on by writing art songs and later by transcribing folk songs for publication in songbooks for adults and children. Feeling challenged by the circumstances of Depression-era America to promote social justice and solidarity, the two women pursued different avenues of musical activism. They nonetheless shared a sense of the political importance of the music of common people, seeing in it moving expressions of daily struggle and triumph. Horton and Crawford consequently became crucial transmitters of this musical legacy to future generations.

As musicians, Crawford and Horton were self-consciously involved in the political arena. Each saw their compositions as capable of directly af-fecting social attitudes and changing society for the better. Both women had observed poverty firsthand and were profoundly influenced by how it discouraged political participation and ultimately disenfranchised the poor. They were committed to notions of equality and justice in a democ-racy, and each worked toward increasing political participation through education. This article presents and contrasts the ways in which Craw-ford and Horton employed music for political purposes. It brings to light three different strategies for communicating political ideas through music: communal performances of labor songs and other folk music at political demonstrations, professional performances of classical music, and tran-scriptions of folk songs.

RUTH CRAWFORD SEEGER

Ruth Crawford Seeger became politically engaged while living in New York during the early Depression years. Returning from a year in Europe sponsored by a Guggenheim fellowship, she moved into Charles Seeger's small apartment in Greenwich Village in November 1931. While her hus-band-to-be taught part time at the New School of Social Research, Ruth found it difficult at first to find professional work (Tick 1997: 181). In fi-nancially strained circumstances and surrounded by the more desperate poverty of countless others, both Crawford and Seeger felt strongly that making art only for aesthetic reasons was absurd: it became, in Seeger's

Ruth Crawford Seeger teaching children in 1950. Peggy Seeger collection.

words, "almost immoral to closet oneself in one's comfortable room and compose music for his own delight" (Tick 1997: 190).

During this time, the couple became increasingly politicized. Charles Seeger's political impulses found expression when he cofounded the Composers' Collective, a coterie of classically trained composers in New York City who dedicated themselves to the task of mobilizing the working class through music. Although Ruth Crawford never joined in the intense debates on the role of music in promoting social change, she visited the group on a few occasions (Pescatello 1992: 111). This exposure to ongoing discussions about music and politics and the spillover such discussions presumably had in her relationship with Charles clearly influenced her thinking.

Crawford started working in 1932 on a commission for the Society of Contemporary Music in Philadelphia: two art songs with political content, which she titled "Two Ricercari." The *ricercari* (from the Italian verb "to seek") is a musical form resembling a fugue. The first song carries the subtitle "Sacco, Vanzetti" and the second "Chinaman, Laundryman." The songs, based on poems by H. T. Tsiang, are composed in an avant-garde musical style. "Sacco, Vanzetti" mourns the death of two Italian anarchists living in Massachusetts, who were tried for a fatal bank robbery and executed in

1927. "Chinaman, Laundryman" describes the exhausting work and exploitation of a laundry worker, who calls his own position "worse than a slave." Both songs feature highly emotional text with many exclamation points. Crawford's primary intention in composing the songs was to compel the audience to absorb the lyrics. In an explanatory note to "Sacco, Vanzetti," she wrote, "It is essential that the audience understand the words. If the effort to secure the pitches as written should interfere with the clear rendition of the words, those pitches should then be regarded as general rather than as specific indications" (Crawford Seeger 1973).

The songs express a political message through both text and music. Voice and piano are composed as opposing elements in both songs, struggling with one another and evoking the musical equivalent of class struggle. In "Sacco, Vanzetti," ongoing chords in a single rhythmic pattern in the piano part contrast with the voice line, which features more freely ranging rhythms. In "Chinaman, Laundryman," a rhythmically relentless piano accompaniment symbolizes an oppressive external force, as well as the worker's unrelenting pace of work (Tick 1997: 192). The song becomes a lament, with the high, disconnected voice part expressing the laundryman's agony. The listener who is confronted with this misery is enlisted as a witness.

"Two Ricercari" are Crawford's only original, explicitly political musical works. Composed for the Society of Contemporary Music, the political message of the compositions was directed toward intellectuals. The songs were performed in 1933 for a mass audience of leftist workers, but they did not resonate with the working class audience (Tick 1997: 193). After the premiere of "Two Ricercari," Crawford moved to Washington, D.C., with her husband, where they worked in the Federal Music Project. In 1936, Crawford started channeling her expertise, artistic sense, and energy in a new direction: toward the collection and transcription of folk songs.

In publishing American folk song transcriptions, Crawford followed in a long tradition of scholarship dedicated to the preservation of folk music. American folk song collections began to appear in the nineteenth century. They were, however, highly selective, and at times music and lyrics were deliberately changed. These collections tended to focus on European—mainly English or Scottish—folk music, neglecting African American music (Filene 2000: 15, 26). One of the first collections to contain folk music of many origins, including African American, was Carl Sandburg's *American Songbag* (1927), to which Crawford contributed several piano accompaniments (Pescatello 1992: 102). This collection differed from the academic collections not only in its criteria of song selection but also in its aim of reaching a popular readership.

Crawford's goal was to provide as authentic a reconstruction of folk performance as possible. Her background as a composer provided the analytical tools and attentiveness to detail needed to transcribe the songs she heard. Pete Seeger recalled an example of the challenges his stepmother faced:

> I remember one week she was asking everybody to listen to a certain work song—some guy was hollering out in the fields, and she said, "Is that an A or an A-sharp there?" And we'd listen to it, and she knew she had to put down one or the other, and you know, what to do, what would be the best thing. (Tick 2001: xxii)

Crawford's transcriptions appeared in two books by John and Alan Lomax. The first collection, *Our Singing Country* (1941), did not sell well and went out of print in just a few years. Alan Lomax blamed the book's failure mostly on Crawford's approach, which he believed to be "too detailed to be used because the notation was so complex. . . . No one could handle it" (Tick 1997: 268). In folklore and classical avant-garde circles, Crawford's work was well received. Marc Blitzstein, who reviewed the book for *Modern Music*, praised Crawford for her meticulousness:

> Mrs. Seeger hears with extraordinary precision and love. In particular, she hears a pause as a pause, not as a tied-over note or as an aimless wait until the next line: some of the rests, as in "God Don't Like It" are really thrilling in the way they evoke the singer's breathing apparatus and niceness of phrasing. . . . The Lomaxes and Mrs. Seeger have let us in on an *alive* musical moment, from which we . . . can reconstruct the variations and the possibilities. (Tick 1997: 269)

This kind of precision and attention to detail is especially evident in her thesis-like work *The Music of American Folk Song*, published posthumously in 2001, which contains information on the transcription process as well as on singing styles. The second Lomax book, *Folk Song USA*, appeared in 1947. Crawford soon published her own pioneering collection, *American Folk Songs for Children* (1948), and *Animal Folk Songs for Children* (1950), which were both designed for use in elementary grades, as well as *American Folk Songs for Christmas* (1953).

ZILPHIA HORTON

Growing up as the daughter of a coal mine owner and operator, Zilphia Johnson's political interest was awakened by the Presbyterian minister Claude Williams, who attempted to organize her father's workers for the Progressive Miners' Union (Carter 1994: 2). She joined the unionization efforts despite her father's disapproval and was disowned by him as a result.

Wanting to deepen her knowledge of the labor movement, she came to the Highlander Folk School in January 1935. Highlander, with strong ties to the labor union movement, was an adult education center founded by Myles Horton and Don West in Monteagle, Tennessee, in the southern Appalachians. The move was a life-changing step for Zilphia; she became both personally and professionally involved in the school's activities, taking on responsibility for the cultural program, which included theater and music. In March 1935, soon after her marriage to Myles Horton, Zilphia attended a workers' theater workshop at the New Theatre School in New York City, where she learned the skills needed to bring the arts into leadership training programs (Glen 1996: 45). Both Hortons maintained connections to New York throughout their lives. The earliest was Myles's association with Union Theological Seminary and Reinhold Niebuhr; in later years, Pete Seeger and other performers became conduits between the Highlander Folk School and the New York folk music scene.

Zilphia Horton arrived at Highlander committed to the idea that music and drama could help organize labor. She saw cultural programs as a means of raising levels of self-confidence in the industrial workers and farmers who were students at Highlander, so that they would have the negotiating skills necessary to meet management as equals. Highlander was preparing union men and women to "organize the South" (Glen 1996: 45–47). Music also became a means to integrate the school into the community in Monteagle. Horton's singing and Ralph Tefferteller's square dance revivals became occasions at which local residents and students could interact.

Nationally known folk musicians like Pete Seeger were regular visitors to Highlander. Seeger, who formed the politically engaged Almanac Singers in New York City in 1940, recalled Horton's musical and organizational skills:

> She had a beautiful alto voice, an unpretentious rare voice, but not the show-off kind. . . . She brought out the talents of her audience

Zilphia Horton singing on the picket line in the 1940s. Highlander Research and Education Center, Resource Center photo collection.

and their enthusiastic participation. Her approach resembled more that of a Black singer and the Black church. (Austin 1991: 50)

Seeger's evocation of the Black church in this retrospective interview is telling, given the integral role of music in Highlander leadership training sessions. When Highlander's mission shifted from labor organizing to civil rights around 1945, music became an even more important means of connecting with students, dovetailing well with the southern Black tradition of song as communication and protest. The Highlander Folk School provided a critical incubator for the civil rights movement, training potential leaders in the Black community, including young ministers, which helped build the churches' capacity to mobilize congregants to act politically. The music program at the Highlander Folk School was a means of bringing an emotional charge to the movements it fostered (Morris 1986).

Horton sought to use music to achieve a sense of common purpose and collective activism. The 1935 textile workers strike in Daisy, Tennessee, stands as an early example of her success in employing song to influence the outcome of a strike. Her account of the event, as quoted by Myles Horton in his autobiography, invites comparison to her later uses of song in the civil rights movement:

We were marching two-by-two with children in the band. They marched past the mill and 400 machine gun bullets were fired into the midst of the group. A woman on the right of me was hit in the leg, and the one on the left was shot in the ankle; I looked around and the police had all disappeared. . . . Well, in about five minutes, a few of us stood up at the mill gates and sang, "We shall not be moved, just like a tree that's planted by the water. . . ." And in ten minutes the marchers began to come out again from behind the garages and little stores that were around in the small town. And they stood there and WERE NOT MOVED and sang. And that's what won their organization. (Horton 1998: 78)

Horton was a pioneer at Highlander in the use of folk music as a tool of political mobilization. She adapted songs to serve in the political struggles—both labor and civil rights—of the mid-twentieth century. Of the many examples of her adaptations of the folk music heritage, one stands out as a powerful demonstration of her success: the transformation of the song "We Shall Overcome." Originally an old Baptist hymn, "I Will Be All Right," the song came to Highlander from the picket lines of the 1945 American Tobacco Company strike by the South Carolina CIO Food and Tobacco Workers Union in Charleston (Glen 1996: 177).

The lyrics of the song had already undergone many changes. In the era of slavery, the line of text was "The Lord will see us through." This was altered by Southern workers after World War II to "The union will see us through," "We will win this fight," and "We're on to victory." Horton saw a broader potential for the music, and in discussion with the Charleston strikers planned new verses for the song to appeal to people other than unionized workers fighting for their rights (Austin 1991: 51). Horton continued to adapt the song's text to suit the occasion. In 1947 she taught the song to Pete Seeger, who changed "will" (the original verb) to "shall" and added some new verses, including, "We shall end Jim Crow / We shall live in peace / All the world around" (Glen 1996: 177). Martin Luther King Jr. first heard the song when Pete Seeger performed it at Highlander's twenty-fifth anniversary celebration. In the 1960s, Guy Carawan, who succeeded Horton as music director of the Highlander Folk School after her untimely death in April 1956, added other verses and further adapted the lyrics (Austin 1991: 51).

In her work at the Highlander Folk School, Horton made it a point not only to transform the songs she encountered but also to preserve them.

The civil rights movement training held at Highlander featured old songs collected by Horton from the South Carolina sea islands: "We Shall Not Be Moved," "Keep Your Eyes on the Prize," "This Little Light of Mine," as well as "We Shall Overcome." She was exposed to a variety of song traditions, including mountain folk music, American labor songs, international songs of political struggle, and Southern spirituals. She notated and published songs in *Highlander Songbook* (Austin 1991: 49) and in a songbook entitled *Labor Songs* published in 1939 (Cohen 2002: 60). While Myles Horton was not directly involved with making music, he recalled, "Song, music, and food are integral parts of education at Highlander. Music is one way for people to express their traditions, longings, and determination" (Horton 1998: 158).

Zilphia Horton's achievements can be seen in her musical legacy. Long before the civil rights movement of the 1960s, the Highlander Folk School had pushed for equality among the races. The school held racially mixed classes as early as 1944, and between 1942 and 1947 worked diligently to build an interracial labor movement in the South (Glen 1996). Given its early commitment to an integrated society, it was only natural that High-lander would be intensively involved in the civil rights struggles of later years. One of Horton's greatest contributions was making available to later generations of activists the musical techniques she developed with her collaborators.

FOLK MUSIC AS POLITICAL ACTION

Understanding the power of folk songs to inspire collective action in politics depends in part on understanding the distinctive qualities of oral tradition. The transmission of oral knowledge requires the involvement of listeners who become part of the realization of the art form, blurring the distinction between performer and audience members. By encourag-ing everybody to be artist-performers, oral tradition tends to give rise to more purely democratic art forms. In art forms that constitute a literate tradition, artists are more solitary. In addition, when knowledge is fixed on a page, its transmission is less flexible and variable than transmission by way of an oral tradition. The process of fixing knowledge on paper, however, as when a song is transcribed into musical notation, does offer other advantages. Knowledge conveyed through literate means fosters a sense of distance or detachment not characteristic of oral traditions: an audience member does not need to be emotionally involved as a recipient of such knowledge. Because the literate tradition does not depend on the context of live performance, it can also be disseminated widely through publications.

The oral tradition in which Horton worked directly promoted political action. Her musical performances had an immediate effect on listeners: they inspired ordinary people to stick together and stay on track toward a goal. The strength of this musical influence is evident in memoirs of the nonviolent protest actions of the civil rights movement. The flexible relationship between words and music helped an oral tradition of political song making to survive for use in a variety of contemporary political struggles.

In contrast, both Crawford's transcriptions of folk songs and her original compositions aimed to communicate a political message to an educated class. They served to preserve an art form that was threatened with extinction, while making folk songs available to an audience not otherwise likely to encounter folk music. Her transcriptions fostered an awareness of the complexity of folk music, which—especially in so-called high art circles—was considered a simplistic form of art. Along with other musicians of her time, Crawford wanted newly discovered folk material to earn consideration as high art and thereby enrich the American tradition of classical music.

Crawford's work helped to convince Americans of the worth of folk music and served to unite people of different class backgrounds. This is especially true of her folk music collections for children, which were widely used in schools to foster feelings of national belonging and heritage. In her introduction to *American Folk Songs for Children*, Crawford wrote:

> [The folksong collection] gives early experience of democratic attitudes and values. . . . This kind of music has crossed and recrossed many sorts of boundaries and is still crossing and recrossing them. It can give the children a glimpse of ways of life and thought different from their own. It can do this in an unself-conscious way—not as a teacher who comes especially to instruct, but as a traveler dropping by with stories to tell about places he has come from. (Crawford Seeger 1948: 22)

The "boundaries" of which Crawford writes are almost certainly class, and perhaps also racial, boundaries. Her argument is that folk music can powerfully convey a sense of different lives and build solidarity. An otherwise unfamiliar content—stories about the works and lives of other people—becomes accessible to the accompaniment of music. The act of singing, which demands collective participation, also triggers identification with the situation described in the lyrics. Or, as Crawford would have it, "the song can come to be an integral part of a child's living" (1948: 22).

It is in this belief in the personally transformative power of music, especially folk music, where Crawford's and Horton's ideas meet. Like Crawford, Horton argued:

> The people can be made aware that many of the songs about their everyday lives . . . are songs of merit. This gives them a new sense of dignity and pride in their cultural heritage. . . . The folk song grows out of reality. It is this stark reality and genuineness which gives the folk song vitality and strength. (Adams 1975: 76)

Both women were idealists who believed that the world could become a better place. Both recognized the long-term importance of musical scores and the written word, expending valuable time and energy on transcriptions. Committed to the ideals of democracy, they employed their music to motivate and educate Americans, and each confronted class-based obstacles to democratic solidarity. Horton chose direct action and succeeded in influencing policy outcomes, promoting unionization and desegregation in the South. Crawford's attempts to use high art in the service of social progress were less successful. Her notion of music education in the service of socializing children for a new national democratic order is nonetheless politically noteworthy and demands further investigation.

WORKS CITED

Adams, Frank. 1975. *Unearthing Seeds of Fire: The Idea of Highlander*. Winston-Salem, N.C.: John F. Blair.

Austin, Aleine. 1991. "Zilphia." *Social Policy* 21 (3): 49–53.

Carter, Vicki. 1994. "The Singing Heart of Highlander Folk School." *New Horizons in Adult Education* 8: 4–24.

Cohen, Ronald. 2002. *Rainbow Quest: The Folk Music Revival and American Society, 1940–1970*. Amherst: University of Massachusetts Press.

Crawford Seeger, Ruth. 1948. *American Folk Songs for Children in Home, School, and Nursery School*. New York: Music Sales Corporation.

———. 1973. "Sacco, Vanzetti." Bryn Mawr, Pa.: Merion Music.

Filene, Benjamin. 2000. *Public Memory and American Roots*. Chapel Hill: University of North Carolina Press.

Glen, John M. 1996. *Highlander: No Ordinary School*. 2nd ed. Knoxville: University of Tennessee Press.

Horton, Myles. 1998. *The Long Haul: An Autobiography*. New York: Teachers College Press.

Morris, Aldon. 1986. *The Origins of the Civil Rights Movement*. New York: The Free Press.

Pescatello, Ann M. 1992. *Charles Seeger: A Life in American Music*. Pittsburgh: University of Pittsburgh Press.

Tick, Judith. 1997. *Ruth Crawford Seeger: A Composer's Search for American Music*. New York: Oxford University Press.

———. 2001. "Historical Introduction." In *The Music of American Folk Song and Selected Other Writings on American Folk Music*, by Ruth Crawford Seeger, xxi–xxix. Edited by Larry Polansky. Rochester, N.Y.: University of Rochester Press.

"Employing Music in the Cause of Social Justice: Ruth Crawford Seeger and Zilphia Horton" was first published in *Voices: The Journal of New York Folklore* 31, nos. 1–2 (Spring–Summer 2005): 32–36.

BURNING MESSAGES

Interpreting African American Fraternity Brands and Their Bearers

SANDRA MIZUMOTO POSEY

Some members of black Greek letter organizations voluntarily scar themselves by branding. Understanding this ritual requires going beyond the brand's physical form and examining the personal and organizational narrative histories that often accompany it. As participants in an ongoing dialogue about what branding means today, fraternity members informally negotiate with brothers who do not support branding, family members who struggle with what it means to their own group identity, and, most importantly, popular culture, which holds negative associations. The men who undergo branding, however, invert the narratives that explain branding as a mark of ownership and slavery and insist on defining its meaning for themselves.

Sam Ryan, Warren Dews, and Richard Pierre belong to the Epsilon Chapter of Omega Psi Phi Fraternity, a black Greek letter organization founded at Howard University in 1911. The Epsilon Chapter followed not long after, in 1919, to serve African American men studying at New York City–area universities (Ryan 2004). Ryan, Dews, and Pierre are in their thirties, college educated, and community minded. Each of them bears between four and ten Omegas branded onto various parts of their bodies.

Neither the method nor the numbers are unusual within the sphere of black fraternities, although branding is often condemned or unacknowledged by official policy. Greek letters seared onto flesh are common among fraternity members and are occasionally found among members of sororities. They are also sometimes found among members of historically white fraternities. Tattoos depicting emblems symbolic of fraternity ties are common among all "Greeks." Often, such markings on the body are considered part of the college experience, as students explore ways to express their new and changing identities. And yet the phenomenon

From left: Fraternity members Sam Ryan, Richard Pierre, Alex Hoag, and Warren Dews proudly display their brands. Photo: Sandra Mizumoto Posey.

of branding cannot be explained or defined solely in this way. Warren Dews, for example, joined Omega Psi Phi Fraternity after graduating from college, as do an increasing number of other individuals. Black Greeks in general are reputed to stay involved, and deeply so, long after graduation. Even among those who join later in life, brands are common. If not the unrestrained imprudence of youth, what do these brands signify?

THE AESTHETICS OF BRANDING

Dews bears brands on each of his arms, two designs created with a total of four "hits" of the iron. On his left arm, two omegas intersect in what some call the Blood Link or Friend-over-Friend pattern. Both the names and the form reinforce the idea of a deep connection between fraternity brothers. On his right arm, Dews has the letter epsilon, representing his chapter, surrounded by a larger omega. The artistry of these brands is exceptional. The raised, or keloid, scars have formed evenly. The intersecting omegas are clearly distinct from each other, creating the effect that one is lying atop the other, and the Epsilon Chapter symbol is small and flat, complementing but subordinate to the larger raised omega.

Branding is an unpredictable process. Some wearers prefer raised scars, such as those on Dews; others do not. Members sometimes try to guide the brand into the desired result by either purposely interrupting the healing process to create a keloid (by picking off scabs), or by cleansing the wound carefully on a regular basis in hopes of creating a flat scar. Unfortunately, how one scars is almost entirely genetically determined, and these methods can affect the resulting scar only minimally at best.

The other factor that determines the form of the resulting brand is the skill of the brander. An uncertain or inexperienced brander may not have the control necessary to apply each part of the form equally on the skin. Rounded surfaces, such as the arm, can be especially difficult in this regard. Expert branders combine a steady hand with careful touch-up hits if necessary, but when poorly done, these touch-ups can add to the unevenness of the brand instead of fixing it. The person being branded must also be able to keep perfectly still during what can be a painful process.

The final result, which can be judged only much later, after the wound has completely healed, is thus determined by the intersection between biology and artistry. Fellow Epsilon Chapter member Sam Ryan, who has acted as the brander for several people, says, "You either have it or you don't. Got to know what you are doing. You don't want to scar someone for life." Ryan himself has experienced the process on the receiving end several times. He bears one brand on each of his arms, one on his left calf, and a "double hit" on his chest.

Ryan's terminology suggests much about the artistry of branding. If we define "scar" as the more or less permanent result of the skin's natural healing process, then the brander actually does want to "scar someone for life." But the word scar as used by Ryan is the antithesis of the result desired by branders and points to the aesthetic rules that govern branding. A brand is not a scar; it is art.

Branding, however, is a complex art form that is half material and half incorporeal. To analyze it, we must go beyond its physical form and understand the personal and organizational narrative histories that often accompany it. For Ryan, the development of his appreciation for branding, and his understanding of what it means to him, began early:

> I learned about the fraternity by seeing brands. My mentor at the Boys Club . . . the way his shirt [was] rolled up, you could see his brands. He was initiated in 1954. As a kid growing up from the age of six on, that's all I would see and I would ask about it and he'd say,

"Well, if you go to college, I'll tell you more about it." So upon entering college, I already knew about the organization because I had spoken to him and he helped write my reference letters, so in more ways than one, I wanted to do the same things that he did, follow the same footsteps, and one of the things I decided to do was that when I did cross [and become a full-fledged fraternity member], I would have myself branded in particular places.

Following in his mentor's footsteps included joining the same fraternity, being branded, and later becoming a director for the Boys Club in New York. If we look at the phrase "follow the same footsteps," its literal interpretation suggests filling a physical space in order to acquire admired traits. Similarly, branding allows the body to fill that same physical space. Branding swells thick with meaning, literally and physically embodying membership in the organization, the organization's commitment to community service, and admiration for a particular individual. After being branded, the body is transformed physically to enter a new psychic space. Narratives enter to bridge the gap and explain to others what the transformation represents. They embody personal histories and organizational histories and are constructed and reconstructed to define what branding means. Ryan's personal branding history complements and reinforces the organizational branding history that he considers the most viable.

One story dates back to when we used to go overseas to fight wars. Help identify bodies. You know, especially with African American soldiers who a lot of times the government did not want to claim, you know, with the brand being on their body, there's a way of Omega calling back her sons and identifying her sons. So that's one story I heard. That goes back to World War II, and I know somebody that personally served that, in the war, and told me that particular story.

SLAVERY VERSUS AGENCY

To George Santayana's saying—"Those who cannot remember the past are condemned to repeat it"—we may add, "We create our history in order to establish our future." There is a difference between history as an interest, a story unfolding, and history as an act of creation, of personal meaning.

They become legends, appearing and proliferating out of contested territory. As Linda Dégh states in *Legend and Belief*, "In regard to its con-
versational, dialectic-polyphonic nature, the legend, more than any other
folklore genre, can make sense only within the crossfire of controversies"
(2001: 2). For example, by pushing aside the narrative histories that tie
branding to marks of ownership and slavery, Pierre asserts that the association and its attendant meaning simply doesn't fit:

> Everyone has their own opinion. And the argument that slaves got
> branded, well, slaves didn't *get* branded. They *were* branded. They did
> not have a choice. This is a choice we have, that we make. I mean,
> we could make the argument, slaves didn't go to college. But they
> weren't allowed to go to college. To be part of this organization, you
> must meet the requirements. You have to have been attending or go-
> ing to college or have attended college and have a certain GPA. And
> I'm not trying to be funny, but, okay, the slaves didn't go to college.

For Pierre, branding is wrapped up in the idea of association, achievement, and agency. Members are quick to name the many extraordinary
individuals who were Omegas. Pierre likes to cite Charles Drew, the doctor who developed long-term storage techniques for blood plasma, making possible the blood banks we know today. He points out the irony that
he died after a car accident because he was denied access to the blood he
needed to survive by hospitals who served only white people. Although
this story is unsubstantiated, like branding motifs in organizational legends, the issue actually is less important than why individual narrators
include it. The idea of agency, of access and choice, is reinforced by this
narrative. The ability to choose for oneself, and to disallow outsiders to
dictate your behavior or what it means, is central to the ability to self-
represent one's identity and to achieve the oft unrecognized potential of
the black male.

There is no known record of the history of the practice among Omega
members, nor is there one narrative that dominates or enjoys consensus.[1]
In fact, the governing body of Omega Psi Phi makes an effort to distance
itself by formally denying that branding has any place in the organization. Instead, there are legend motifs that are arranged and rearranged
by individuals according to what makes sense to them in light of their
personal world view. Any motif or unsubstantiated narrative history that
does not seem likely must be discarded or reconstructed by the individual

proponent because it fails to reflect a foundation for the truth of what branding means to him today, even if it goes against what the organization dictates. As Dégh notes,

> Evidently, the legend touches upon the most sensitive areas of our existence, and its manifest forms cannot be isolated as simple and coherent stories. Rather, legends appear as products of conflicting opinions, expressed in conversation. They manifest in discussions, contradictions, additions, implementations, corrections, approvals, and disapprovals during some or all phases of their transmission, from their inception through various courses of elaboration, variation, decline, and revitalization. (2001: 2)

Another potent demonstration of this process can be seen in the dog as a symbol that is widely used by individuals and chapters, even though Omega Psi Phi does not acknowledge it as part of fraternity culture. Dews explains that "the fraternity's against that, but personally I like the dog symbol . . . the dog means something different to me. . . . He's bold, he's tenacious. And that's what I am."

IMPOSED NARRATIVES

The most familiar narratives constructed by outsiders involve the branding of slaves to denote ownership and relegate the slave to a status more animal than human. Of late, branding has also become a practice associated with neotribalists, an often marginalized group interested in preserving and promoting the tribal values of earlier eras. Common practices within this subculture include tattooing, piercing, cutting, and branding, which are rarely viewed positively by outsiders—much as tattoos were once associated with motorcycle gangs and dissolute sailors.

Media narratives about branding are even more striking. For example, in the science fiction series *Stargate SG-1* (2003), human males are used by a parasitic alien race as incubators for their young. The brand here is a mark of ownership, and as such it indicates the bearer's primary worth in this society as a vehicle rather than as a sentient being in his own right. Interestingly, the symbol used by one of the alien contingents is the Japanese-Chinese character for "within" or "inside," underscoring their men's status as mere carriers.

In the short-lived series *John Doe* (2002), the lead character is found nude with no recollection of his true identity. A keloid scar on his chest is the only clue—one that evokes a mysterious and perhaps sinister truth. Once again, the brand-like scar evokes suspicion, fear, and possible ownership.

In the series *Charmed* (2001), a human's progress toward becoming a demon is recorded by a series of chevrons appearing as raised scars on his arm. The bodily change symbolizes the process of dehumanization.

In his DVD commentary on *School Daze* (1988), Spike Lee (2001) states that the Gammas were his conflation of the worst characteristics of all the African American fraternities. He makes no secret of his disdain for these organizations: "It always amazed me, the amount of abuse and punishment people put up with just to belong to a group, to any organization. Broken limbs, I mean they will fuck you up, just hit you with paddles, all types of stuff, just so they can belong to an organization." Lee's film places branding in the African American fraternity context, but his particular perspective is evident. The significant keloid brand is sexualized and visible only on the film's most unethical character. It evokes the stereotype of the black man as overly sexual and dangerous.

PUBLIC PERCEPTIONS

Some years ago, news stories appeared about a custom in the U.S. Marine Corps known as "blood wings," in which the wings pin of the group is pinned not only through the member's shirt but deep into his skin. A videotape showing footage of this rite caused a public uproar about hazing in the military. Yet participation in the rite is said to be voluntary, and in the wider sphere of American culture, many people voluntarily undergo processes that are both unnecessary and painful—body piercing, tattooing, even plastic surgery. Such activities are often disapproved of but rarely inspire the outcries of torture that were heard about blood wings among the Marines—and that are heard about branding in African American fraternities.

Public acceptance of brands as a positive statement or work of art seems almost impossible. Stories about the perils of hazing and the pain and cruelty often associated with these rituals appeal to people for the same reason that reality shows and *Jerry Springer* do: by viewing these spectacles, viewers define themselves by what they are not. The distance between the observer and the observed makes it easy to divest the other of humanity and thus forget to turn the analytic eye to our own behavior. Whether laughing or cringing, the viewer has no need to understand because the other has become living kitsch. Put another way, to be civilized and avoid challenging existing world views, people need barbarians to compare themselves with.

Not surprisingly, Springer himself frames his show differently. Where some might see chair throwing, hair pulling, prostitutes, or proponents of incest and marital infidelity (to name but a few examples) as participants in a modern-day Roman Colosseum death struggle, Springer says, "Being a talk show host gives me a chance to meet all kinds of people from all walks of life, hear about the problems that affect each of us and learn to develop an insight and sensitivity into issues that we may not have had before. I want my viewers to feel that they've been touched by and learned something about life that they may not have known before watching our show" (William Morris Agency, n.d.: 1).

Jerry Springer may or may not be helping society achieve greater insight into human nature, but in the media, some headway is being made. When well-respected public figures such as Michael Jordan appear with brands, the ritual becomes associated more with the perceived character of the bearer. Bell hooks, however, argues that Jordan does more harm than good to the public image of black men. She argues that, instead of changing public perception, he is "the quintessential symbol of the fetishized eroticized black male body" (1995: 207), dehumanizing himself by appearing in cartoons, his photographic image juxtaposed with animated characters. She also points to instances where photographs of Jordan's sexualized male body are paired with quotes that refer to his aggressive tactics on the basketball court. If hooks is correct in these assertions, we can extrapolate that these stereotypic and demeaning portrayals will by extension also apply to Omega men, especially given that Jordan's Omega brand is clearly visible.

If we disagree with hooks's interpretations of Jordan specifically, we can still agree with her statement that "as the diversity and multiplicity of perspectives emerges, the vision of radical black male subjects claiming their bodies will stand forever in resistance, calling us to contestation and interrogation, calling us all to release the black male body and let it live again" (1995: 212). As members of Omega Psi Phi, Warren Dews, Sam Ryan, and Richard Pierre represent thousands more who take it upon themselves to challenge media narratives with personal ones, allowing only themselves to define what branding is and who they are. It is they who "release the black male body and let it live again."

NOTES

1. The *Omega Bulletin* 9, no. 1 (January 1931) references branding with the statement: "The Test Numbered Four (Branding Test) has been deleted from the ritual and it shall be illegal to use this test in initiations hereafter. The Supreme Council is to review and revise the ritual." This suggests that some form of branding was indeed an official part of rituals prior to 1931. Freemasons, however, were known around this era to use fake branding as part of their rituals, and whether the Omegas used something similar to this or real branding as part of their rituals is not known.

WORKS CITED

Interviews with Sam Ryan, Warren Dews, and Richard Pierre were conducted at the Omega Psi Phi Grand Conclave in Los Angeles during summer 1996.
Charmed. 2001. "Wrestling with Demons," season 3, episode 56. Written by Sheryl J. Anderson. Directed by Joel J. Feigenbaum. Spelling Television.
Dégh, Linda. 2001. *Legend and Belief: Dialectics of a Folklore Genre*. Bloomington: Indiana University Press.
Dreer, Herman. 1940. *The History of the Omega Psi Phi Fraternity: A Brotherhood of Negro College Men, 1911 to 1939*. N.p.: Omega Psi Phi Fraternity, Inc.
Gill, Robert L. 1963. *The Omega Psi Phi Fraternity and the Men Who Made Its History: A Concise History*. N.p.: Omega Psi Phi Fraternity, Inc.
hooks, bell. 1995. "Representing the Black Male Body." In *Art on My Mind: Visual Politics*. New York: The New Press.
John Doe. 2002. Pilot, season 1, episode 1. Brandon Camp, Mimi Leder, and Mike Thompson, executive producers. Fox Television Studios.
John H. Williams Historical Committee. 1994. *Omega Psi Phi Fraternity, Inc.: A Pictorial History*. N.p.: Omega Psi Phi Fraternity, Inc.
Jones, Michael Owen. 1995. "Why Material *Behavior*?" Paper presented at the American Folklore Society Conference, Lafayette, La., October.
———. 1996. "Studying Organizational Symbolism." *Qualitative Research Methods* 39.
Lee, Spike. 2001. Director's Commentary. *School Daze*. DVD. Culver City, Calif.: Columbia Tri-Star Home Entertainment.
Omega Psi Phi Fraternity, Inc. 1995. *Commemorative Souvenir Journal*. Omega World Center Dedication Festival, Decatur, Ga., December 5–9.
———. n.d. "Policy on Branding." Procedures Manual.
———. n.d. "Statement of Position against Canine Reference." Procedures Manual.
Ryan, Sam. n.d. "Epsilon Chapter History." Available at www.angelfire.com/ny2/might yepsilon/Ehist.html. Accessed May 30, 2004.

School Daze. 1988. Written and directed by Spike Lee. 40 Acres and a Mule Filmworks; Columbia Pictures Corporation.

Stargate SG-1. 2003. "Fallen," season 7, episode 1. Written by Robert C. Cooper. Directed by Martin Wood. Metro-Goldwyn-Mayer.

William Morris Agency. n.d. "Jerry Springer: Biography." Available at www.wma.com/ jerry_springer/bio/JERRY_SPRINGER.pdf. Accessed May 23, 2004.

"Burning Messages: Interpreting African American Fraternity Brands and Their Bearers" was first published in *Voices: The Journal of New York Folklore* 30, nos. 3–4 (Fall–Winter 2004): 42–45.

FOOD

WILD GAME COOKING

KAY KENNEDY, GUS HEDLUND, AND EDITH BILLS
COMPILED BY VARICK CHITTENDEN

In the mountains and woods of northern New York, wild game has been a significant part of the diets of many residents, beginning with the wandering Iroquois tribes before the permanent white settlements of two centuries ago. The bounty of native wildlife has been described in many of the accounts of life here. Early families depended on wild meat for survival. Today, it's more of a delicacy, and one can only look forward to it occasionally. Certain cooks in logging camps, hunting lodges, and restaurants have become known for their mastery of the peculiar textures and tastes of wild game.

Campers and catch at Camp 13, Dry Brook, deer season, 1982. Photo: Courtesy of Melissa Ladenheim. Photo provided by Robert Hill; photographer unknown.

Kay Kennedy is one of these cooks. She grew up in a family of hunters and learned a great deal from her mother about cooking game. For twenty years, Kay was the cook at the Birches Restaurant in Hannawa Falls, where she often prepared special meals for the hunters who brought game there. In this article she offers tips on preparing rabbit and bear.

Cooks in the region have prepared venison in almost every way one would prepare beef, including canning it, grinding it into hamburger, making mincemeat, or, as Native Americans did long ago, curing it as jerked venison. Gus Hedlund, a long-time deer hunter from Saint Lawrence County, describes making jerked venison.

Edith Bills was born and raised on a farm on Roaring Brook Road outside the town of Stony Creek in the southeastern Adirondacks. For fifteen years she wrote a weekly column for the *Adirondack Journal/Warrensburg–Lake George News* relating stories collected from her family and neighbors and offering her readers details about foodways, work, and other aspects of daily life in the rural parts of the Adirondacks. The following is from an interview made in 1995.

RABBIT STEW

Kay Kennedy

Some of the kids from Crarys Mills used to bring rabbit. I'd have a refrigerator full before I would get to do it, you know. Every weekend they'd go, and they'd keep bringing it, and I'd get where I almost couldn't shut the door I'd have so many in there. And then I would take them and—I had great big kettles—and I would parboil them with a couple teaspoons of baking soda. That would bring this residue that's on rabbits, you know, up to the top, and then I would put it in clear water, and maybe I'd boil it for another half hour. I'd have a great big iron skillet that I had, and I'd just put the butter in it, salt and pepper, just keep adding hot water, just let it keep simmering, simmering in its own juice, until it almost comes off the bone, you know. Then I would add the onions, and the green peppers and then on to the grill again. When I got it done I'd put it on the grill or put it in a roaster to keep warm, and they would come about five o'clock or so, and I'd have maybe a baked potato with it or make salads or something like that to go with it. It was a grand time.

BEAR

Kay Kennedy

I've used Mogen David on bear meat, and I would cook it maybe about an hour, an hour and twenty minutes. A lot of people think that bear meat is, I don't know, coarse, or has a different taste to it. And I would do it that way, and it was almost—it was a delicacy, you know?

JERKED VENISON

Gus Hedlund

I don't know for sure exactly what makes it, but I know that most venison and rabbits and these certain things have a gamey taste, whatever you want to call it. I suppose it's from eating the different things it eats in the woods, but to me it's not strong. See, I like it. In fact, I like the taste of venison better than any meat there is. Up at Stillwater, up at camp and several other places, we've had jerked venison. The venison is cut up in chunks, and then it's buried in a swamp in the hide. You put salt and pepper on it, and you wrap it up in the hide and bury it for two or three or four days in the swamp or in a mud hole. And then the venison chunks are grilled slowly over a charcoal fire and covered with hemlock bark chips to create a flavored smoke. It took, oh, the better part of a day to prepare a batch of jerked venison. It's wonderful. It's really like eating peanuts, you can't stop.

CANNED VENISON

Edith Bills

How do you can venison? Well, you just have to cut it in smaller pieces. Pack it in your jars. Don't put any water or anything on it, it makes its own juice. It's raw when it goes into the cans. And you cut it into pieces, I always did anyway. About two-by-two-inch cubes. Just so you can get it down into the can. Then you'd put the canning salt. Be sure you always put canning salt in. Never put anything other, because all this other salt has got iodine, this and that, and something else, and it won't keep. And you put that, one tablespoon in a quart can. And you just put it in your cans, cover them up, and put them in a big kettle of water on the stove. If it's a pint can, boil it for an hour and a half, if it's a quart can you boil it for three hours. And it made its own juice, and it was delicious. You could use that stuff so many ways. You could use it for sandwiches, right out of the jar. It was just like—you know, you make your cold roast beef sandwich or something, it was just like that! Delicious! You could make gravy out of it, you could make a main meal out of it. You could make gravy with that juice, and it was delicious. It was great for potatoes and stuff like that.

VENISON STEW RECIPE

Gus Hedlund, courtesy of Varick Chittenden

Toward the end of deer season, hunters in the North Country will often get together and share their bounty in a big venison feed. Gus Hedlund, a longtime member of a local hunting club, got the idea to have a public feed for charity, after attending many of these private feeds. For years now, Gus and his friends have donated their venison and their time to this event, the proceeds of which go to the American Heart Association. Gus prepares the traditional steaks and makes gallons upon gallons of his version of venison stew. Normally he uses twenty-five to thirty pounds of cubed meat for the feed, but here's a reduced version, based on three pounds of venison, which will feed a family.

Ingredients

Salt pork	Sliced celery
Flour	Minced cloves
Salt	Carrots cut into 2-inch pieces
Pepper	Rutabagas
2 cups water	10 allspice
Butter	Wine
Chopped onions	Worcestershire sauce
Diced pepper	

You fry the salt pork to get the fat out over low heat until it starts to brown. And then you put flour, salt, and pepper in a paper bag, and you shake to mix it up. And then you add the venison and shake until it's well coated. Then you add the venison to the salt pork in the pot and brown the chunks of venison over medium heat. You add two cups of water, and you simmer for an hour. In a large skillet, sauté three tablespoons of butter, the chopped onions, diced pepper, sliced celery, and minced cloves until barely crisp. Add vegetables to the pot with carrots cut in two-inch pieces and the rutabagas. Add ten whole allspice. Simmer for one more hour; add wine during last half hour and Worcestershire sauce. And that does it.

Except for the section "Canned Venison," this article is adapted from the radio series Home Cooking, the Art of Good Food, *produced by Traditional Arts of Upstate New York and North Country Public Radio.*

"Wild Game Cooking" was first published in the *New York Folklore Society Newsletter* 9, no. 4 (1998): 10.

FOODWAYS

LYNN CASE EKFELT

COMMUNITY MEALS IN RURAL NEW YORK

In the days following September 11, 2001, the media seemed fascinated by Americans' turn to comfort foods and social evenings with friends. Arugula at the trendy bistro was out, and meatloaf at the kitchen table was in. Those horrible days may have marked the only time that rural New Yorkers have found themselves at the forefront of any trend; around here, cooks have always been judged by the creaminess of the scalloped potatoes, and communal meals have been the cornerstone of social structure.

Where I live in the North Country, and I suspect in other rural areas of the state as well, it is possible to eat out every day of the week simply by attending fund-raising dinners put on by churches and service organizations. Clearly, they've found a formula that works. In our village alone, we have the biweekly VFW breakfasts, the Church and Community Worker Lenten lunches, the Hospital Guild soup lunch, the Rotary and the Day Care Center spaghetti suppers, the Friends of the Canton Fire Station chili cook-off, the Presbyterian church international smorgasbord, the Zonta pie sale, and countless Methodist church dinners. And that's just Canton; the surrounding towns offer equally varied possibilities.

To some extent, the menus are seasonal: maple syrup festivals and bullhead feeds in the spring, strawberry or ice cream socials and chicken barbecues in the summer, turkey dinners in the fall, pastry sales around the holidays. But other foods know no season. Ham, spaghetti, cabbage rolls, roast beef, and chicken-and-biscuits can show up any time.

What makes these dinners and bake sales so successful? Their appeal is that they offer something to everyone involved. Sponsoring organizations like them because people are generally more willing to contribute money if they get something in return. It's easier to find two hundred people to eat a six-dollar ham dinner than to find two hundred people who'll put six dollars into a collection jar. Since the labor and most of the food are donated, the proceeds go straight to the organization's coffers.

More important, though, is the way these events act to strengthen the group itself. Many have been going on for half a century or more. The wise old lady tasting the gravy and directing the kitchen operations probably began as a girl helping set the tables, then graduated to cutting vegetables and mashing potatoes under strict supervision. Along the way she learned the oral traditions of her organization and built strong ties to the other members—ties that make her a more loyal member of the group.

The organizations are not the only ones to benefit from these meals. As we were reminded by September 11, humans are social creatures who need to feel connected to friends and family. One good way to achieve this connection is to work together for a common cause. That work might be as draining as standing for several hours stirring a cauldron of gravy or as pleasant as tucking into a piece of homemade peach pie in the church hall. In any case it provides a sense of belonging to something bigger than oneself.

Since time immemorial, breaking bread together has been a way of building community. Preparing and sharing traditional foods smoothes the entrance of a new member into a group and can cement the bonds between that group's established members. There's a reason why radicchio has not made it onto the menu at the DePeyster Methodist Church's election night supper. Not that no one ever introduces a new dish or ingredient to the repertoire, but it takes a long time to change the values of a community. Who is—and who isn't—a good cook and what defines good food are part of a group's shared aesthetic, and threats to the comfort that belonging brings are not to be taken lightly.

The following selection from *Good Food, Served Right* (Canton, N.Y.: Traditional Arts in Upstate New York, 2000) describes some of the preparations for the semiannual chicken-and-biscuit dinner given by the Pierrepont Fire Department Ladies' Auxiliary. In the account of Judy Hoyt, the president, we see the pride of belonging, the shared system of values, and the sense of tradition that underlie all community meals.

Our Election Day dinner started many years ago. People know about us, and some travel for miles to eat our chicken and biscuits. We usually serve 360 to 400 people between 4 p.m. and 7 p.m. The dinner includes mashed potatoes, chicken, biscuits, gravy, coleslaw, peas and pearl onions, a raw veggie tray (carrots, celery, radishes,

SCALLOPED POTATOES

Scalloped potatoes are a staple of community dinners. Every cook has a favorite addition—a bit of ham, some grated cheese, more onion. It would be possible to eat ten different helpings of scalloped potatoes from ten cooks and never find one that duplicated another. This recipe is a favorite of Ruth Trudell of Lisbon, New York, and her family.

    6–8 medium potatoes, peeled and sliced
    1 medium onion, sliced
    1½ teaspoons black pepper
    1 teaspoon salt
    3–4 cups milk
    4 tablespoons butter or margarine
    2 cups cooked ham, diced
    ½ cup flour
    1 cup grated sharp cheddar (optional)

Mix all the ingredients together in a large greased baking dish. Pour in enough milk to cover the potatoes. If desired, add a cup of grated cheddar. Bake at 350 degrees for one hour.

and green peppers), pickles (dill and sweet), olives, cranberry sauce, and cake or pie.

Preparing the dinner is a two-day process. We cook all the chicken the day before, then at a night work detail we debone it and refrigerate it. I keep all the broth and chicken fat for my gravy. That day we also put the cabbages and carrots for the coleslaw through the food processor and mix them together, but we do not mix up the slaw until the next morning.

The day of the dinner I spend the whole morning making gravy; it's usually a three-hour job for me. I use large restaurant pots—two full ones for the dinner. For thickening the gravy I use cornstarch because I feel that flour makes it too pasty for such a large amount. It will take twelve boxes of cornstarch to make this much gravy. I mix one box at a time in a smaller kettle until it is a perfect consistency. Then I mix all the batches together in the big pots so the gravy is all flavored the same. Sometimes after you get it all done, you have to add more of some ingredients; you just have to taste it and keep working until it's right.

We make the coleslaw the morning of the dinner, too, so it can season through. We chop the Spanish onions fine, then add them to the carrots and cabbage we shredded the day before, along with salt, pepper, and sugar to taste. Then we mix the whole thing very well with Hellmann's mayonnaise; don't use any other kind! Finally we taste it and adjust the seasonings to perfection.

We are usually ready to serve at 3:30 or 3:45. We use a steam table and people help themselves. We serve the coffee, Kool-Aid, and water once people are seated. This is an auxiliary function, but the firemen help us serve. We are proud of our dinner, but we sure are tired at the end!

IT WOULDN'T BE EASTER IN BUFFALO WITHOUT BUTTER LAMBS

Buffalo's Broadway Market is a mere shadow of its former self since the Polish community migrated from downtown to Cheektowaga. Now the endless rows of stalls selling baked goods, vegetables, and meat to ladies with market baskets over their arms have shrunk to just a few. But there's one time of year when visitors can sense the place's former splendor. During the weeks before Easter, the huge hall is packed with people selling molded chocolates, painted Polish Easter eggs, horseradish, pussy willows for Dyngus Day, and—of course—butter lambs.

I stopped by Malczewski's Chicken Shoppe to admire the rows of cute little lambs adorned with red ribbons and flags, in sizes ranging from a couple of ounces up to almost as big as a real newborn lamb. The friendly woman behind the counter, Beverly, told me that, since all their lambs are made by hand, they have to start molding right after New Year's in order to supply all the Wegmans and Tops stores around the city and still have enough for their own market stand. They work in a specific sequence of steps, first molding the lambs, then adding the eyes to signify God's lighting of the world, and finally adding the red ribbon around the neck representing Christ's blood and the little flag saying Happy Easter.

Bulk lamb making must immunize you against sentiment. When I told Beverly I couldn't imagine actually eating something so cute, she said, "We

Butter lamb at the Broadway Market in Buffalo. Photo: Lynn Ekfelt.

call them Marie Antoinette lambs—the head goes first." Be that as it may, in my friend Denise Szafran's home, there is always a regular stick of butter available for the bread. The lamb sits on the table, then moves to the refrigerator until May or June, when someone finally gets up the nerve to take that first bite.

Denise, displaced to Canton from Niagara Falls, kindly took a break from her preparations for the holiday to describe a Polish Easter dinner for me. The menu is set in stone: sausage (smoked and fresh), ham, horseradish to represent the bitter aspects of life, both hard-boiled eggs with shells dyed red and peeled hard-boiled eggs pickled in beet juice, and the classic Polish gifts of welcome to guests—the life-sustaining staples, bread and salt. The centerpiece on the table is always the same: the butter lamb, a symbol of the Lamb of God watching over the meal, sitting on a bed of greens. The day before Easter, all of these foods are carefully packed into a basket and taken to the church to be blessed by the priest and sprinkled with holy water. (Because the church's exodus to Cheektowaga made it difficult for the older people who remained in Buffalo to find a priest to bless their baskets, the priest now travels to them, meeting them at the market on Saturday.)

In spite of the thousands of butter lambs sold at the market and in grocery stores around the city, many more are made at home by women either using molds handed down in their families or working freehand. Denise showed me her mold, the little flag reading *wesolego alleluja* (Happy Easter), and the beautifully embroidered cloth she uses to cover the basket on its way to be blessed. In her family, ethnicity trumps religion. She was planning to make her lamb as soon as she got to her mother's house in Niagara Falls, so the basket could go to the church for its blessing—this in spite of the fact that neither she nor her mother is Catholic. When I asked why, she replied, "It's part of being Polish; you just have to do it."

NICK TAHOU'S GARBAGE PLATE

Warning: Those suffering from high cholesterol should avoid reading this column. The descriptions alone may cause fatal clogging of the arteries.

Nick Tahou (pronounced like Nevada's Lake Tahoe) is no longer alive, but the "garbage plate" served at his restaurant is still a mainstay of Rochester cuisine—primarily of the late-at-night-after-the-bars-close variety. Still, when my husband and I stopped for lunch at the original downtown Nick Tahou's (yes, there now is a suburban branch), we found the place filled with customers, most of whom were happily tearing into garbage plates, although there are plenty of other items on the menu.

We had been just a bit apprehensive, having learned that the restaurant was no longer open twenty-four hours because there had been so many incidents there involving various weapons. However, a friend who is a native Rochesterian assured us we'd be fine eating there in the daytime and that we *had* to go to the original restaurant to get the authentic atmosphere. The clientele proved to be a happy multiracial mix of young businessmen in suits and ties, teens in baggy pants or sweats with baseball caps, old men in neatly pressed khakis and windbreakers, office workers, and three-generation families, with everyone much too busy eating to cause trouble.

My husband put me in charge of ordering, so while he grabbed a seat for us at one of the Formica-topped tables, I went up to the busy counter and threw myself at the mercy of the young woman taking orders, explaining that I had no idea how to go about arranging a garbage plate. She very kindly walked me through the vast number of choices. You don't just order a plate—you build one. For the bottom layer, you have a choice of two starches from the following list: cold baked beans, home fries, French fries, and macaroni salad. The next layer consists of any two of the following (again, your choice): cheeseburger, hamburger, steak, hotdog, white hot, red hot, grilled cheese, eggs, fried ham, chicken, or fish. Next come the optional chopped onions and mustard. Finally the entire plate is smothered in the secret meat sauce and served with Frank's Red Hot sauce.

After some consideration, I selected the beans and home fries base, topped with red hots and a cheeseburger, and, of course, the onions and mustard. When I carried the plate and its accompanying bread and butter back to the table, we stared at the mound of food and congratulated ourselves on our foresight in ordering just one plate to share. As I understand plate etiquette, the real aficionados stir everything together before eating it. That seemed excessive, since the individual items were already fairly indistinguishable, so we settled for shaking Frank's over the whole thing and tucking into it with our plastic forks. Interesting—although I don't expect I'll ever become a real fan of cold baked beans.

A sign over the counter proclaims that this restaurant, the home of the original garbage plate, was established in 1918. Apparently the roots of the plate lie in a dish called "hots and potatoes," consisting of two hot dogs accompanied by either cold baked beans or home fries—very filling for hungry workmen during the Depression, according to Becky Mercuri in *Sandwiches That You Will Like* (2002). It wasn't until the early 1980s that a college boy in the wee hours of the morning ordered "the plate with all that garbage on it," giving it the name that stuck and became so popular that the restaurant now has trademarked it.

On her web site "What's Cooking America," Linda Stradley tells us that, although many other restaurants in the area have jumped on the bandwagon and serve similar plates, all have been legally required to give their dishes other names such as Dumpster Plate, Dog Dish, and my favorite: Plat du Refuse. There's even a web site—Rochester Wiki, Garbage Plates (http://rocwiki.org/Garbage_Plates)—that rates all such plates in the city, should you be planning a visit and want to sample the best of the best. Doubtless the many fine chefs in Rochester cringe to think that their city is best known for its garbage plates, but generations of returning alumni from colleges as far away as Ithaca can't wait to stop in Rochester for a plate—by whatever name.

GARBAGE PLATE MEAT SAUCE

It goes without saying that Nick Tahou's sauce recipe is a secret. Should you want to try making your own garbage plate, however, the following recipe is a ballpark approximation.

½ pound twice-ground beef
½ teaspoon chili powder
¼ teaspoon cayenne pepper
½ teaspoon paprika
½ teaspoon cinnamon
¼ teaspoon ground cloves
½ teaspoon dry mustard
½ teaspoon black pepper
¼ teaspoon salt
1¼ cups water

Combine the ingredients and simmer for two hours, replacing water as needed to keep the meat from drying out. Serve over your choice of meats and starches.

THE NORTH COUNTRY BULLHEAD FEED

Forget about robins and crocuses. In the North Country you know it's spring when the newspaper begins to carry ads for bullhead feeds at VFW posts, volunteer fire companies, and sporting clubs. These dinners are so ubiquitous that it seems as if there couldn't possibly be any bullhead left in the streams after the end of May. The secret? Most local organizations buy their bullhead from Canadian fish farms. State regulations say that the fish must be alive when they cross the border, so middlemen along the Saint Lawrence clean them and sell the cleaned fish in bags. No, the sponsoring groups are not too lazy to catch their own fish—although the size of many feeds would make that a full-time job for their members. The problem is trematodes, little parasites that are basically harmless but quite unappetizing to find in your supper. The farm-raised fish are free of these parasites as well as any pollutants that the bottom-feeding bullhead might ingest from local waterways.

If you've ever seen a bullhead, you'll wonder how anything so ugly can possibly taste so good. Members of the catfish family, they have wide, flat heads with prominent whiskers and thick skin instead of scales. There is no designated season for bullhead fishing and no limit on how many you can bring home. Local bullheading experts tell me, however, that the best time to catch your own bullhead is in the early spring, and the best time of day to fish for them is after dark. You take a lantern or the makings of a fire, a carton of worms or a pail of minnows, something to sit on, a few beers, and a friend or two, and suddenly the fishing is a social event, as well as a way to provide dinner for the family. By confining your fishing to the early spring, you can avoid the trematodes and the muddy taste of bullhead caught later in the season. Once you've caught your fish, you clean it differently than a trout or bass. Rather than filleting it, you simply cut off the head, remove the insides, and skin it. Then you fry the remainder whole and enjoy.

Wanting to savor the sweet bullhead meat without fighting the mosquitoes, we decided to drive over to South Colton for the Racquette Valley Fish and Game Club's twentieth annual bullhead feed. We got there at about 2:15 for a meal advertised as running from "2:00 p.m. until all are served." The room was already filled with contented customers at long, paper-covered tables, plates piled high with coleslaw, potato salad, baked beans, pasta salad, rolls, and two or three crisp, golden-brown bullhead. Many had already chosen their desserts from the well-stocked table by the kitchen; I grabbed the last piece of blackberry pie to round off my feast.

After twenty years, the club has their preparations down to a science. The women come over the day before to make salads; the men arrive at ten on the day of the feed to start heating the oil in two different pots. (By using separate pots for large and small fish, they can ensure that all the fish from a given pot will be ready to take out at the same time.) During the meal, two men sort the five hundred pounds of fish by size; two dip the fish into a mixture of flour, salt, and pepper before dropping them into the bubbling oil; and one keeps an eye on the cooking fish. It's a congenial group—hard working but still managing to catch up on local gossip and tell jokes. (Actually, I didn't get to hear the joke. Just as I arrived, one of the workers looked up and said, "Uh-oh. Lady!" and the raconteur broke off in midsentence. Chivalry lives in South Colton.) There isn't much time for relaxing, though, when you're expecting four hundred guests for dinner.

Although the feed is a fundraiser for the Racquette Valley Fish and Game Club, it is also very much a community event. Many local women who are not members of the club generously contribute pies, cakes, salads, and baked beans to the event, probably well aware that the club members will reciprocate when the ladies hold church suppers or bake sales for *their* organizations. Fried bullhead may be tender, but they provide good cement to hold together a small community.

DEEP-FRIED NORTHERN BULLHEAD

This recipe, used by Dads Post 80 of the Gouverneur VFW at their bullhead feed, is slightly more complicated than the Racquette Valley Fish and Game Club's flour coating.

    1 cup fine cornmeal
    1 cup Italian-seasoned bread crumbs
    ½ teaspoon salt
    1 teaspoon lemon pepper
    2 pounds cleaned bullhead
    1 quart water
    Canola oil for frying

Heat the oil to 375 degrees. Combine the cornmeal, crumbs, salt, and lemon pepper in a shallow pan. Place the cleaned fish in a pan of water, splitting them in half if they are large. Drain them. While they are still moist, roll them in the crumb mixture until they are completely covered, then shake off the excess coating and gently drop them into the oil. Cook the fish until they are golden brown, approximately four to eight minutes, depending on their size. They are done when the meat is white, with no blood showing.

These "Foodways" columns were first published in *Voices: The Journal of New York Folklore*. "Community Meals in Rural New York" appeared in vol. 28, nos. 1–2 (Spring–Summer 2002): 22–23; "It Wouldn't Be Easter in Buffalo without Butter Lambs" appeared in vol. 33, nos. 3–4 (Fall–Winter 2007): 31; "Nick Tahou's Garbage Plate" appeared in vol. 33, nos. 1–2 (Spring–Summer 2007): 31; and "The North Country Bullhead Feed" appeared in vol. 32, nos. 3–4 (Fall–Winter 2006): 33.

FREE MARKET FLAVOR

STEVE ZEITLIN

> Human beings feed on metaphors [of food]: we hunger for, cannibalize, spice
> it up, sugar coat, hash things out, sink our teeth into, and find something
> difficult to swallow or hard to digest so we cough it up and then have a bone
> to pick with someone.
> —MICHAEL OWEN JONES, "FOOD CHOICE, SYMBOLISM, AND IDENTITY"

"I am the accumulated memory and waistline of the dead restaurants of
New York," writes the poet Bob Hershon, "and the dishes that will never
be set before us again, the snow pea leaves in garlic at the Ocean Palace,
the blini and caviar at the Russian Tea Room, the osso buco at the New
Port Alba, the kasha varnishkes at the Second Avenue Deli, the veal ra-
gout at C'ent Anni."[1] I'm with Hershon—for where but in memory can I
ever again find the spicy taste of the *pla phrik sot* at Siam Square, with
its unique mix of lemongrass and spiced peppers? Ingested into our very
beings, these tastes imbue our social gatherings and, later, can define our
fondest memories.

Whenever my wife, Amanda, and our children, Ben and Eliza, ate at
Ubol's Kitchen, a Thai restaurant on Steinway Street in Astoria, Queens,
the owner, perhaps prodding us to try something new, joked that she could
put in our order as soon as we walked through the door. We celebrated
every birthday and special occasion with their spicy barbeque beef, flaming
chicken, and *pad thai*—we finally did try something new and added Pork in
the Garden. Ubol's was what my daughter Eliza calls a "re-creatable good
experience," like riding the Cyclone on Coney Island. Re-creatable until the
sad day we sat down to eat, a little disconcerted not to see the familiar staff.
We tasted the pork only to realize that the chef had left the garden.

Changes in the U.S. immigration law in the mid-1960s, and subsequent
events in world history such as the end of the war in Vietnam and the
breakup of the Soviet Union, ushered in a new wave of immigrants and

expanded the American palate. Culinary entrepreneurs confronted the marketability of their heritage—their cuisine as currency—as they tried to compete against the long-standing Chinese, Greek, and Italian restaurants and the newer ones from Asia, South America, and Africa in the vast open marketplace of New York.

As two books by Mark Kurlansky—*Cod: The Biography of a Fish that Changed the World* and *Salt: A World History*—attest, the entire history of the world can be told through a single food.[2] Foodways provide a window into geography and cultural history. On a recent visit to a Filipino bakery in Queens, New York, folklorist Bill Westerman ordered a traditional dessert, *halo halo*, from the Tagalog word *halò*, meaning "mix." "You can see the history of the Philippines in this dish," he said. He explained that the purple yam, plantains, garbanzos, mangos, and *macapuno* (sweetened coconut meat) are the indigenous and Asian ingredients; the ice cream and crème caramel come from Europeans, beginning with Magellan, who arrived in the Philippines in 1521.

Our family first heard of the restaurant Cendrillon from the Chinese scholar Jack Tchen, who brought a friend of ours to this Filipino restaurant on Mercer Street in Manhattan. "I am going to order a dessert," he told her. "It's called the mango tart. It's big enough for four people—but do not ask me to share. If you want some, you'll have to order your own." When we first ate there, well, we made the same mistake: ordered one for the table to split four ways, then promptly ordered another.

A few weeks ago, I sat in a booth at Cendrillon with Romy Dorotan, the owner and head chef, whose unusual story speaks to the unique qualities of each individual's immigrant experience. He came to Philadelphia in the 1970s to study economics at Temple University. He and his wife Amy were activists, organizing against the Marcos dictatorship. He started out as a dishwasher, moved on to cook, then moved to New York. He opened Cendrillon in 1995. A strong advocate of using fresh, local ingredients, he built the menu around his own unique cooking style. But as critics visited, "they started calling us a Filipino restaurant," he said, "so we added more Filipino dishes."

I asked about the origin of our family's favorite appetizer, the goat curry. "Where in the Philippines does that come from?"

Romy laughed. "The origin of the goat curry is that we lived in Flatbush, Brooklyn, and it's a West Indian community. So that's my own take on the goat roti. I used a scallion pancake instead of the roti—the bread. It's what I call 'fusion confusion.'"

"Filipino restaurants," he continued, "have lagged behind the other Asian foods. We have been here since the nineteenth century, but there are not many Filipino restaurants. For one, the Filipino restaurants mostly cater to other Filipinos; secondly, a lot of Filipinos are not entrepreneurs, and they can get jobs because they speak English. They can go into nursing and other services."

The Cambodian, Thai, and Vietnamese restaurants, he said, "use a tremendous amount of sweetness, which always attracts people—it's the most accessible taste, sweetness—far more than in their home countries. Filipino is different from the other Asian cuisines. We love anything sour—tamarind, vinegar, citrus. Sweetness is not a big thing, but it's starting to encroach."

Romy's Cendrillon restaurant is moving. Now that his SoHo neighborhood attracts mostly tourists—who, unlike the priced-out artists, are looking for more standard fare—he is seeking more hospitable environs in Brooklyn. The city's eateries are in perpetual motion. In the vast culinary marketplace of New York, the spring rolls face off against the empanada. The Brazilian *caipirinha* takes on the Mexican margarita. The Puerto Rican *piragua* water ice cart takes to the streets against Mr. Softee. Yonah Schimmel's adjusts to the competition by inventing the cheddar and jalapeño knish. Chinese restaurants serve fried chicken in African American neighborhoods. "The Koreans," says Romy, "now serve a hot dog smothered with *bulgogi*."

World history, immigrant history, and shifting New York City demographics create an ever-changing range of eateries offering a panoply of tastes, often concocting new flavors by mixing ingredients like the colors of an artist's palette. In the Zeitlin fold, our deepest shared family memories waft back to a tangle of lemongrass, peppers and fish sauce, or goat curry, combined in dishes cooked from half remembered, reimagined, and reconstituted recipes from Thailand, other parts of Asia, or the Caribbean via the Philippines, by immigrant cooks and entrepreneurs trying to match home country and American ingredients, Asian and American tastes, in a flavorful combination for New York City's global palate. As we tuck the goat curry into the scallion pancake, bringing it to our lips, currents of world and immigrant history seem to swirl around a single point on the tip of our tongues, the taste ineffable.

NOTES

1. Written by Bob Hershon as an "I Am" poem, "New York City Epic," produced by City Lore and the Bowery Poetry Club for the People's Poetry Gathering in 2006.

2. See Mark Kurlansky, *Cod: The Biography of a Fish that Changed the World* (New York: Penguin, 1997); and *Salt: A World History* (New York: Penguin, 2002).

A version of "Free Market Flavor" was published in *Voices: The Journal of New York Folklore* 35, nos. 1–2 (Spring–Summer 2009): 19. The epigraph is taken from Michael Owen Jones, "Food Choice, Symbolism, and Identity: Bread and Butter Issues for Folkloristics and Nutrition Studies," *Journal of American Folklore* 120, no. 476 (Spring 2007): 129–177.

NEW YORK FOLKLORE ARCHIVES

[Editors' note: these are among the most important resources for folklorists; not all archives in New York State are listed here].

Alan Lomax Archives
Association for Cultural Equity
New York City
http://www.culturalequity.org

Archive of Vietnam Veterans Oral History and Folklore Project
Department of Anthropology
Buffalo State College
http://www.nyfolklore.org/pubs/voic30-3-4/vietvets.html

Center for Traditional Music and Dance Archives
New York City
http://www.ctmd.org/archives.htm

Crandall Public Library
Center for Folklife, History, and Cultural Programs
http://crandalllibrary.org/folklife/

Edith Cutting Papers
Norman Studer Papers
M.E. Grenander Department of Special Collections and Archives
University at Albany
http://library.albany.edu/speccoll/findaids/ua902.001.htm

Federal Writers' Project Files
Library of Congress
Washington, D.C.
http://lcweb2.loc.gov/wpaintro/wpafwp.html

Louis C. Jones Folklore Archives
Special Collections, Research Library
New York Historical Association
http://www.nysha.org

New York State Library
Albany
Special Collections include:
New York Folklore Society Collection
Papers of Dr. Bruce Buckley
http://www.nysl.nysed.gov/mssdesc.htm

Niagara Frontier Folklore Archive
Department of Anthropology
Buffalo State College
http://buffalolore.buffalonet.org/archives/FolkloreArchives.htm

Rensselaer County Historical Society
Troy
http://www.rchsonline.org

Schomberg Center for Research in Black Culture
New York City
http://www.nypl.org/locations/schomberg

Traditional Arts of Upstate New York
Canton
Papers of Edith Cutting, Robert Bethke, Richard Lunt, and other North
    Country Collections
http://tauny.org/index.php

Urban Archives, City Lore
New York City
http://www.citylore.org/urbanarchive.html

A CALENDAR OF NEW YORK FOLK FESTIVALS

[Editors' note: these listings represent the many festivals that take place in New York State]

January:
Three Kings Celebration and Parade (New York City)
Traditional Arts in Upstate New York Music Jam (Canton)
Vietnamese Tet/Lunar New Year Festival (Syracuse and other locations)

February:
Chinese New Year Celebration (Manlius and other locations)
Dance Flurry (Saratoga Springs)
Karen New Year Celebration (Utica)
Millers Mills Old-Fashioned Ice Harvest (West Winfield)
Russian Winter Festival (Albany)

March:
Maple Festival (Marathon)
Saint Patrick's Day Parade (New York City, Syracuse, Binghamton, and
    other locations)

April:
Easter Egg Hunt (Palmyra and other locations)
Fifth Avenue Easter Parade (New York City)
Powwow and Smokedance (Ithaca)
Riverway Storytelling Festival (public libraries in Albany and Rensselaer
    Counties)

May:
Cinco de Mayo Celebration (New York City)
Haitian Day Parade and Spring Fest (Brooklyn)
Irish Dance Festival (New York City)
Motorcycle Blessing Ceremonies (Buffalo)

Pinkster Festival (Sleepy Hollow)
Riverspark Canal Festival, Erie Canalway (Waterford)

June:
Brooklyn Folk Festival (Brooklyn)
Clearwater Festival (Croton on Hudson)
Gay Pride Celebration (New York City)
Greek Festival (Rochester)
Juneteenth (Rochester)
Museum at Eldridge Street's Egg Roll and Egg Cream Festival (New York City)
Old Songs Festival (Altamont)
Yonkers Puerto Rican and Hispanic Parade (Yonkers)

July:
Balloon Rally (Wellsville)
Canal Fest of the Tonawandas (Tonawanda and North Tonawanda)
Catskills Irish Arts Week (East Durham)
Cranberry Dulcimer and Autoharp Gathering (Cobleskill)
Falcon Ridge Folk Music Festival (Hillsdale)
Finger Lakes International Dragon Boat Festival (Ithaca)
Grassroots Festival of Music and Dance (Trumansburg)
Grey Fox Bluegrass Festival (Oak Hill)
Highbanks Celtic Gathering (Castile)
Native American Dance and Music Festival (Victor)
New York State Old Tyme Fiddlers' Association's Annual Fiddlers' Picnic Festival (Osceola)
Schoharie River Day (Esperance)
Sons of Italy Festival (Geneva)

August:
Adirondack Folk Music Festival (Schroon Lake)
Canal Splash, Erie Canalway (Waterford)
Cortland Celtic Festival (Cortland)
Festa Italiana (Peekskill)
Italian-American Festival (Watkins Glen)
Main Street Music Fest (Wellsville)
Mohegan Colony Storytelling and Music Festival (Westchester County)
Pickin' in the Pasture (Lodi)

Spiedie Fest and Balloon Rally (Binghamton)
Saint Josaphat's Ukrainian Festival (Rochester)
Saint Stanislaus Polish Arts Festival (Rochester)
Top of the Hill Bluegrass Festival (Canisteo)

September:
Blues on the Bridge (Binghamton)
Falling Leaves Festival (Salamanca)
Genundowa, the Festival of Lights (Hammondsport)
Heritage Harvest Festival (Gowanda)
Irish Fest (Syracuse)
Jewish Festival (Syracuse)
Klezmerfest (New York City)
La Festa Italiana (Syracuse)
Red, White, and Blues Festival (Fredonia)
Springwater Fiddlers Fair (Springwater)

October:
Diwali Festival (New York City)
Festival of Iroquois Arts (Howes Cave)
Fiddlers 17! (Roxbury)
Halloween (New York City and other locations)
Oktoberfest (New York City)
Saratoga Native American Festival (Saratoga Springs)
Schweinfurth Multicultural Festival (Auburn)

November:
Barksgiving (Buffalo)
Eisteddfod (Kerhonkson)
Dio de los Muertes/Day of the Dead (New York City)
1863 Thanksgiving Holiday (Old Bethpage)
Five Dutch Days (New York City)
O Tannenbaum Holiday Festival (Owego)
Roberson Center's Multicultural Christmas Forest (Binghamton)
Tibetan Cultural Day (Ithaca)

December:
Christmas in the Village (Wellsville)
Gilded Age Christmas (Staatsburg)

It's a Wonderful Life Celebration (Seneca Falls)
Kwanzaa Celebration (New York City and other locations)
Plowshares Craftsfair and Winter Peace Festival (Syracuse)
Winter Celebration at Lindenwald (Kinderhook)

CONTRIBUTORS

ROBERT BARON is the founding director of the Folk Arts Program of the New York State Council on the Arts (NYSCA). The NYSCA Folk Arts Program fosters the sustainability of folklore throughout New York State through its funding of the presentation of folk artists, field research, and services to artists and arts organizations. It has been a catalyst for the development of a number of regional traditional arts programs and organizations, and organizes the annual New York State Folk Arts Roundtable in collaboration with the New York Folklore Society. Baron also directs the Music Program at NYSCA, serves as a senior program officer in the Arts Education Program, and is on the faculty of the Master's Program in Cultural Sustainability at Goucher College. He has also served as folklore administrator of the National Endowment for the Humanities, senior research specialist in the Education Division of the Brooklyn Museum, adjunct lecturer at Rutgers University in Newark, and nonresident fellow of the W. E. B. Du Bois Institute for African and African American Research at Harvard University. Baron received the Benjamin A. Botkin Prize for outstanding achievement in public folklore from the American Folklore Society; grants from the Wenner-Gren Foundation, Asian Cultural Council, and Japan Foundation; and a Smithsonian Fellowship in Museum Practice. He has been a Fulbright senior specialist in Finland and the Philippines. Baron's research interests include Afro-Atlantic cultures, Creolization, cultural policy, the history of folklore studies, and public folklore. He has carried out field research in New York City, Haiti, Japan, and Saint Lucia. His publications include *Public Folklore*, edited with Nick Spitzer; *Creolization as Cultural Creativity*, edited with Ana Cara; and articles in *Curator*, *Journal of American Folklore*, *New York Folklore*, *Voices: The Journal of New York Folklore*, *Western Folklore*, and the *Journal of Folklore Research*. Baron received a Ph.D. in folklore and folklife from the University of Pennsylvania and an A.B. from the University of Chicago.

EDITH BILLS was a weekly columnist for the *Adirondack Journal/Warrensburg–Lake George News* for fifteen years, writing stories of her family and neighbors and detailing foodways, work, and other aspects of daily life in the rural Adirondacks.

DR. DEBORAH BLINCOE, before her untimely death in 2007 at the age of fifty-two, was a folklorist and anthropologist who spent several years as the folklorist for the Delaware Valley Arts Alliance in Narrowsburg, New York. A former coeditor of *New York Folklore* (1991–1993) with her husband, Dr. John Forrest, Blincoe helped to develop new directions for the publications of the New York Folklore Society, including giving a platform for community scholars in their "Voices of Tradition" project. This idea was later expanded to become an important focus for the New York Folklore Society's current journal, *Voices: The Journal of New York Folklore.*

DEE BRITTON is an assistant professor and academic area coordinator in social science at Empire State College (SUNY). She teaches studies and courses in research methods, social aspects of disaster, perspectives in terrorism, and collective memory. Her primary research focus is in collective memory, and she has created an analytic framework, "Memorial Worlds," which is used to analyze the construction of identity through commemoration. Britton is a regular presenter at a number of international conferences including the International Sociological Association, the International Visual Sociology Association, and the International Institute of Sociology.

MARTHA COOPER is a photographer whose images have appeared in museum exhibitions, books, and magazines. She has a diploma in ethnology from Oxford University and specializes in shooting urban vernacular art and architecture, street life, graffiti, and hip hop in New York City, Baltimore, and worldwide. She has been the director of photography at City Lore since its inception in 1986.

VARICK CHITTENDEN, senior folklorist, director of special projects, and founder of Traditional Arts in Upstate New York (TAUNY), has particular research and programming interests in regional culture, folk art, traditional crafts, foodways, and oral storytelling traditions. Retired after thirty-six years of teaching, he is professor emeritus of English and folklore at the State University of New York at Canton. He has an M.A. in American folk culture from the Cooperstown graduate program and a B.A. and M.Ed. from Saint Lawrence University. He has been curator of several exhibitions of folk art, including "Found in the North Country: The Folk Art of a Region" (1982) and "Out of the Ordinary: Community Tastes and Values in Contemporary New York State Folk Art" (1995). His publications include articles in scholarly journals and general interest magazines, and the books *The Danes of Yates County* (1985) and *Vietnam Remembered: The Folk Art of Marine Combat Veteran Michael D. Cousino, Sr.* (1985). He is currently responsible for TAUNY's signature projects: the Register of Very Special Places and the North Country Heritage Awards.

LYNN CASE EKFELT is retired from her position as a special collections librarian and university archivist at Saint Lawrence University. She is the author of *Good Food Served Right: Traditional Recipes and Food Customs from New York's North Country* (2000).

VALÉRIE FESCHET teaches anthropology at the Université de Provence in Aix-en-Provence, France. She is a researcher at the Institut d'Ethnologie Méditerranéenne, Européenne et Comparative (IDEMEC). Intrigued by the expanding success of petanque—an emblematic game of Provençal identity—in the United States, she did fieldwork in New York's petanque community from 2009 to 2012.

RYN GARGULINSKI is a journalist, poet, cartoonist, and humorist. She wrote her master's thesis on the occupational folklore of New York City subway workers for Brooklyn College (CUNY), where she received a B.F.A. in creative writing. She contributes a monthly column, poems, and illustrations to 12gauge.com.

CURTIS HARRIS was on the staff at the American Indian Community House (AICH) in New York City.

GUS HEDLUND is a long-time deer hunter from Saint Lawrence County, New York.

DALE W. JOHNSON, a lifelong musician, spent many years as a professional musician, playing guitar in R&B, rock and roll, and country bands and working as a Nashville-based performer, studio musician, songwriter, and producer. In the 1990s, he graduated from Western Kentucky University with a B.A. and then an M.A. in folk studies. Johnson's work as a folklorist includes work for the Kentucky Arts Council and as director of services for the New York Folklore Society. After moving to eastern Kentucky, he received an M.Ed. in exceptional education in 2010. Besides folklore research, teaching, and music interests, Johnson is chairman of the Carcassonne Community Center, which sponsors the longest running community square dance in Kentucky. He sometimes plays guitar at the square dances with banjo great Lee Sexton. He also serves in local government on the Letcher County Parks and Recreation Committee.

KAY KENNEDY was the cook for twenty years at the Birches Restaurant in Hannawa Falls, New York, where she often prepared special meals for the hunters who brought game there.

LEOTA LONE DOG served on the American Indian Community House (AICH) Board of Directors.

ELENA MARTÍNEZ received an M.A. in anthropology and an M.A. in folklore at the University of Oregon. Since 1997, she has been a folklorist at City Lore. She coproduced the video documentary *From Mambo to Hip Hop: A South Bronx Tale*, which aired on PBS in September 2006 and won the National Council of La Raza's (NCLR) 2007 ALMA Award for Best TV Documentary. Elena curated the exhibition *"¡Que bonita bandera! The Puerto Rican Flag as Folk Art,"* which traveled through New York, New Jersey, and Pennsylvania, and was the assistant curator for the exhibit "Nueva York: 1613–1945" at El Museo del Barrio. She was a contributor to *Latinas in the United States: A Historical Encyclopedia* by Virginia Sánchez Korrol and Vicki L. Ruiz.

KAREN M. McCURDY is an associate professor of political science at Georgia Southern University. She studies policy change in the American political arena, with a particular interest in understanding how policy preferences from new constituents are integrated into the legislative process. Her cross-disciplinary research includes music as well as the geosciences and has appeared in outlets including *Legislative Studies Quarterly*, *PS: Political Science and Politics*, and *Reviews in Engineering Geology*.

ELLEN McHALE is the executive director of the New York Folklore Society, a position she's held since 1999. Since 2000, she has been researching the folk arts and folklife of the thoroughbred racetrack in partnership with the National Museum of Racing and Hall of Fame. Her work in 2012 was supported through an Archie Green Fellowship awarded by the American Folklife Center at the Library of Congress. A Fulbright scholar to Sweden, McHale holds a Ph.D. in folklore and folklife from the University of Pennsylvania.

FELICIA McMAHON earned a Ph.D. in folklore and folklife studies at the University of Pennsylvania and currently teaches in the Renée Crown Honors Program at Syracuse University. She was awarded the 2008 Chicago Folklore Prize for her book-length ethnography, *Not Just Child's Play: Emerging Tradition and the Lost Boys of Sudan* (2007), and was coeditor (with Brian Sutton-Smith et al.) of *Children's Folklore: A Source Book* (1995), which won the 1996 Opie Prize for Best Edited Book. Her current work with Somali Bantu refugees was recently a feature story in *Syracuse University Magazine* (Spring/Summer 2012).

MICHAEL L. MURRAY is a member of the English faculty, Bard High School Early College Newark. A graduate of the University of Pennsylvania's graduate program in folklore and folklife and the University of North Carolina at Chapel Hill's curriculum in folklore, Murray's research interests include traditional culture in the American suburbs, vernacular art and artists, and public culture studies. He has taught folklore and writing at Princeton University and Bard College, in addition to stints as a public folklorist with the Westchester Arts Council and the Rockland County Historical Society.

BARBARA MYERHOFF (1935–1985) was an anthropologist who devoted her scholarly life to the study of women and "domestic Judaism," two areas of study that had not previously received much attention from scholars. As described by biographer Riv-Ellen Prell, Myerhoff "was a pioneer in challenging the notion that religion can only or best be understood from an elite perspective, usually dominated by males. Rather, her work demonstrated a well-articulated religious system for women that ran parallel to men's sacred worlds. These early insights have been used effectively by a variety of writers and scholars to understand religion from a woman's perspective." Myerhoff was one of a group of scholars in the 1970s that studied narrative and storytelling within communities, and she was interested in the interplay of age, ethnicity, and gender. With filmmaker Lynn Littman, Myerhoff made the award-winning documentary film *Number Our Days*, which earned a 1977 Oscar for Best Documentary Short Film and two Emmy awards. *Number Our Days* was later published as a book, chosen by both the *New York Times* and *Psychology Today* as among the ten best so-cial science books of 1979. Myerhoff's interest in documentary filmmaking led her to found the Department of Visual Anthropology at the University of Southern California, and she served as chair of that department from 1976 to 1980. Barbara Myerhoff died in 1985 from cancer, at the age of fifty. In 2000, the Jewish Women's Archive named her a "Woman of Valor."

SANDRA MIZUMOTO POSEY is the director of Learning Communities and First Year Success at the Metropolitan State University of Denver, where she is also an associate professor at the Institute of Women's Studies and Services. She received her Ph.D. in folklore and mythology at the University of California at Los Angeles. Previous publications include *Rubber Soul: Rubber Stamps and Correspondence Art* (1996), part of the University Press of Mississippi's Folk Art and Artists series.

CATHY RAGLAND is an assistant professor in the Division of Music History, Theory, and Ethnomusicology in the College of Music at the University of North Texas. Her book *Música Norteña: Mexican Migrants Creating a Nation between Nations* (2009) is a study of the Mexican immigrant experience as told through music and performance. She has conducted research among the Mexican immigrant population and a number of ethnic communities in New York. She has served as project director at several arts organizations in New York, most significantly the Center for Traditional Music and Dance (CTMD). While at the CTMD, she cofounded the Mariachi Academy of New York. She has also been a music critic for the *Seattle Times*, the *Austin American-Statesman*, and the *San Antonio Express-News*.

LINDA ROSEKRANS teaches in the English department at the State University of New York College at Cortland and Tompkins Cortland Community College. She worked with Cornell University's American Indian Program from 1996 to 2007 and continues to serve local Native communities through volunteer service work.

PUJA SAHNEY served as graduate intern at the Dutchess County Arts Council in Poughkeepsie, New York, during the summer of 2005, thanks to a grant provided by New York State Council on the Arts and the New York Folklore Society. Sahney is currently a Ph.D. candidate in the folklore program at Indiana University, Bloomington. Her essay is written in honor of the people she met and the love she received at the Kagyu Thubten Choling monastery.

JULIA SCHMIDT-PIRRO is a German-trained musicologist specializing in American avant-garde music. She founded the Paideia Women's Chorus and directed it for seven years. She has taught at Georgia Southern University and Armstrong Atlantic State University and currently works as an independent scholar, piano teacher, and translator in Savannah, Georgia.

BRIAN SUTTON-SMITH is professor emeritus, University of Pennsylvania. He is the author of *The Folkgames of Children* (1972), *The Folkstories of Children* (1981), *Toys as Culture* (1986), *The Ambiguity of Play* (1997), and many other publications.

ELIZABETH TUCKER, professor of English at Binghamton University, has been a member of the New York Folklore Society's executive board. Her previous books are *Campus Legends: A Handbook* (2005), *Haunted Halls: Ghostlore of American College Campuses* (2007), *Children's Folklore: A Handbook* (2008), and *Haunted Southern Tier* (2011). She also edits the journal *Children's Folklore Review* and is president of the International Society for Contemporary Legend Research. She is proud to follow in Louis C. Jones's footsteps as a chronicler of New York State's folklore of the supernatural and feels fortunate to have gotten to know so many wonderful New Yorkers while doing folklore fieldwork.

KAY TURNER directs the Folk Arts Program at the Brooklyn Arts Council (BAC). As part of an annual 9/11 memorial project she presented at the BAC from 2005 to 2011, she curated the photography exhibition "Here *Was* New York: Memorial Images of the Twin Towers" in 2006 for the fifth anniversary of September 11th. For a special issue of *Western Folklore* dedicated to September 11th, Turner published "September 11 and the Burden of the Ephemeral" (2009). Turner is currently working on "Harborlore: Where the River Meets the Sea in Brooklyn's Folk Imagination," a festival slated for spring 2013. She also teaches courses on temporality, gender, and oral narrative theory in the Performance Studies Department at New York University.

TOM VAN BUREN is director of the Folk Arts Program for ArtsWestchester, the arts council of Westchester County, New York. A folk arts and music presenter with extensive public sector folk arts experience in field research, performance programs, and media productions, he earned a doctorate in ethnomusicology from the University of Maryland (2001), writing on the practice of music and dance in the Francophone West African immigrant community of New York City. His areas of cultural expertise include the expressive cultures of the Caribbean and the Middle East, as well as the wider topic of cultural migration and transnational communities. From 1994 to 2003, he worked on cultural programs related to immigrant communities of the New York metropolitan area for the Center for Traditional Music and Dance, including concert and festival productions and audiovisual documentation projects. From 1996 to 2000, he was project director of the Dominican Community Cultural Initiative, which founded the Quisqueya en el Hudson Festival in Washington Heights, New York. He was coeditor and compiler of the *Global Beat of the Boroughs* CD series for Smithsonian Folkways Recordings, for which he also produced two other albums: *Badenya: Manden Music in New York City* (2002) and *Quisqueya en el Hudson: Dominican Music in New York* (2004). Since 2003, he has produced public programs for ArtsWestchester, including concerts, festivals, and material arts exhibitions featuring primarily immigrant community–based artists of the lower Hudson Valley. He has also curated exhibitions of material arts, including "Folk Arts of the Spirit," presenting folk religious expressions in 2007. The following year, he organized the exhibit "Set in Stone," which presented field research conducted over the previous decade, beginning with work done by folklorist Amanda Dargan. Currently, he is developing a 2013 exhibition on boat builders, in partnership with Long Island Traditions.

STEVE ZEITLIN is the founding director of City Lore in New York City.

INDEX

CPSIA information can be obtained
at www.ICGtesting.com
Printed in the USA
FSHW021633100719
59879FS

9 781496 814852